Illinois Voices

Illinois Voices

AN ANTHOLOGY OF TWENTIETH-CENTURY POETRY

Edited by Kevin Stein and G. E. Murray

University of Illinois Press

Urbana and Chicago

Library of Congress Cataloging-in-Publication Data
Illinois voices : an anthology of twentieth-century poetry /
edited by Kevin Stein and G. E. Murray.
p.   cm.
Includes index.
ISBN 0-252-02658-6 (cloth : acid-free paper)
ISBN 0-252-06978-1 (paper : acid-free paper)
1. American poetry—Illinois.
2. American poetry—20th century.
3. Illinois—Poetry.
I. Stein, Kevin, 1954–   .
II. Murray, G. E., 1945–   .
PS571.I3I45   2001
811'.50809773—dc21   00-012666

to our wives—Deb and Joanne
for their patience, faith, and love

Contents

Introduction

Kevin Stein and G. E. Murray

To assemble an anthology for an entire century and an entire state—not a specific literary movement, period, or theme—offers a slew of intrinsic merits and peculiar difficulties. That we are considering the twentieth century—an era of nearly unfathomable literary evolution—complicates matters considerably. That this is Illinois—home to urban, suburban, and rural communities, as well as startling ethnic and racial blends—heightens both the challenge and the rewards that issue from it. This challenge we relished as both timely and acute, especially in 2001, as Illinois definitively enters a new century and a new millennium.

—◊◊◊—

In striking but not surprising ways, the history of twentieth-century Illinois poetry mirrors that of the United States as a whole. As the century turned, the genteel, often didactic, and still largely romantic poetry characteristic of the nineteenth century smashed headlong into the horror of World War I and the stultifying effects of industrialized culture. Victorian social and moral order collapsed into the lap of modernism. The moderns brusquely tossed the husks aside, feeling no sympathy for what Ezra Pound called a "botched civilization." Among poets, the impulse to "make it new" fueled radical changes in subject matter, language, and form. The old order fell before the wrecking ball of the modern, and our country's most familiar poetic voices at the time—say, the Fireside Poets Longfellow, Whittier, and Holmes—seemed hopelessly outdated in this suddenly strange terrain.

Usually viewed as stolidly midwestern, Illinois may seem at first glance distant from the epicenter of such literary rebellion, yet much of that revolt was fomented by writers of the Chicago Renaissance, such as Vachel Lindsay, Edgar Lee Masters, and Carl Sandburg. In addition, fiction writers Ernest Hemingway, Sherwood Anderson, and Nelson Algren stretched their literary wings on Chicago's Near North Side before flying off to Paris and other exotic places. In fact, one may argue that modern American poetry's initial bell rang in Chicago's own *Poetry: A Magazine of Verse*, the little magazine Harriet Monroe founded in 1912 and which continues today as a benchmark for poetry worldwide. When Monroe published T. S. Eliot's "The Love Song of J. Alfred Prufrock" in 1915, modernism found its consummate voice. Not only Pound and Eliot but also Illinoisans Lindsay, Masters, and Sandburg got their literary starts in *Poetry*. That magazine and the troop of writers associated with the Chicago Renaissance worked feverishly to make the city a cultural center not merely for the state but also for the nation.

If the century's aesthetic evolution began with the moderns' storming of the nineteenth-century sentimentalists' castle, arguably Edgar Lee Masters's *Spoon River Anthology* kicked a brick or two from that castle wall. Masters, ensconced at safe distance in a Chicago law office, scrutinized his childhood years in Lewiston (near Springfield) and his grandparents' experience in rural Petersburg. From that remove, he created a town not of the living but of the dead, many of whose citizens spoke openly of their shabby failures and illicit doings. No wonder he named the place after the turbid waters of a central Illinois river and not either of the real towns that served as his models. When his version of the era's "revolt from the village" revealed the often thwarted lives found there, small-town life could not be envisioned as quaint or innocent again. One citizen, "Margaret Fuller Slack" (the name perhaps poking fun at the moon-eyed first editor of the Transcendentalist journal *The Dial*), even glints with feminist edge. Angry at being "lured" into marrying the "rich druggist" with "the promise of leisure" in which to write her novel, she laments her life of tending not to her writing but instead to her eight children—a fate that left her "no time to write." Here's her summation and cautionary note: "Hear me, ambitious souls, / Sex is the curse of life!"

Carl Sandburg took a similarly hard look at life's vicissitudes, especially those played out in the lives of the working poor he saw in Chicago. For instance, Mrs. Pietro Giovannitti, whose husband died at work in a horrific "tunnel explosion," now supports herself by picking onions "ten . . . sometimes twelve" hours a day for a wealthy landowner. Refusing to sentimentalize, Sandburg honors rather than pities this woman who, three months with child, remains "far from desperate about life." He honors as well the woman's elderly mother-in-law, Mrs. Gabrielle Giovannitti, kindling piled atop her head every morning trundling "along Peoria Street." While his fellows suggest "here's good stuff for a novel or / . . . a good play," Sandburg, the populist, prefers a less parasitic and more reverential approach. His wonderful poem "I Am the People, the Mob," speaks the notion cleanly:

I am the people—the mob—the crowd—the mass.
Do you know that all the great work of the world is done through me? . . .
When I, the People, learn to remember, when I, the People, use the
 lessons of yesterday and no longer forget who robbed me last year,
 who played me for a fool—then there will be no speaker in all the
 world say the name: "The People," with any fleck of a sneer in his
 voice or any far-off smile of derision.

All the while, the century's great gear caught its teeth and spun. Emerging perspectives and new focuses required a shift in style. As Harriet Monroe exhibited in her magazine much of the era's aesthetic and cultural changes, she wrought similar changes in her own work, moving from formal odes to compact image poems such as "The Garden." Monroe's poem "The Meeting" even boldly figures the clash of these old and new-fangled cultures, describing the prophetic encounter of the "ox-team and the automobile." In fact, Monroe's "The Meeting" fittingly opens this anthology by illustrating the collision of traditional and modern values that would serve as a hallmark of this century. Such games of cultural tug-of-war are discernible in the work of poets early in the century such as Vachel Lindsay, whose talents span the gamut from sidewalk poetry performance to motion picture criticism. On the one hand, Lindsay can memorialize the "mourning" of Abraham Lincoln over the "sick world" of war while on the other hand shamelessly praise actress Mary Pickford as "One dear lily-girl demure, / Saucy, dancing, cold and pure." In short, these poets straddle the line dividing nineteenth- and twentieth-century technologies, morals, and aesthetics.

By the time Oak Park's Ernest Hemingway had arrived, both feet of Illinois poetry were planted firmly in the modern era—an age, he bitterly suggested, that "demanded that we sing / And cut away our tongue." The result? Here's the closing couplet of Hemingway's "The Age Demanded"—a far cry from nineteenth-century positivism and propriety: "And in the end the age was handed / The sort of shit that it demanded." Contentious as ever, impious, impetuous, and impatient, Hemingway imbues his poems with the era's profound "shock of the modern." By midcentury, Illinois poets had fashioned a variety of responses to this dispiriting notion. Some, like Kenneth Fearing, the tough-guy Chicago reporter, embraced the subjects and style of that bustling city. Some took a more worldly view, as did Archibald MacLeish, two-time Pulitzer Prize winner and later our nation's assistant secretary of state during 1944–45. Still others looked toward renewed formalism and scholarly decorum in the face of modernism's uncertainty, as Yvor Winters demonstrated through his leading role among the formidable New Critics. With such an immense poetic overture, the stage was thus set for the stunning appearance of Gwendolyn Brooks.

In manifest ways, Gwendolyn Brooks became a central figure of twentieth-century American poetry. From her earliest ballads about daily life among the downtrodden, misunderstood, and invisible to her later oracular visions of revolutionary proportions, Brooks led the way in establishing our multiracial, multiethnic American artistic heritage. After five decades of poetic achievement, she earned an honored place in that realm of American poetic originals that includes Eliot, Frost, Stevens, Pound, Moore, Williams, Crane, Bishop.

In 1950, quite amazingly and somewhat surprisingly considering the conformist American literary community that had honored few women and no African Americans, she won the Pulitzer Prize for her gem of a collection *Annie Allen*, which forever lends loving and serious interpretation to the lives of those "who are poor, / Who are adjudged the leastwise of the land, / Who are my sweetest lepers" ("the children of the poor"). Whether from the perspective of mother, daughter, wife, or guardian for the black community, Brooks is steadfast in her ability to balance insights into desire and disillusionment, humor and injustice. From looking down hard streets to looking for the true self amid remnants and ruins, the poet takes strength:

> I hold my honey and I store my bread
> In little jars and cabinets of my will.
> I label clearly, and each latch and lid
> I bid, Be firm till I return from hell.
> ("Gay Chaps at the Bar")

Throughout a dozen important collections, Brooks's exceptional assessments of life's commonalities—however sentimental or savage—developed into an ever-deepening oeuvre, at once clear-eyed, self-sacrificing, unrelenting:

> It has been a
> hard trudge, with fainting, bandaging and death.
> There have been startling confrontations.
> There have been tramplings. Tramplings
> of monarchs and of other men.
>
> But there remain large countries in your eyes.
> ("To Black Women")

Large countries, indeed, but never larger than the singular spirit and voice

Brooks added to American literature. In 1968, she succeeded Carl Sandburg as the poet laureate of Illinois. In retrospect, that passing of the torch from the last living son of the Chicago Renaissance to a new heroic voice intent upon singing the virtues of diversity and the blessings of being black signaled expansion in both style and content. In small but definite ways, America was waking up to the almost endless possibilities of poetic expression, from the mantras of Allen Ginsberg to the wrenching confessions of Sylvia Plath to the revolutionary proclamations of Amiri Baraka—and in the wake of Gwendolyn Brooks's dominant achievement, mainstream poetry in Illinois was branching out in fresh and distinctive ways too.

Among those emerging talents was the German-born Lisel Mueller, who migrated with her family to the Midwest just before the outbreak of World War II. Over the last third of the century, Mueller's subtle explorations of family and cultural histories, along with her fascination for the discoveries offered by language, earned her the Pulitzer Prize and the American Book Award. Seemingly rooted in revelations of the routine, Mueller's finest poems elevate to landscapes of larger implications and lessons, where private and public realms converge as they do in her "Highway Poems":

> The narrow black veins on the map
> will get you there, but the fat
> red arteries will get you there quicker
> and without pain;
> you can go from the head
> to the toes of America
> without seeing
> a hospital or a jail
> without ever coming on tears
> > toys
> > wrinkles
> > scars
> > fists
> > guns
> > crossed fingers
> > broken teeth.

This highway vision of America unfolding also reminds of the pure, often miraculous poetry of John Knoepfle, who from his central Illinois viewpoint speaks so simply (devoid even of punctuation or capitalization) about what is complex and essential about existence:

the sun eye gleams on the burnt black prairie
the winter blackened moraines of all conclusions
and the white egret
ascetic alone with his promise
knowing where the river is
threads a fiery needle.
    ("confluence")

Not all prominent Illinois poets dwell on themes rooted in the native soil. Laurence Lieberman, with his ornate and illuminating tales of island life, has become a preeminent poetic voice on the Caribbean. Similarly, Lucien Stryk has adopted Japanese settings for much of his original poetry and translations.

Michael Anania's locales are decidedly "heartland," but his purposes seem more cosmic and at times existential (take, for instance, his classic "The Fall"). And while Michael Van Walleghen blends humor with unfailingly sound judgments about life's perils, Mary Kinzie's philosophical narratives leave one emotionally extended and better off for the experience.

Clearly, the Illinois poetic troika of Carl Sandburg, Vachel Lindsay, and Edgar Lee Masters laid substantial flooring for the walls and beams that followed. *Poetry* magazine's presence in Chicago since its inception has brought in even more bright light in the form of its notable editors, including Karl Shapiro, John Frederick Nims, and Daryl Hine. Another of its editors, George Dillon, won the Pulitzer Prize at the unlikely age of twenty-two.

Each poet and every poem included here pays special witness to the vast integrated fabric we have come to understand as Illinois poetry at the end of the twentieth century. Certainly influences can be traced. Just as Dave Etter's rural characterizations echo those of Edgar Lee Masters, Haki R. Madhubuti has learned vital lessons from Gwendolyn Brooks, as has Angela Jackson and Carolyn M. Rodgers. And so on, and so on.

Still, the purpose here is not just to appreciate the past and its intriguing lineages. Equally important is to glimpse the possibilities of new directions. In this we believe the future of Illinois poetry will as be rich and varied as its heritage. We have little doubt that readers will be hearing a great deal more from Illinois-connected poets the likes of Edward Hirsch, Albert Goldbarth, Paul Hoover, Li-Young Lee, Maxine Chernoff, Sandra Cisneros, Rodney Jones, and Brigit Pegeen Kelly, among many others.

These new writers are the descendants of a twentieth-century Illinois poetry that survived the transition from didacticism to modernism and then evolved through Imagism and surrealism to the erudition and decorum of poetry inspired by New Criticism to the instigations of the Beats to the experiments of Objectivism to the evocative Deep Image to the sincere manner of the "plain style" to the prominence of African American, Latino/Latina, and Asian American voices to the emotional vulnerability of Confessionalism to feminism and those concerned with marital and gender issues to gay and lesbian poetics and politics to recent (though backward-glancing) developments of the New Narrative and New Formalism to the verbal and theoretical play of LANGUAGE and "performance" poetry. What comes next—for Illinois and perhaps for our nation as a whole—looms incandescent just below the brightening horizon of this new century.

—〰—

We believe the unfolding of twentieth-century Illinois poetry offers a gloss for that of the nation at large, and thus we have striven to offer readers a diverse gathering depicting that development in all its variety. In sum, we have attempted to recreate the multicolored weave of this literary—as well as social—fabric.

As with all anthologies, a note on how we chose these poets is obligatory. Initially, we faced the thorny problem of defining just what constitutes an "Illinois" poet. We auditioned a number of working definitions either narrow or broad in scope. Finding some fatal flaw in each, we settled finally on these loose parameters: that the poet was born in Illinois or produced a considerable body of significant work while living there. Those many fine poets whose residence seemingly lasted only long enough to transfer planes at O'Hare Airport were eliminated. To simplify matters further, we excluded translators and poets writing in languages other than English.

We have considered issues of time and geography, seeking a representative sample from throughout the century's span as well as the state's urban and rural sprawl. In our research, we discovered with delight that beyond the noteworthy contributions of Chicago area poets, virtually every enclave and corner of the state offered its own singular poetic achievements.

We have in addition sought an expansive range of poetic styles and aesthetics. We like the notion that this anthology, as well as this state, can embrace the formalist and the avant-garde poet, the jazz-inspired and the rural plain speaker, the African American, Latino/Latina, and Asian voice. Finally, we trust readers will find within these pages something new—a poem that challenges definitions, a mode of writing that stretches their idea of what a poem is and might become, a new side of a familiar voice. Any anthology, even a retrospective one like this, must both surprise and confirm, instruct and delight.

One final aspect of this selection process warrants explanation. Because both editors are also poets, we envisioned a process that sought our contributors' input in a way rarely pursued by anthologizers. We wondered, "Why not ask the poets to suggest what they believe is their most representative work?" Therefore, after finalizing our list of contributors, an exhaustive process consuming nearly three years, we asked our living poets to suggest their own noteworthy poems. Our idea was to compile our lists without looking at the poets' lists and then compare the two. How often our choices closely reflected the poets' suggestions surprised us both. And, in fairness, how strange on occasion one's choices seemed to the other. In the end, the project demanded the usual editorial picking and choosing, but that process—we happily discovered—was deeply enriched by the flavor of our authors' nominations. Finally, having chosen poets and their work, we organized the contributors chronologically by date of birth so that the anthology might reflect our poetry's development over the century.

—※—

Thanks are due to myriad folks who contributed to this adventure. Two poets whose untimely deaths came while the project was underway contributed largely to its success. John Frederick Nims provided invaluable leads on poets writing in the early and midcentury, and Gwendolyn Brooks generously offered us her best work and ample support for this anthology. We are grateful as well for support offered at Bradley University, particularly the administrative help of Willie Heberer and Tracy Anderson, without whom this project might easily have foundered among the choppy seas of correspondence, typing, record keeping, and permissions granting. Thanks also to Richard Wentworth, retired director of the University of Illinois Press, for his support of this project. Thanks to our wives and families who endured tottering piles of files, dusty books, and endless phone calls. Thanks most to the poets who responded with good cheer to our requests for their work. Without them, this book's pages would be as blank as what follows this period.

Illinois Voices

HARRIET MONROE

The Meeting

The ox-team and the automobile
Stood face to face on the long red road.
The long red road was narrow
At the turn of the hill,
And below was the sun-dancing river
Afoam over the rocks.

The mild-mannered beasts stood pat, chewing their cud.
The stubble-bearded man from the mountains,
Rustier than his wagon,
Unmoving eyed the proud chauffeur.
The little ragged girl
With sun-bleached hair,
Sitting on a hard, yellow-powdery bag,
Looked across at the smart motor hats of the ladies,
And their chiffon scarfs
That the light breeze fingered.
The proud chauffeur blew his horn,
But nothing moved—
Except the foaming, sun-dancing river down below.

Then he jerked his head,
And turned his wheel.
And slowly, carefully,
The automobile moved back over the long red road.

And the mild-mannered beasts lifted their feet,
And the stubble-bearded man flipped his rein,
And the ragged little girl looked ahead up the hill.
And the ox-team lumbered and limped over the long red road.

These Two

Maurice Pretyman: 1891–1915

Franklin Remington Pretyman: 1893–1917

They died, these two—
The little boys I knew—
One at Gallipoli and one in France.
Long ago—
Oh, twenty years or so—
They used to romp and dance
Over the grass, under the trees.
One toddling brother
Had golden curls
Fine as a girl's,
And funny little round fat cheeks the other.
They liked me, used to climb
Into my lap, and tease
For stories before bed-time, tugging close
With little arms and knees.

It seems too short a time
For these two to grow tall
Of body and soul,
Grow into men, and hear the iron call,
And give their youth's bright hoard.

Brief was their story
As sunlight on a sword.

Rubens

Here you are, grand old sensualist!
And here are the three goddesses
    displaying their charms to Paris.
It was all one to you—goddesses, saints, court ladies—
Your world was all curves of flesh,
    rolling curves repeated like a shell.

Mary Magdalen was almost as good copy as Venus,
Angels might be as voluptuous as nymphs.

It was a rich old gorgeous world you painted—
For kings or prelates, what mattered!—palace or church!
You had a wonderful glorious time!—
And no doubt the ladies loved you.

The Garden

Hiding under the hill,
Heavy with trailing robes and tangled veils of green,
Till only its little haggard face was visible,
The garden lay shy and wistful,
Lovelorn for summer departing,
Blowing its little trickling fountain tune into the air.
And over all, hushing, soothing,
Lay the clematis
Like early snow.

Edgar Lee Masters

The Hill

Where are Elmer, Herman, Bert, Tom and Charley,
The weak of will, the strong of arm, the clown, the boozer, the fighter?
All, all are sleeping on the hill.

One passed in a fever,
One was burned in a mine,
One was killed in a brawl,
One died in a jail,
One fell from a bridge toiling for children and wife—
All, all are sleeping, sleeping, sleeping on the hill.

Where are Ella, Kate, Mag, Lizzie and Edith,
The tender heart, the simple soul, the loud, the proud, the happy one?—
All, all are sleeping on the hill.

One died in shameful child-birth,
One of a thwarted love,
One at the hands of a brute in a brothel,
One of a broken pride, in the search for heart's desire;
One after life in far-away London and Paris
Was brought to her little space by Ella and Kate and Mag—
All, all are sleeping, sleeping, sleeping on the hill.

Where are Uncle Isaac and Aunt Emily,
And old Towny Kincaid and Sevigne Houghton,
And Major Walker who had talked
With venerable men of the revolution?—
All, all are sleeping on the hill.

They brought them dead sons from the war,
And daughters whom life had crushed,

And their children fatherless, crying—
All, all are sleeping, sleeping, sleeping on the hill.

Where is Old Fiddler Jones
Who played with life all his ninety years,
Braving the sleet with bared breast,
Drinking, rioting, thinking neither of wife nor kin,
Nor gold, nor love, nor heaven?
Lo! He babbles of the fish-frys of long ago,
Of the horse-races of long ago at Clary's Grove,
Of what Abe Lincoln said
One time at Springfield.

Trainor, the Druggist

Only the chemist can tell, and not always the chemist,
What will result from compounding
Fluids or solids.
And who can tell
How men and women will interact
On each other, or what children will result?
There were Benjamin Pantier and his wife,
Good in themselves, but evil toward each other:
He oxygen, she hydrogen,
Their son, a devastating fire.
I Trainor, the druggist, a mixer of chemicals,
Killed while making an experiment,
Lived unwedded.

Minerva Jones

I am Minerva, the village poetess,
Hooted at, jeered at by the Yahoos of the street
For my heavy body, cock-eye, and rolling walk,
And all the more when "Butch" Weldy

Captured me after a brutal hunt.
He left me to my fate with Doctor Meyers;
And I sank into death, growing numb from the feet up,
Like one stepping deeper and deeper into a stream of ice.
Will someone go to the village newspaper
And gather into a book the verses I wrote?—
I thirsted so for love!
I hungered so for life!

Doctor Meyers

No other man, unless it was Doc Hill,
Did more for people in this town than I.
And all the weak, the halt, the improvident
And those who could not pay flocked to me.
I was good-hearted, easy Doctor Meyers.
I was healthy, happy, in comfortable fortune,
Blest with a congenial mate, my children raised,
All wedded, doing well in the world.
And then one night, Minerva, the poetess,
Came to me in her trouble, crying.
I tried to help her out—she died—
They indicted me, the newspapers disgraced me,
My wife perished of a broken heart,
And pneumonia finished me.

Mrs. Meyers

He protested all his life long
That newspapers lied about him villainously;
That he was not at fault for Minerva's fall,
But only tried to help her.
Poor soul so sunk in sin he could not see
That even trying to help her, as he called it,
He had broken the law human and divine.
Passers-by, an ancient admonition to you:

If your ways would be ways of pleasantness,
And all your pathways peace,
Love God and keep his commandments.

Margaret Fuller Slack

I would have been as great as George Eliot
But for an untoward fate.
For look at the photograph of me made by Penniwit,
Chin resting on hand, and deep-set eyes—
Gray, too, and far-searching.
But there was the old, old problem:
Should it be celibacy, matrimony or unchastity?
Then John Slack, the rich druggist, wooed me,
Luring me with the promise of leisure for my novel,
And I married him, giving birth to eight children,
And had no time to write.
It was all over with me, anyway,
When I ran the needle in my hand
While washing the baby's things,
And died from lock-jaw, an ironical death.
Hear me, ambitious souls,
Sex is the curse of life!

Fiddler Jones

The earth keeps some vibration going
There in your heart, and that is you.   \
And if the people find you can fiddle,
Why, fiddle you must, for all your life.
What do you see, a harvest of clover?
Or a meadow to walk through to the river?
The wind's in the corn; you rub your hands
For beeves hereafter ready for market;
Or else you hear the rustle of skirts
Like the girls when dancing at Little Grove.

To Cooney Potter a pillar of dust
Or whirling leaves meant ruinous drouth;
They looked to me like Red-Head Sammy
Stepping it off, to "Toor-a-Loor."
How could I till my forty acres
Not to speak of getting more,
With a medley of horns, bassoons and piccolos
Stirred in my brain by crows and robins
And the creak of a wind-mill—only these?
And I never started to plow in my life
That someone did not stop in the road
And take me away to a dance or picnic.
I ended up with forty acres;
I ended up with a broken fiddle—
And a broken laugh, and a thousand memories,
And not a single regret.

Sexsmith the Dentist

Do you think that odes and sermons,
And the ringing of church bells,
And the blood of old men and young men,
Martyred for the truth they saw
With eyes made bright by faith in God,
Accomplished the world's great reformations?
Do you think that the "Battle Hymn of the Republic"
Would have been heard if the chattel slave
Had crowned the dominant dollar,
In spite of Whitney's cotton gin,
And steam and rolling mills and iron
And telegraphs and white free labor?
Do you think that Daisy Fraser
Had been put out and driven out
If the canning works had never needed
Her little house and lot?
Or do you think the poker room
Of Johnnie Taylor and Burchard's bar
Had been closed up if the money lost

And spent for beer had not been turned,
By closing them, to Thomas Rhodes
For larger sales of shoes and blankets,
And children's cloaks and gold-oak cradles?
Why, a moral truth is a hollow tooth
Which must be propped with gold.

Lucinda Matlock

I went to the dances at Chandlerville,
And played snap-out at Winchester.
One time we changed partners,
Driving home in the moonlight of middle June,
And then I found Davis.
We were married and lived together for seventy years,
Enjoying, working, raising the twelve children,
Eight of whom we lost
Ere I had reached the age of sixty.
I spun, I wove, I kept the house, I nursed the sick,
I made the garden, and for holiday
Rambled over the fields where sang the larks,
And by Spoon River gathering many a shell,
And many a flower and medicinal weed—
Shouting to the wooded hills, singing to the green valleys.
At ninety-six I had lived enough, that is all,
And passed to a sweet repose.
What is this I hear of sorrow and weariness,
Anger, discontent and drooping hopes?
Degenerate sons and daughters,
Life is too strong for you—
It takes life to love Life.

Starved Rock

As a soul from whom companionships subside
The meaningless and onsweeping tide

Of the river hastening, as it would disown
Old ways and places, left this stone
Of sand above the valley, to look down
Miles of the valley, hamlet, village, town.

—w—

It is a head-gear of a chief whose head,
Down from the implacable brow,
Waiting is held below
The waters, feather decked
With blossoms blue and red,
With ferns and vines;
Hiding beneath the waters, head erect,
His savage eyes and treacherous designs.

—w—

It is a musing memory and memorial
Of geologic ages
Before the floods began to fall;
The cenotaph of sorrows, pilgrimages
Of Marquette and LaSalle.
The eagles and the Indians left it here
In solitude, blown clean
Of kindred things: as an oak whose leaves are sere
Fly over the valley when the winds are keen,
And nestle where the earth receives
Another generation of exhausted leaves.

—w—

Fatigued with age its sleepless eyes look over
Fenced fields of corn and wheat,
Barley and clover.
The lowered pulses of the river beat
Invisibly by shores that stray
In progress and retreat
Past Utica and Ottawa,

And past the meadow where the Illini
Shouted and danced under the autumn moon,
When toddlers and papooses gave a cry,
And dogs were barking for the boon
Of the hunter home again to clamorous tents
Smoking beneath the evening's copper sky.
Later the remnant of the Illini
Climbed up this Rock, to die
Of hunger, thirst, or down its sheer ascents
Rushed on the spears of Pottawatomies,
And found the peace
Where thirst and hunger are unknown.

—⚋—

This is the tragic and the fateful stone
Le Rocher or Starved Rock,
A symbol and a paradigm,
A sphinx of elegy and battle hymn,
Whose lips unlock
Life's secret, which is vanishment, defeat,
In epic dirges for the races
That pass and leave no traces
Before new generations driven in the blast
Of Time and Nature blowing round its head.
Renewing in the Present what the Past
Knew wholly, or in part, so to repeat
Warfare, extermination, old things dead
But brought to life again
In Life's immortal pain.

—⚋—

What Destinies confer,
And laughing mock
LaSalle, his dreamings stir
To wander here, depart
The fortress of Creve Coeur,
Of broken heart,

For this fort of Starved Rock?
After the heart is broken then the cliff
Where vultures flock;
And where below its steeps the savage skiff
Cuts with a pitiless knife the rope let down
For water. From the earth this Indian town
Vanished and on this Rock the Illini
Thirsting, their buckets taken with the knife,
Lay down to die.

This is the land where every generation
Lets down its buckets for the water of Life.
We are the children and the epigone
Of the Illini, the vanished nation.
And this starved scarp of stone
Is now the emblem of our tribulation,
The inverted cup of our insatiable thirst,
The Illini by fate accursed,
This land lost to the Pottawatomies,
They lost the land to us,
Who baffled and idolatrous,
And thirsting, spurred by hope
Kneel upon aching knees,
And with our eager hands draw up the bucketless rope.

This is the tragic, the symbolic face,
Le Rocher or Starved Rock,
Round which the eternal turtles drink and swim
And serpents green and strange,
As race comes after race,
War after war.
This is the sphinx whose Memnon lips breathe dirges
To empire's wayward star,
And over the race's restless urges,
Whose lips unlock
Life's secret which is vanishment and change.

Vachel Lindsay

An Indian Summer Day on the Prairie

IN THE BEGINNING
The sun is a huntress young,
The sun is a red, red joy,
The sun is an Indian girl,
Of the tribe of the Illinois.

MID-MORNING
The sun is a smoldering fire,
That creeps through the high gray plain,
And leaves not a bush of cloud
To blossom with flowers of rain.

NOON
The sun is a wounded deer,
That treads pale grass in the skies,
Shaking his golden horns,
Flashing his baleful eyes.

SUNSET
The sun is an eagle old,
There in the windless west.
Atop of the spirit-cliffs
He builds him a crimson nest.

To Mary Pickford—Moving Picture Actress
(On hearing she was leaving the moving-pictures for the stage.)

Mary Pickford, doll divine,
Year by year, and every day
At the moving-picture play,
You have been my valentine.

Once a free-limbed page in hose,
Baby Rosalind in flower,
Cloakless, shrinking, in that hour
How our reverent passion rose,

How our fine desire you won.
Kitchen-wench another day,
Shapeless, wooden every way.
Next, a fairy from the sun.

Once you walked a grown-up strand
Fish-wife siren, full of lure,
Snaring with devices sure
Lads who murdered on the sand.
But on most days just a child
Dimpled as no grown-folk are,
Cold of kiss as some north star,
Violet from the valleys wild.
Snared as innocence must be,
Fleeing, prisoned, chained, half-dead—
At the end of tortures dread
Roaring cowboys set you free.

Fly, O song, to her today,
Like a cowboy cross the land.
Snatch her from Belasco's hand
And that prison called Broadway.

All the village swains await
One dear lily-girl demure,
Saucy, dancing, cold and pure,
Elf who must return in state.

Abraham Lincoln Walks at Midnight
(In Springfield, Illinois)

It is portentous, and a thing of state
That here at midnight, in our little town

A mourning figure walks, and will not rest,
Near the old court-house pacing up and down,

Or by his homestead, or in shadowed yards
He lingers where his children used to play,
Or through the market, on the well-worn stones
He stalks until the dawn-stars burn away.

A bronzed, lank man! His suit of ancient black,
A famous high top-hat and plain worn shawl
Make him the quaint great figure that men love,
The prairie-lawyer, master of us all.

He cannot sleep upon his hillside now.
He is among us:—as in times before!
And we who toss and lie awake for long
Breathe deep, and start, to see him pass the door.

His head is bowed. He thinks on men and kings.
Yea, when the sick world cries, how can he sleep?
Too many peasants fight, they know not why,
Too many homesteads in black terror weep.

The sins of all the war-lords burn his heart.
He sees the dreadnoughts scouring every main.
He carries on his shawl-wrapped shoulders now
The bitterness, the folly and the pain.

He cannot rest until a spirit-dawn
Shall come;—the shining hope of Europe free:
The league of sober folk, the Workers' Earth,
Bringing long peace to Cornland, Alp and Sea.

It breaks his heart that kings must murder still,
That all his hours of travail here for men
Seem yet in vain. And who will bring white peace
That he may sleep upon his hill again?

Carl Sandburg

The Right to Grief

To Certain Poets about to Die

Take your fill of intimate remorse, perfumed sorrow,
Over the dead child of a millionaire,
And the pity of Death refusing any check on the bank
Which the millionaire might order his secretary to scratch off
And get cashed.

    Very well,
You for your grief and I for mine.
Let me have a sorrow my own if I want to.

I shall cry over the dead child of a stockyards hunky.
His job is sweeping blood off the floor.
He gets a dollar seventy cents a day when he works
And it's many tubs of blood he shoves out with a broom day by day.

Now his three year old daughter
Is in a white coffin that cost him a week's wages.
Every Saturday night he will pay the undertaker fifty cents till the debt is
    wiped out.

The hunky and his wife and the kids
Cry over the pinched face almost at peace in the white box.

They remember it was scrawny and ran up high doctor bills.
They are glad it is gone for the rest of the family now will have more to eat
    and wear.

Yet before the majesty of Death they cry around the coffin
And wipe their eyes with red bandanas and sob when the priest says, "God
    have mercy on us all."

I have a right to feel my throat choke about this.

You take your grief and I mine—see?

To-morrow there is no funeral and the hunky goes back to his job sweeping blood off the floor at a dollar seventy cents a day.

All he does all day long is keep on shoving hog blood ahead of him with a broom.

Onion Days

Mrs. Gabrielle Giovannitti comes along Peoria Street every morning at nine o'clock

With kindling wool piled on top of her head, her eyes looking straight ahead to find the way for her old feet.

Her daughter-in-law, Mrs. Pietro Giovannitti, whose husband was killed in a tunnel explosion through the negligence of a fellow-servant,

Works ten hours a day, sometimes twelve, picking onions for Jasper on the Bowmanville road.

She takes a street car at half-past five in the morning, Mrs. Pietro Giovannitti does,

And gets back from Jasper's with cash for her day's work, between nine and ten o'clock at night.

Last week she got eight cents a box, Mrs. Pietro Giovannitti, picking onions for Jasper,

But this week Jasper dropped the pay to six cents a box because so many women and girls were answering the ads in the *Daily News*.

Jasper belongs to an Episcopal church in Ravenswood and on certain Sundays

He enjoys chanting the Nicene creed with his daughters on each side of him joining their voices with his.

If the preacher repeats old sermons of a Sunday, Jasper's mind wanders to his 700-acre farm and how he can make it produce more efficiently

And sometimes he speculates on whether he could word an ad in the *Daily News* so it would bring more women and girls out to his farm and reduce operating costs.

Mrs. Pietro Giovannitti is far from desperate about life; her joy is in a child she knows will arrive to her in three months.

And now while these are the pictures for today there are other pictures of the
　　Giovannitti people I could give you for to-morrow,
And how some of them go to the county agent on winter mornings with their
　　baskets for beans and cornmeal and molasses.
I listen to fellows saying here's good stuff for a novel or it might be worked up
　　into a good play.
I say there's no dramatist living can put old Mrs. Gabrielle Giovannitti into a
　　play with that kindling wood piled on top of her head coming along
　　Peoria Street nine o'clock in the morning.

Happiness

I asked professors who teach the meaning of life to tell me what is happiness.
And I went to famous executives who boss the work of thousands of men.
They all shook their heads and gave me a smile as though I was trying to fool
　　with them.
And then one Sunday afternoon I wandered out along the Desplaines river
And I saw a crowd of Hungarians under the trees with their women and
　　children and a keg of beer and an accordion.

A Teamster's Farewell

Sobs en Route to a Penitentiary

Good-by now to the streets and the clash of wheels and locking hubs,
The sun coming on the brass buckles and harness knobs.
The muscles of the horses sliding under their heavy haunches,
Good-by now to the traffic policeman and his whistle,
The smash of the iron hoof on the stones,
All the crazy wonderful slamming roar of the street—
O God, there's noises I'm going to be hungry for.

Halsted Street Car

Come you, cartoonists,
Hang on a strap with me here
At seven o'clock in the morning
On a Halsted street car.

Take your pencils
And draw these faces.

Try with your pencils for these crooked faces,
That pig-sticker in one corner—his mouth—
That overall factory girl—her loose cheeks.

Find for your pencils
A way to mark your memory
Of tired empty faces.

After their night's sleep,
In the moist dawn
And cool daybreak,
    Faces
Tired of wishes,
Empty of dreams.

I Am the People, the Mob

I am the people—the mob—the crowd—the mass.
Do you know that all the great work of the world is done through me?
I am the workingman, the inventor, the maker of the world's food and
    clothes.
I am the audience that witnesses history. The Napoleons come from me and
    the Lincolns. They die. And then I send forth more Napoleons and
    Lincolns.
I am the seed ground. I am a prairie that will stand for much plowing.
    Terrible storms pass over me. I forget. The best of me is sucked out and
    wasted. I forget. Everything but Death comes to me and makes me work
    and give up what I have. And I forget.

Sometimes I growl, shake myself and spatter a few red drops for history to
remember. Then—I forget.

When I, the People, learn to remember, when I, the People, use the lessons of
yesterday and no longer forget who robbed me last year, who played me
for a fool—then there will be no speaker in all the world say the name:
"The People," with any fleck of a sneer in his voice or any far-off smile of
derision.

The mob—the crowd—the mass—will arrive then.

Murmurings in a Field Hospital

*[They picked him up in the grass where he had lain two
days in the rain with a piece of shrapnel in his lungs.]*

Come to me only with playthings now . . .
A picture of a singing woman with blue eyes
Standing at a fence of hollyhocks, poppies and sunflowers . . .
Or an old man I remember sitting with children telling stories
Of days that never happened anywhere in the world . . .

No more iron cold and real to handle,
Shaped for a drive straight ahead.
Bring me only beautiful useless things.
Only old home things touched at sunset in the quiet . . .
And at the window one day in summer
Yellow of the new crock of butter
Stood against the red of new climbing roses . . .
And the world was all playthings.

Washerwoman

The washerwoman is a member of the Salvation Army.
And over the tub of suds rubbing underwear clean
She sings that Jesus will wash her sins away
And the red wrongs she has done God and man
Shall be white as driven snow.
Rubbing underwear she sings of the Last Great Washday.

Chicago

> Hog Butcher for the World,
> Tool Maker, Stacker of Wheat,
> Player with Railroads and the Nation's Freight Handler;
> Stormy, husky, brawling,
> City of the Big Shoulders:

They tell me you are wicked and I believe them, for I have seen your painted women under the gas lamps luring the farm boys.

And they tell me you are crooked and I answer: Yes, it is true I have seen the gunman kill and go free to kill again.

And they tell me you are brutal and my reply is: On the faces of women and children I have seen the marks of wanton hunger.

And having answered so I turn once more to those who sneer at this my city, and I give them back the sneer and say to them:

Come and show me another city with lifted head singing so proud to be alive and coarse and strong and cunning.

Flinging magnetic curses amid the toil of piling job on job, here is a tall bold slugger set vivid against the little soft cities;

Fierce as a dog with tongue lapping for action, cunning as a savage pitted against the wilderness,

> Bareheaded,
> Shoveling,
> Wrecking,
> Planning,
> Building, breaking, rebuilding,

Under the smoke, dust all over his mouth, laughing with white teeth,

Under the terrible burden of destiny laughing as a young man laughs,

Laughing even as an ignorant fighter laughs who has never lost a battle,

Bragging and laughing that under his wrist is the pulse, and under his ribs the heart of the people,

> Laughing!

Laughing the stormy, husky, brawling laughter of Youth, half-naked, sweating, proud to be Hog Butcher, Tool Maker, Stacker of Wheat, Player with Railroads and Freight Handler to the Nation.

Archibald MacLeish

Ars Poetica

A poem should be palpable and mute
As a globed fruit,

Dumb
As old medallions to the thumb,

Silent as the sleeve-worn stone
Of casement ledges where the moss has grown—

A poem should be wordless
As the flight of birds.

—⁓—

A poem should be motionless in time
As the moon climbs,

Leaving, as the moon releases
Twig by twig the night-entangled trees,

Leaving, as the moon behind the winter leaves,
Memory by memory the mind—

A poem should be motionless in time
As the moon climbs.

—⁓—

A poem should be equal to:
Not true.

For all the history of grief
An empty doorway and a maple leaf.

For love
The leaning grasses and two lights above the sea—

A poem should not mean
But be.

Cook County

The northeast wind was the wind off the lake
Blowing the oak-leaves pale side out like
Aspen: blowing the sound of the surf far
Inland over the fences: blowing for
Miles over smell of the earth the lake smell in.

The southwest wind was thunder in afternoon.
You saw the wind first in the trumpet vine
And the green went white with the sky and the weather-vane
Whirled on the barn and the doors slammed all together.
After the rain in the grass we used to gather
Wind-fallen cold white apples.

                        The west
Wind was the August wind, the wind over waste
Valleys, over the waterless plains where still
Were skulls of the buffalo, where in the sand stale
Dung lay of wild cattle. The west wind blew
Day after day as the winds on the plains blow
Burning the grass, turning the leaves brown, filling
Noon with the bronze of cicadas, far out falling
Dark on the colorless water, the lake where not
Waves were nor movement.

                    The north wind was at night
When no leaves and the husk on the oak stirs
Only nor birds then. The north wind was stars

Over the whole sky and snow in the ways
And snow on the sand where in summer the water was . . .

The Old Men in the Leaf Smoke

The old men rake the yards for winter
Burning the autumn-fallen leaves.
They have no lives, the one or the other.
The leaves are dead, the old men live
Only a little, light as a leaf,
Left to themselves of all their loves:
Light in the head most often too.
Raking the leaves, raking the lives,
Raking life and leaf together,
The old men smell of burning leaves,
But which is which they wonder—whether
Anyone tells the leaves and loves—
Anyone left, that is, who lives.

Autumn

Sun smudge on the smoky water

ERNEST HEMINGWAY

Champs d'Honneur

Soldiers never do die well;
    Crosses mark the places—
Wooden crosses where they fell,
    Stuck above their faces.
Soldiers pitch and cough and twitch—
    All the world roars red and black;
Soldiers smother in a ditch,
    Choking through the whole attack.

Valentine
    For a Mr. Lee Wilson Dodd and Any of His Friends Who Want It.

Sing a song of critics
pockets full of lye
four and twenty critics
hope that you will die
hope that you will peter out
hope that you will fail
so they can be the first one
be the first to hail
any happy weakening or sign of quick decay.
(All very much alike, weariness too great,
sordid small catastrophes, stack the cards on fate,
very vulgar people, annals of the callous,
dope fiends, soldiers, prostitutes,
men without a gallus)
If you do not like them lads
One thing you can do
Stick them up your ———— lads
My Valentine to you.

The Lady Poet with Footnotes

One lady poet was a nymphomaniac and wrote for Vanity Fair. (1)
One lady poet's husband was killed in the war. (2)
One lady poet wanted her lover but was afraid of having a baby. When she
    finally got married she found she couldn't have a baby. (3)
One lady poet slept with Bill Keely, got fatter and fatter and made half a
    million dollars writing bum plays. (4)
One lady poet had enough to eat. (5)
One lady poet was big and fat and no fool. (6)

———————————

(1) College nymph. Favorite lyric poet of leading editorial writer N.Y. Tribune.
(2) It sold her stuff.
(3) Favorite of State University male virgins. Wonderful on unrequited love.
(4) Stomach's gone bad from liquor. Expects to do something really good
    soon.
(5) It showed in her work.
(6) She smoked cigars all right, but her stuff was no good.

The Age Demanded

The age demanded that we sing
And cut away our tongue.

The age demanded that we flow
And hammered in the bung.

The age demanded that we dance
And jammed us into iron pants.

And in the end the age was handed
The sort of shit that it demanded.

JANET LEWIS

The Indians in the Woods

Ah, the woods, the woods
Where small things
Are distinct and visible,

The berry plant,
The berry leaf, remembered
Line for line.

There are three figures
Walking in the woods
Whose feet press down
Needle and leaf and vine.

The Grandmother Remembers

Ah, the cold, cold days
When we lived
On wintergren berries and nuts,
On caraway seeds.

The deer went over the grass
With wet hooves
To the river to drink.

Their shadows passed
Our tent.

Yvor Winters

To My Infant Daughter

I

Ah, could you now with thinking tongue
Discover what involved lies
In flesh and thought obscurely young,
What earth and age can worst devise!

Then I might thread my path across
Your sin and anguish; I might weigh
Minutely every gain and loss,
And time each motion of my day—

So break the impact of my wrath
To change some instant of your pain,
And clear the darkness from my path
That your decay were not in vain.

Whose hands will lay those hands to rest,
Those hands themselves, no more the same,
Will weeping lay them on the breast,
A token only and a name?

II

Alas, that I should be
So old, and you so small!
You will think naught of me
When your dire hours befall.

Take few men to your heart!
Unstable, fierce, unkind,
The ways that men impart.
True love is slow to find.

True art is slow to grow.
Like a belated friend,
It comes to let one know
Of what has had an end.

For My Father's Grave

Here lies one sweet of heart.
Stay! Thou too must depart.
In silence set thy store—
These ashes speak no more.

KENNETH FEARING

Obituary

Take him away, he's as dead as they die,
Hear that ambulance bell, his eyes are staring straight at death;
Look at the fingers growing stiff, touch the face already cold, see the stars in
the sky, look at the stains on the street,

Look at the ten-ton truck that came rolling along fast and stretched him out
cold,

Then turn out his pockets and make the crowd move on.
Sergeant, what was his name? What's the driver's name? What's your name,
sergeant?
Go through his clothes,
Take out the cigars, the money, the papers, the keys, take everything there is,

And give a dollar and a half to the Standard Oil. It was his true-blue friend.
Give the key of his flat to the D.A.R. They were friends of his, the best a man
ever had.
Take out the pawnticket, wrap it, seal it, send it along to the People's Gas.
They were life-long pals. It was more than his brother. They were just like
twins.

Give away the shoes,
Give his derby away. Donate his socks to the Guggenheim fund,
Let the Morgans hold the priceless bills, and leaflets, and racing tips under
lock and key,
And give Mr. Hoover the pint of gin,
Because they're all good men. And they were friends of his.

Don't forget Gene Tunney. Don't forget Will Hays. Don't forget Al Capone.
Don't forget the I.R.T.
Give them his matches to remember him by.
They lived with him, in the same old world. And they're good men, too.

Twentieth-Century Blues

What do you call it, bobsled champion, and you, too, Olympic roller-coaster
     ace,
High-diving queen, what is the word,
Number one man on the Saturday poker squad, motion-picture star
     incognito as a home girl, life of the party or you, the serious type, what is
     it, what is it,

When it's just like a fever shooting up and up and up but there are no chills
     and there is no fever,
Just exactly like a song, like a knockout, like a dream, like a book,

What is the word, when you know that all the lights of all the cities of all the
     world are burning bright as day, and you know that some time they all go
     out for you,
Or your taxi rolls and rolls through streets made of velvet, what is the feeling,
     what is the feeling when the radio never ends, but the hour, the swift, the
     electric, the invisible hour does not stop and does not turn,
What does it mean, when the get-away money burns in dollars big as moons,
     but where is there to go that's just exactly right,
What have you won, plunger, when the 20-to-1 comes in; what have you won,
     salesman, when the dotted line is signed; irresistible lover, when her
     eyelids flutter shut at last, what have you really, finally won;
And what is gone, soldier, soldier, step-and-a-half marine who saw the whole
     world; hot-tip addict, what is always just missed; picker of crumbs, how
     much has been lost, denied, what are all the things destroyed
Question mark, question mark, question mark, question mark,
And you, fantasy Frank, and dreamworld Dora and hallucination Harold, and
     delusion Dick, and nightmare Ned,

What is it, how do you say it, what does it mean, what's the word,
That miracle thing, the thing that can't be so, quote, unquote, but just the
     same it's true,
That third-rail, million-volt exclamation mark, that ditto, ditto, ditto,
That stop, stop, go.

Any Man's Advice to His Son

If you have lost the radio beam, then guide yourself by the sun or the stars.
(By the North Star at night, and in daytime by the compass and the sun.)
Should the sky be overcast and there are neither stars nor a sun, then steer by
dead reckoning.
If the wind and direction and speed are not known, then trust to your wits
and your luck.

Do you follow me? Do you understand? Or is this too difficult to learn?
But you must and you will, it is important that you do,
Because there may be troubles even greater than these that I have said.

Because, remember this: Trust no man fully.
Remember: If you must shoot at another man squeeze, do not jerk the
trigger. Otherwise you may miss and die, yourself, at the hand of some
other man's son.
And remember: In all this world there is nothing so easily squandered, or
once gone, so completely lost as life.
I tell you this because I remember you when you were small,
And because I remember all your monstrous infant boasts and lies,
And the way you smiled, and how you ran and climbed, as no one else quite
did, and how you fell and were bruised,
And because there is no other person, anywhere on earth, who remembers
these things as clearly as I do now.

GEORGE DILLON

The Hours of the Day

The city stirred about me softly and distant.
Its iron voice flew upward into the air.
All day I wondered that I walked and listened
As if in freedom there—

And wondered how love so led me and removed me:
My breath coming deep and glad, for she had drawn it;
My eyes being wild with pride because she loved me;
My heart being shielded with her beauty upon it.

Snow

I

Amid the holy weather of winter, one speaks
Wisely of many things, believing nothing.
Truth only does not cringe from the cold. She passes
Clear and incredible through the white weeks.

Lovers, love growing a little gaunt and gay,
Become articulate on a winter day,
When flashing firelight captures and composes.
He has brought flowers, as if to say,
"See,—there are flowers even when it snows.
What if the wind has blown a few petals away?
What if we cry a little for one lost rose?
There are so many roses."

II

"As white and noiseless as snow," she says; and he,
"Roses and snow are very much the same.

White roses are, at least; and as I came
Hurrying here, roses occurred to me.

"Sometimes when people dream, seeing the snow,
They dream of roses, and are taken with dread
And an old, innocent pity for the dead,
And carry garlands to their snowy graves,
Feeling somehow they will awake and know."

She smiles and stares, as if she had not heard
Each aimless, inescapable word.
"Can you recall that morning by blue waves
You told me how, beholding death, you knew
No faith in it, but only grief? Do you
Believe death now?"

                          "I think that I believe
Only what I can make no answer to;
And what can not engage me, can not grieve,—
This snow, for instance, blowing down the window.
And there is nothing nearer death than snow."

Has she not heard? Or does her converse flow
Not with the word, but with the innuendo?

"When I recall it, sitting here to-day,
That extreme spring seems very long ago,
And all its beauties very far away;
And I can hardly remember, watching the snow,
What lost enchantment guided us amid
What lost delight,—so beautiful and so
Remote, and like a dream it seems, as though
It never happened. Perhaps it never did."

III
"One understands so much, believing nothing,"
He says; "and many things must be forgot.
There will be snow wherever I walk tomorrow
Whether it snows or not.

"We speak truly of what is dead and gone,
But of the other things we have nothing to say.
Now we shall always feel the snow coming on,
No matter how fair the day.

"You will remember what I have prophesied.
After a few more winters we shall meet
Again; I'll come again down this white street
And talk to you,—and there will be more to be said,
We having lived a little longer, and died;
For we are always dying till we are dead."

IV
He is not sure of this. All he is sure of
Is the snow sidling softly along the pane,
Drifting away and blowing back again,
And falling, wordless, and resolute, and slow.

Not stars above the sea, not wind or rain
Inhabits so enormously the brain.

There is nothing nearer nothing than snow.

ELDER OLSON

The Presence

How absence becomes presence
After death!
Not here, no; no, but near: in the next room
Sleeping, or reading; only outdoors
—The light step almost heard? A fragrance lingering?
The air still stirring
As a curtain drifts back with a failing breeze?

Seen, even, sometimes—instantly vanishing?
Always in a *there* so close to *here;*
Making no sound
But surely, surely faint
Echoes of echoes; or silence, silence, yes,
But silence just before,
Just after, speech.

The absent, present still
As though—as though
What love loses, love itself restores.

JOHN FREDERICK NIMS

Love Poem

My clumsiest dear, whose hands shipwreck vases,
At whose quick touch all glasses chip and ring,
Whose palms are bulls in china, burrs in linen,
And have no cunning with any soft thing

Except all ill-at-ease fidgeting people:
The refugee uncertain at the door
You make at home; deftly you steady
The drunk clambering on his undulant floor.

Unpredictable dear, the taxi drivers' terror,
Shrinking from far headlights pale as a dime
Yet leaping before red apoplectic streetcars—
Misfit in any space. And never on time.

A wrench in clocks and the solar system. Only
With words and people and love you move at ease;
In traffic of wit expertly manoeuvre
And keep us, all devotion, at your knees,

Forgetting your coffee spreading on our flannel,
Your lipstick grinning on our coat,
So gayly in love's unbreakable heaven
Our souls on glory of spilt bourbon float.

Be with me, darling, early and late. Smash glasses—
I will study wry music for your sake.
For should your hands drop white and empty
All the toys of the world would break.

The Young Ionia

If you could come on the late train for
  The same walk
Or a hushed talk by the fireplace
  When the ash flares
As a heart could (if a heart would) to
  Recall you,
To recall all in a long
  Look, to enwrap you
As it once had when the rain streamed on the
  Fall air,
And we knew, then, it was all wrong,
  It was love lost
And a year lost of the few years we
  Account most—
But the bough blew and the cloud
  Blew and the sky fell
From its rose ledge on the wood's rim to
  The wan brook,
And the clock read to the half-dead
  A profound page
As the cloud broke and the moon spoke and the
  Door shook—

If you could come, and it meant come at the
  Steep price
We regret yet as the debt swells
  In the nighttime
And the *could come, if you could* hum in
  The skull's drum
And the limbs writhe till the bed
  Cries like a hurt thing—
If you could—ah but the moon's dead and the
  Clock's dead.
For we know now: we can give all
  But it won't do,
Not the day's length nor the black strength nor
  The blood's flush.

What we took once for a sure thing,
    For delight's right,
For the clear eve with its wild star in
    The sunset,
We would have back at the old
    Cost, at the old grief
And we beg love for the same pain—for a
    Last chance!
Then the god turns with a low
    Laugh (as the leaves hush)
But the eyes ice and there's no twice: the
    Benign gaze
Upon some woe but on ours no.
    And the leaves rush.

Tide Turning

Through salt marsh, grassy channel where the shark's
A rumor—lean, alongside—rides our boat;
Four of us off with picnic-things and wine.
Past tufty clutters of the mud called *pluff,*
Sun on the ocean tingles like a kiss.
About the fourth hour of the falling tide.

The six-hour-falling, six-hour-rising tide
Turns heron-haunts to alleys for the shark.
Tide-waters kiss and loosen; loosen, kiss.
Black-hooded terns blurt kazoo-talk—our boat
Now in midchannel and now rounding pluff.
Lolling, we eye the mud-tufts. Eye the wine.

The Atlantic, off there, dazzles. Who said wine—
Dark sea? Not this sea. Not at noon. The tide
Runs gold as chablis over sumps of pluff.
Too shallow here for lurkings of the shark,
His nose-cone, grin unsmiling. *Cr-ush!* The boat
Shocks, shudders—grounded. An abrupt tough kiss.

Our outboard's dug a mud-trough. Call that kiss?
Bronze knee bruised. A fair ankle gashed. With "wine-
Dark blood" a bard's on target here. The boat
Swivels, propeller in a pit, as tide
Withdraws in puddles round us—shows the shark-
Grey fin, grey flank, grey broadening humps of pluff.

Fingers that trailed in water, fume in pluff.
Wrist-deep, they learn how octopuses kiss.
Then—shark fins? No. Three dolphins there—shhh!—arc
Coquettish. As on TV. Cup of wine
To you, slaphappy sidekicks! with the tide's
Last hour a mudflat draining round the boat.

The hourglass turns. Look, tricklings toward the boat.
The first hour, poky, picks away at pluff.
The second, though, swirls currents. Then the tide's
Third, fourth—abundance! The great ocean's kiss.
The last two slacken. So? We're free, for wine
And gaudier mathematics. Toast the shark,

Good shark, a no-show. Glory floats our boat.
We, with the wine remaining—done with pluff—
Carouse on the affluent kisses of the tide.

Trick or Treat

Holy and hokey, Hallowe'en.
That kindergarten of witches in the street,
Skeletons (but with tummies) doorbell high
Piping up, "Trick or treat!"

A hoyden by Goya with her Breughel chum
Scrabbles black-orange jelly beans—then scoots.
—To think I saw *you*, spangled so,
Rouged in your Puss-in-Boots

Some forty and more years ago!
Memory: the reruns in full color seem
As three-dimensional as *now*.
Could it be *now's* the dream

We've been bewitched by?—spirited
Into this crinkled skin, this ashy hair,
Starch at the joints—this hand-me-down
Raggedy gear we wear?

We've dealt with clothes before; know well
Just what they hallow, and how they fall away
Strewing the floor in moonlight; yes,
Into and past midday.

Good costumes then. But now let's play
Pretend with those glittering infants at the door,
Now that our autumn's come and soon
The snows arrive—before

We're out of costumes and a place to play,
Of zest for the zany carnival in the street,
Out of breath, out of world and time
Teasing with "Trick or treat!"

KARL SHAPIRO

V-Letter

I love you first because your face is fair,
    Because your eyes Jewish and blue,
Set sweetly with the touch of foreignness
Above the cheekbones, stare rather than dream.
Often your countenance recalls a boy
    Blue-eyed and small, whose silent mischief
Tortured his parents and compelled my hate
        To wish his ugly death.
Because of this reminder, my soul's trouble,
And for your face, so often beautiful,
        I love you, wish you life.

I love you first because you wait, because
    For your own sake, I cannot write
Beyond these words. I love you for these words
That sting and creep like insects and leave filth.
I love you for the poverty you cry
    And I bend down with tears of steel
That melt your hand like wax, not for this war
        The droplets shattering
Those candle-glowing fingers of my joy,
But for your name of agony, my love,
        That cakes my mouth with salt.

And all your imperfections and perfections
    And all your magnitude of grace
And all this love explained and unexplained
Is just a breath. I see you woman-size
And this looms larger and more goddess-like
    Than silver goddesses on screens.
I see you in the ugliness of light,
        Yet you are beautiful,

And in the dark of absence your full length
Is such as meets my body to the full
            Though I am starved and huge.

You turn me from these days as from a scene
        Out of an open window far
Where lies the foreign city and the war.
You are my home and in your spacious love
I dream to march as under flaring flags
        Until the door is gently shut.
Give me the tearless lesson of your pride,
            Teach me to live and die
As one deserving anonymity,
The mere devotion of a house to keep
            A woman and a man.

Give me the free and poor inheritance
        Of our own kind, not furniture
Of education, nor the prophet's pose,
The general cause of words, the hero's stance,
The ambitions incommensurable with flesh,
        But the drab makings of a room
Where sometimes in the afternoon of thought
            The brief and blinding flash
May light the enormous chambers of your will
And show the gracious Parthenon that time
            Is ever measured by.

As groceries in a pantry gleam and smile
        Because they are important weights
Bought with the metal minutes of your pay,
So do these hours stand in solid rows,
The dowry for a use in common life.
        I love you first because your years
Lead to my matter-of-fact and simple death
            Or to our open marriage,
And I pray nothing for my safety back,
Not even luck, because our love is whole
            Whether I live or fail.

The Bourgeois Poet

The bourgeois poet closes the door of his study and lights his pipe. Why am I in this box, he says to himself (although it is exactly as he planned). The bourgeois poet sits down at his inoffensive desk—a door with legs, a door turned table—and almost approves the careful disarray of books, papers, magazines and such artifacts as thumbtacks. The bourgeois poet is already out of matches and gets up. It is too early in the morning for any definite emotion and the B.P. smokes. It is beautiful in the midlands: green fields and tawny fields, sorghum the color of red morocco bindings, distant new neighborhoods, cleanly and treeless, and the Veterans Hospital fronted with a shimmering Indian Summer tree. The Beep feels seasonal, placid as a melon, neat as a child's football lying under the tree, waiting for whose hands to pick it up.

Crossing Lincoln Park

Dit le corbeau, jamais plus.
  —Mallarmé

Car locked, I started home across the grass,
A kind of island with a stand of oaks
Washed round on all sides by the swish of cars,
To where I lived, a hundred yards in view.
Quarried apartments rose on every hand,
Scoriac Gothic shouldering solid glass
Hemming me in, reflecting a blank sky.
Briefcase and I happily homeward strode
Through ankle-grass, when something at my shoe
Darkly turned over, what I never knew,
For down came the crow and with a sudden blow,
Its great wings beating, slashed at my face
With croak and scream and yellow beak
Screeching me out. I did not stop to think
But leapt and sprinted toward the curb, the bird
Cursing, crisscrossing, driving at my face,
Crashing my shoulders with its filthy wings.

Ugly, omnivorous offal-eating crow,
Bird of ill omen,
Eater of turd and dead fish, get thy beak
From out my heart! My eyeglasses flew off,
I stumbled forward, clutching my briefcase,
Fanning away the bird with naked hand,
Until I reached the street where solid cars
Bumper to bumper blocked my flight,
And still the crow surrounded me and struck
Till I broke through and in the door and up
The elevator to the velvet hall
And to the door and in, where your bright smile
Changed instantly to—"White!" you said.
"Your face whiter than chalk!"

Editing Poetry

Next to my office where I edit poems ("Can poems be edited?") there is the Chicago Models Club. All day the girls stroll past my door where I am editing poems, behind my head a signed photograph of Rupert Brooke, handsomer than any movie star. I edit, keeping one eye peeled for the models, straining my ears to hear what they say. In there they photograph the girls on the bamboo furniture, glossies for the pulsing facades of night spots. One day the manager brings me flowers, a huge and damaged bouquet: hurt gladiolas, overly open roses, long-leaping ferns (least hurt), and bruised carnations. I accept the gift, remainder of last night's opening (where?), debut of lower-class blondes. I distribute the flowers in the other poetry rooms, too formal-looking for our disarray.

Now after every model's bow to the footlights the manager brings more flowers, hurt gladiolas, overly open roses, long-leaping ferns, and bruised carnations. I edit poems to the click of sharp high heels, flanked by the swords of lavender debut, whiffing the cinnamon of crepe-paper-pink carnations of the bruised and lower-class blondes.

Behind me rears my wall of books, most formidable of human barriers. No flower depresses me like the iris but these I have a fondness for. They bring stale memories over the threshold of the street. They bring the night of cloth palm trees and soft plastic leopard chairs, night of sticky drinks, the shining rhinestone hour in the dark-blue mirror, the peroxide chat of models and photogenic morn.

Today the manager brings all gladioli. A few rose petals lie in the corridor. The mail is heavy this morning.

HENRY RAGO

A Child's Birthday

1

A Switzerland upon
 The continent of our years
Your two years

The heap of blocks
 With burrowing trains and traffic
In the floor's traffic

Shine, a holiday
 Whose lights plunge to surprise
A child's blue lakes

Whose hours sing out from toy
 Prisons of clocks
A chorus of surprise.

2

Two years a land, its seasons
Jeweled: glacier of sun!
Held beyond holding,
Bright neutrality, free
Of the risk you are, being
What we risk, being
What we ask,

Yield only, clear
In all your lights,
Dearly this
Clearest
Diminutive
Of mountains tossed
In a fiercer love.

The Distances

This house, pitched now
The dark wide stretch
Of plains and ocean
To these hills over
The night-filled river,
Billows with night,
Swells with the rooms
Of sleeping children, pulls
Slowly returns, pulls and holds,
Is held where we
Lock all distances!

Ah, how the distances
Spiral from that
Secrecy:
Room,
Rooms, roof
Spun to the huge
Midnight, and into
The rings and rings of stars.

JOHN DICKSON

The Aragon Ballroom

I could hear the music as I waited to be born—
Wayne King the Waltz King and his golden sax
rolling across the roofs and through the alleys
and into our windows down the street
making my feet move, making me wonder
what sort of planet I'd come to anyway.
And later as I crawled through Persian patterns of the rugs
and later still as I memorized my night paths
behind the stores and through the shadowy streets,
clarinets and trumpets heralded my way.

But in less time than you'd think I'd learned that place—
by day how it slept through roars of the passing L's,
through sooty pigeons cooing at the windows
and by night how it turned to plaster Spain inside—
gold statues of caballeros and their senoritas
and the thick red carpet stretching from the ticket taker
into the illusion paradise of yellow balconies
with vines and bright balloons and tiled roofs
that scraped the Spanish sky of faint electric stars.

And all the Lorettas and Teresas, Margies and Maries
half floosie, half madonna in their first high heels,
the smell of soap, the smell of sharp cologne,
drawn there on those nights to come alive
with some Sam or Tony, Mario or Fred,
lanky, muscle-bound, or Mr. Five-by-Five
but necessarily capable of serious dancing—
either to the organ shuddering through the building
or to a wispy saxophone, snare drum and brushes
for drifting and weaving around the floor.

And off in the haze beyond the dancers
or up in the shadows of the balcony
the crewcuts and greasers busy as scheming roosters,
surveying the crop, considering anything fair game—
girls who lived for their mothers
or those with whom no one would dance.
Girls still homesick for small town families
or those who could barely look up from their shyness
lost in their loneliness of makeup and corsage,
blaming themselves for even being there.

And always on the fire escape of summer nights,
the bright dress and dark suit of intermission.
And always at the tables of the soft drink stand
those long conversations of serious intent.
And always the ultimate weddings of relatives and wine
held in the Halls for All Occasions,
always the painted wedding photographs
of responsible grooms and basic brides—
eyes blue, lips red, and cheeks unnatural pink.

But now only the whisper of those lives
rushes through the empty building
with echoes of Old Black Magic and Small Hotel,
Take the A-Train, Adios, and Blue Room.
And all those nights, as though embedded in amber,
kept safe or worn as charms,
through hospitals or wars or blahs
as a reminder of those nights in Spain
or just of partners who could really dance.

Poemectomy

The trouble was they left her too much alone,
feeding on books and dreaming of love
and watching willow tree shadows
sway across the polluted river.

Instead of running about and laughing
and talking of everything with her friends,
she grew wistful and wan and dangerously thin
and after hours of pondering such things as
frost on a window
or the frail filament of an old nun on a bus,
she would look weaker than ever
and complain of a terrible pain in her chest.

Until late one night when they rushed her to the hospital
and worked over her for hours in Emergency,
removing a huge tumorous verse
so horrible that even the nurses grew sick when they saw it.
For days afterwards
she was draining words where the stitches were
and then only a few letters now and then
until finally the wound was completely healed.
But there's still a large scar where they made the incision
and even now when she sees things
like a bird on a twig
or the shadow of leaves on the sand
or a butterfly wing washed up on the shore,
the scar turns pink or a livid red
and you almost wonder
if they succeeded in getting out all the infection.

GWENDOLYN BROOKS

The Coora Flower

Today I learned the *coora* flower
grows high in the mountains of Itty-go-luba Bésa.
Province Meechee.
Pop. 39.

Now I am coming home.
This, at least, is Real, and what I know.

It was restful, learning nothing necessary.
School is tiny vacation. At least you can sleep.
At least you can think of love or feeling your boy friend against you
(which is not free from grief.)

But now it's Real Business.
I am Coming Home.

My mother will be screaming in an almost dirty dress.
The crack is gone. So a Man will be in the house.

I must watch myself.
I must not dare to sleep.

The Lovers of the Poor

              arrive. The Ladies from the Ladies' Betterment League
Arrive in the afternoon, the late light slanting
In diluted gold bars across the boulevard brag
Of proud, seamed faces with mercy and murder hinting
Here, there, interrupting, all deep and debonair,
The pink paint on the innocence of fear;

Walk in a gingerly manner up the hall.
Cutting with knives served by their softest care,
Served by their love, so barbarously fair.
Whose mothers taught: You'd better not be cruel!
You had better not throw stones upon the wrens!
Herein they kiss and coddle and assault
Anew and dearly in the innocence
With which they baffle nature. Who are full,
Sleek, tender-clad, fit, fiftyish, a-glow, all
Sweetly abortive, hinting at fat fruit,
Judge it high time that fiftyish fingers felt
Beneath the lovelier planes of enterprise.
To resurrect. To moisten with milky chill.
To be a random hitching-post or plush.
To be, for wet eyes, random and handy hem.
       Their guild is giving money to the poor.
The worthy poor. The very very worthy
And beautiful poor. Perhaps just not too swarthy?
Perhaps just not too dirty nor too dim
Nor—passionate. In truth, what they could wish
Is—something less than derelict or dull.
Not staunch enough to stab, though, gaze for gaze!
God shield them sharply from the beggar-bold!
The noxious needy ones whose battle's bald
Nonetheless for being voiceless, hits one down.
       But it's all so bad! and entirely too much for them.
The stench; the urine, cabbage, and dead beans,
Dead porridges of assorted dusty grains,
The old smoke, *heavy* diapers, and, they're told,
Something called chitterlings. The darkness. Drawn
Darkness, or dirty light. The soil that stirs.
The soil that looks the soil of centuries.
And for that matter the general oldness. Old
Wood. Old marble. Old tile. Old old old.
Not homekind Oldness! Not Lake Forest, Glencoe.
Nothing is sturdy, nothing is majestic,
There is no quiet drama, no rubbed glaze, no
Unkillable infirmity of such
A tasteful turn as lately they have left,
Glencoe, Lake Forest, and to which their cars

Must presently restore them. When they're done
With dullards and distortions of this fistic
Patience of the poor and put-upon.

They've never seen such a make-do-ness as
Newspaper rugs before! In this, this "flat,"
Their hostess is gathering up the oozed, the rich
Rugs of the morning (tattered! The bespattered....),
Readies to spread clean rugs for afternoon.
Here is a scene for you. The Ladies look,
In horror, behind a substantial citizeness
Whose trains clank out across her swollen heart.
Who, arms akimbo, almost fills a door.
All tumbling children, quilts dragged to the floor
And tortured thereover, potato peelings, soft-
Eyed kitten, hunched-up, haggard, to-be-hurt.

Their League is allotting largesse to the Lost.
But to put their clean, their pretty money, to put
Their money collected from delicate rose-fingers
Tipped with their hundred flawless rose-nails seems . . .

They own Spode, Lowestoft, candelabra,
Mantels, and hostess gowns, and sunburst clocks,
Turtle soup, Chippendale, red satin "hangings,"
Aubussons and Hattie Carnegie. They Winter
In Palm Beach; cross the Water in June; attend,
When suitable, the nice Art Institute;
Buy the right books in the best bindings; saunter
On Michigan, Easter mornings, in sun or wind.
Oh Squalor! This sick four-story hulk, this fibre
With fissures everywhere! Why, what are bringings
Of loathe-love largesse? What shall peril hungers
So old old, what shall flatter the desolate?
Tin can, blocked fire escape and chitterling
And swaggering seeking youth and the puzzled wreckage
Of the middle passage, and urine and stale shames
And, again, the porridges of the underslung
And children children children. Heavens! That
Was a rat, surely, off there, in the shadows? Long
And long-tailed? Gray? The Ladies from the Ladies'
Betterment League agree it will be better
To achieve the outer air that rights and steadies,

To hie to a house that does not holler, to ring
Bells elsetime, better presently to cater
To no more Possibilities, to get
Away. Perhaps the money can be posted.
Perhaps they two may choose another Slum!
Some serious sooty half-unhappy home!—
Where loathe-love likelier may be invested.
　　　　　Keeping their scented bodies in the center
Of the hall as they walk down the hysterical hall,
They allow their lovely skirts to graze no wall,
Are off at what they manage of a canter,
And, resuming all the clues of what they were,
Try to avoid inhaling the laden air.

We Real Cool

The Pool Players.
Seven at the Golden Shovel.

We real cool. We
Left school. We

Lurk late. We
Strike straight. We

Sing sin. We
Thin gin. We

Jazz June. We
Die soon.

The Near-Johannesburg Boy

> *In South Africa the Black*
> *children ask each other:*
> *"Have you been detained yet?*
> *How many times have you been*
> *detained?"*

> _____

> *The herein boy does not live*
> *in Johannesburg. He is not*
> *allowed to live there. Perhaps*
> *he lives in Soweto.*

My way is from woe to wonder.
A Black boy near Johannesburg, hot
in the Hot Time.

Those people
do not like Black among the colors.
They do not like our
calling our country ours.
They say our country is not ours.

Those people.
Visiting the world as I visit the world.
Those people.
Their bleach is puckered and cruel.

It is work to speak of my Father. My Father.
His body was whole till they Stopped it.
Suddenly.
With a short shot.
But, before that, physically tall and among us,
he died every day. Every moment.
My Father. . . .
First was the crumpling.
No. First was the Fist-and-the-Fury.
Last was the crumpling. It is
a little used rag that is Under, it is not,
it is not my Father gone down.

About my Mother. My Mother
was this loud laugher
below the sunshine, below the starlight at festival.
My Mother is still this loud laugher!
Still moving straight in the Getting-It-Done (as she names it.)
Oh a strong eye is my Mother.
Except when it seems we are lax in our looking.

Well, enough of slump, enough of Old Story.
Like a clean spear of fire
I am moving. I am not still. I am ready
to be ready.
I shall flail
in the Hot Time.

Tonight I walk with
a hundred of playmates to where
the hurt Black of our skin is forbidden.
There, in the dark that is our dark, there,
a-pulse across earth that is our earth, there,
there exulting, there Exactly, there redeeming, there Roaring Up
(oh my Father)
we shall forge with the Fist-and-the-Fury:
we shall flail in the Hot Time:
we shall
we shall

The Mother

Abortions will not let you forget.
You remember the children you got that you did not get,
The damp small pulps with a little or with no hair,
The singers and workers that never handled the air.
You will never neglect or beat
Them, or silence or buy with a sweet.
You will never wind up the sucking-thumb
Or scuttle off ghosts that come.
You will never leave them, controlling your luscious sigh,
Return for a snack of them, with gobbling mother-eye.

I have heard in the voices of the wind the voices of my dim killed children.
I have contracted. I have eased
My dim dears at the breasts they could never suck.
I have said, Sweets, if I sinned, if I seized
Your luck
And your lives from your unfinished reach,
If I stole your births and your names,
Your straight baby tears and your games,
Your stilted or lovely loves, your tumults, your marriages, aches, and your
    deaths,
If I poisoned the beginnings of your breaths,
Believe that even in my deliberateness I was not deliberate.
Though why should I whine,
Whine that the crime was other than mine?—
Since anyhow you are dead.
Or rather, or instead,
You were never made.

But that too, I am afraid,
Is faulty: oh, what shall I say, how is the truth to be said?
You were born, you had body, you died.
It is just that you never giggled or planned or cried.

Believe me, I loved you all.
Believe me, I knew you, though faintly, and I loved, I loved you
All

Gay Chaps at the Bar

    Souvenir for Staff Sergeant Raymond Brooks and Every Other Soldier

    gay chaps at the bar

. . . and guys I knew in the States, young officers, return from the front crying and
trembling. Gay chaps at the bar in Los Angeles, Chicago, New York. . . .
    —Lieutenant William Couch in the South Pacific

We knew how to order. Just the dash
Necessary. The length of gaiety in good taste.
Whether the raillery should be slightly iced
And given green, or served up hot and lush.
And we knew beautifully how to give to women
The summer spread, the tropics, of our love.
When to persist, or hold a hunger off.
Knew white speech. How to make a look an omen.
But nothing every taught us to be islands.
And smart, athletic language for this hour
Was not in the curriculum. No stout
Lesson showed how to chat with death. We brought
No brass fortissimo, among our talents,
To holler down the lions in this air.

still do I keep my look, my identity . . .

Each body has its art, its precious prescribed
Pose, that even in passion's droll contortions, waltzes,
Or push of pain—or when a grief has stabbed,
Or hatred hacked—is its, and nothing else's.
Each body has its pose. No other stock
That is irrevocable, perpetual
And its to keep. In castle or in shack.
With rags or robes. Through good, nothing, or ill.
And even in death a body, like no other
On any hill or plain or crawling cot
Or gentle for the lilyless hasty pall
(Having twisted, gagged, and then sweet-ceased to bother),
Shows the old personal art, the look. Shows what
It showed at baseball. What it showed in school.

my dreams, my works, must wait till after hell

I hold my honey and I store my bread
In little jars and cabinets of my will.
I label clearly, and each latch and lid
I bid, Be firm till I return from hell.
I am very hungry, I am incomplete.
And none can tell when I may dine again.

No man can give me any word but Wait,
The puny light. I keep eyes pointed in;
Hoping that, when the devil days of my hurt
Drag out to their last dregs and I resume
On such legs as are left me, in such heart
As I can manage, remember to go home,
My taste will not have turned insensitive
To honey and bread old purity could love.

To Black Women

Sisters,
where there is cold silence—
no hallelujahs, no hurrahs at all, no handshakes,
no neon red or blue, no smiling faces—
prevail.
Prevail across the editors of the world
who are obsessed, self-honeying and self-crowned
in the seduced arena.

    It has been a
hard trudge, with fainting, bandaging and death.
There have been startling confrontations.
There have been tramplings. Tramplings
of monarchs and of other men.

But there remain large countries in your eyes.
Shrewd sun.

The civil balance.
The listening secrets.
And you create and train your flowers still.

Malcolm X

For Dudley Randall

Original.
Ragged-round.
Rich-robust.

He had the hawk-man's eyes.
We gasped. We saw the maleness.
The maleness raking out and making guttural the air
and pushing us to walls.

And in a soft and fundamental hour
a sorcery devout and vertical
beguiled the world.

He opened us—
who was a key,

who was a man.

From *The Blackstone Rangers*

GANG GIRLS

A Rangerette

Gang Girls are sweet exotics.
Mary Ann
uses the nutrients of her orient,
but sometimes sighs for Cities of blue and jewel
beyond her Ranger rim of Cottage Grove.
(Bowery Boys, Disciples, Whip-Birds will
dissolve no margins, stop no savory sanctities.)

Mary is
a rose in a whiskey glass.

Mary's
Februaries shudder and are gone. Aprils
fret frankly, lilac hurries on.
Summer is a hard irregular ridge.
October looks away.
And that's the Year!
                    Save for her bugle-love.
Save for the bleat of not-obese devotion.

Save for Somebody Terribly Dying, under
the philanthropy of robins. Save for her Ranger
bringing
an amount of rainbow in a string-drawn bag.
"Where did you get the diamond?" Do not ask:
but swallow, straight, the spirals of his flask
and assist him at your zipper; pet his lips
and help him clutch you.

Love's another departure.
Will there be any arrivals, confirmations?
Will there be gleaning?

Mary, the Shakedancer's child
from the rooming-flat, pants carefully, peers at
her laboring lover. . . .
                    Mary! Mary Ann!
Settle for sandwiches! settle for stocking caps!
for sudden blood, aborted carnival,
the props and niceties of non-loneliness—
the rhymes of Leaning.

Uncle Seagram

My uncle likes me too much.

I am five and a half years old, and in kindergarten.
In kindergarten everything is clean.

My uncle is six feet tall with seven bumps on his chin.
My uncle is six feet tall, and he stumbles.
He stumbles because of his Wonderful Medicine
packed in his pocket all times.

Family is ma and pa and my uncle,
three brothers, three sisters, and me.

Every night at my house we play checkers and dominoes.
My uncle sits *close.*
There aren't any shoes or socks on his feet.
Under the table a big toe tickles my ankle.
Under the oilcloth his thin knee beats into mine.
And mashes. And mashes.

When we look at TV
my uncle picks *me* to sit on his lap.
As I sit, he gets hard in the middle.
I squirm, but he keeps me, and kisses my ear.

I am not even a girl.

Once, when I went to the bathroom,
my uncle noticed, came in, shut the door,
put his long white tongue in my ear,
and whispered "We're Best Friends, and Family,
and we know how to keep Secrets."

My uncle likes me too much. I am worried.

I do not like my uncle anymore.

A Bronzeville Mother Loiters in Mississippi. Meanwhile, a Mississippi Mother Burns Bacon

From the first it had been like a
Ballad. It had the beat inevitable. It had the blood.
A wildness cut up, and tied in little bunches,

Like the four-line stanzas of the ballads she had never quite
Understood—the ballads they had set her to, in school.

Herself: the milk-white maid, the "maid mild"
Of the ballad. Pursued
By the Dark Villain. Rescued by the Fine Prince.
The Happiness-Ever-After.
That was worth anything.
It was good to be a "maid mild."
That made the breath go fast.

Her bacon burned. She
Hastened to hide it in the step-on can, and
Drew more strips from the meat case. The eggs and sour-milk biscuits
Did well. She set out a jar
Of her new quince preserve.
. . . But there was a something about the matter of the Dark Villain.
He should have been older, perhaps.
The hacking down of a villain was more fun to think about
When his menace possessed undisputed breadth, undisputed height,
And a harsh kind of vice.
And best of all, when his history was cluttered
With the bones of many eaten knights and princesses.

The fun was disturbed, then all but nullified
When the Dark Villain was a blackish child
Of fourteen, with eyes still too young to be dirty,
And a mouth too young to have lost every reminder
Of its infant softness.

That boy must have been surprised! For
These were grown-ups. Grown-ups were supposed to be wise.
And the Fine Prince—and that other—so tall, so broad, so
Grown! Perhaps the boy had never guessed
That the trouble with grown-ups was that under the magnificent shell of
    adulthood, just under,
Waited the baby full of tantrums.

It occurred to her that there may have been something
Ridiculous in the picture of the Fine Prince

Rushing (rich with the breadth and height and
Mature solidness whose lack, in the Dark Villain, was impressing her,
Confronting her more and more as this first day after the trial
And acquittal wore on) rushing
With his heavy companion to hack down (unhorsed)
That little foe.
So much had happened, she could not remember now what that foe had
    done
Against her, or if anything had been done.
The one thing in the world that she did know and knew
With terrifying clarity was that her composition
Had disintegrated. That, although the pattern prevailed,
The breaks were everywhere. That she could think
Of no thread capable of the necessary
Sew-work.

She made the babies sit in their places at the table.
Then, before calling Him, she hurried
To the mirror with her comb and lipstick. It was necessary
To be more beautiful than ever.
The beautiful wife.
For sometimes she fancied he looked at her as though
Measuring her. As if he considered, Had she been worth It?

Had *she* been worth the blood, the cramped cries, the little stuttering
    bravado,
The gradual dulling of those Negro eyes,
The sudden, overwhelming *little-boyness* in that barn?
Whatever she might feel or half-feel, the lipstick necessarily was something
    apart. He must never conclude
That she had not been worth It.

He sat down, the Fine Prince, and
Began buttering a biscuit. He looked at his hands.
He twisted in his chair, he scratched his nose.
He glanced again, almost secretly, at his hands.
More papers were in from the North, he mumbled. More meddling
    headlines.
With their pepper-words, "bestiality," and "barbarism," and
"Shocking."

The half-sneers he had mastered for the trial worked across
His sweet and pretty face.

What he'd like to do, he explained, was kill them all.
The time lost. The unwanted fame.
Still, it had been fun to show those intruders
A thing or two. To show that snappy-eyed mother,
That sassy, Northern, brown-black —————

Nothing could stop Mississippi.

He knew that. Big Fella
Knew that.
And, what was so good, Mississippi knew that.
Nothing and nothing could stop Mississippi.
They could send in their petitions, and scar
Their newspapers with bleeding headlines. Their governors
Could appeal to Washington. . . .

"What I want," the older baby said, "is 'lasses on my jam."
Whereupon the younger baby
Picked up the molasses pitcher and threw
The molasses in his brother's face. Instantly
The Fine Prince leaned across the table and slapped
The small and smiling criminal.

She did not speak. When the Hand
Came down and away, and she could look at her child,
At her baby-child,
She could think only of blood.
Surely her baby's cheek
Had disappeared, and in its place, surely,
Hung a heaviness, a lengthening red, a red that had no end.
She shook her head. It was not true, of course.
It was not true at all. The
Child's face was as always, the
Color of the paste in her paste-jar.

She left the table, to the tune of the children's lamentations, which were
    shriller
Than ever. She
Looked out of a window. She said not a word. That
Was one of the new Somethings—
The fear,
Tying her as with iron.

Suddenly she felt his hands upon her. He had followed her
To the window. The children were whimpering now.
Such bits of tots. And she, their mother,
Could not protect them. She looked at her shoulders, still
Gripped in the claim of his hands. She tried, but could not resist the idea
That a red ooze was seeping, spreading darkly, thickly, slowly,
Over her white shoulders, her own shoulders,
And over all of Earth and Mars.

He whispered something to her, did the Fine Prince, something
About love, something about love and night and intention.

She heard no hoof-beat of the horse and saw no flash of the shining steel.

He pulled her face around to meet
His, and there it was, close close,

For the first time in all those days and nights.
His mouth, wet and red,
So very, very, very red,
Closed over hers.

Then a sickness heaved within her. The courtroom Coca-Cola,
The courtroom beer and hate and sweat and drone,
Pushed like a wall against her. She wanted to hear it.
But his mouth would not go away and neither would the
Decapitated exclamation points in that Other Woman's eyes.

She did not scream.
She stood there.
But a hatred for him burst into glorious flower,

And its perfume enclasped them—big,
Bigger than all magnolias.

The last bleak news of the ballad.
The rest of the rugged music.
The last quatrain.

RAY BRADBURY

Byzantium I Come Not From

Byzantium
I come not from
But from another time and place
Whose race is simple, tried and true;
As boy
I dropped me forth in Illinois,
A name with neither love nor grace
Was Waukegan. There I came from
And not, good friends, Byzantium.
And yet in looking back I see
From topmost part of farthest tree
A land as bright, beloved and blue
As any Yeats found to be true.
The house I lived in, hewn of gold
And on the highest market sold
Was dandelion-minted, made
By spendthrift bees in bee-loud glade.
And then of course our finest wine
Came forth from that same dandelion,
While dandelion was my hair
As bright as all the summer air;
I dipped in rainbarrels for my eyes
And cherries stained my lips, my cries,
My shouts of purest exaltation:
Byzantium? No. That Indian nation
Which made of Indian girls and boys
Spelled forth itself as Illinois.
Yet all the Indian bees did hum:
Byzantium.
Byzantium.

So we grew up with mythic dead
To spoon upon midwestern bread
And spread old gods' bright marmalade
To slake in peanut-butter shade.
Pretending there beneath our sky
That it was Aphrodite's thigh;
Pretending, too, that Zeus was ours
And Thor fell down in thundershowers.
While by the porch-rail calm and bold
His words pure wisdom, stare pure gold
My grandfather a myth indeed
Did all of Plato supersede;
While Grandmama in rocking-chair
Sewed up the raveled sleeve of care,
Crocheted cool snowflakes rare and bright
To winter us on summer night.
And uncles gathered with their smokes
Emitted wisdoms masked as jokes,
And aunts as wise as Delphic maids
Dispensed prophetic lemonades
To boys knelt there as acolytes
On Grecian porch on summer nights.
Then went to bed there to repent
The evils of the innocent
The gnat-sins sizzling in their ears
Said, through the nights and through the years
Not Illinois nor Waukegan
But blither sky and blither sun;
Though mediocre all our Fates
And Mayor not as bright as Yeats
Yet still we knew ourselves. The sum?
Byzantium.
Byzantium.

JOHN KNOEPFLE

Harpe's Head

Harpe's dead.
He twangs hell's gut maybe.
He won't badger cabins
for new widows
or cheat sons of any more fathers.
We left the worthless part of him
fouled in mudflats
south of Redbanks,
but of Harpe's head,
we took that off gentle,
like a quail's is knuckled.
Goddam Harpe,
we spit there in the noon heat,
we'll wrap you up better than pharaoh.
We scooped stone ledges
below a creek bend
for blue cool clay
and thickened his flame of face with that.
It held him firm for Natchez
for some who knew him there,
down Ohio's shoaling
in a sloshed oak bucket.
Senators priced his took head
and cold-bedded women cursed it.
Oh, God, we booted that pumpkin
through Natchez-under-the-hill
until the blue clay cracked
and his withered head
leered at us.
Then we flung him
down a chuckhole full of blowflies
where hogs wallowed in the heat.

late winter in menard county

1

new salem in patches of snow
I see how the culture
spoke in its hand tools
smooth curves of grain cradles
handles in good polish
for apple butter paddles
and things of strict importance
flails reap hooks tarbuckets

then there are the fabrics
those subtle colors
native elderberry and walnut
subdued horizons of goldenrod
woven after patience
that must have been godly
with flax hackles teasels
drop spindles

and the quilts and spreads
their thimbled excellence
stitchery that explained the years
bear paw maple leaf ohio star
abstractions of secret hands

2

well everybody in petersburg
got out of the house by eleven
they turned up at the middle school
where the kiwanis
had a pancake and sausage day
people were tired of winter
like braid rugs slung over porch rails

politics in the cafeteria
hello Im running for supreme court
how are you today

not bad for a gentile
are you related to the state senator
I am the state senator

3
edgar lee masters your town
has a new day-care center
it is going up on the back rear wall
of mentor grahams old house
you must have known it the one
with the port wine brick
and the clumsy gingerbread
holding up so well for a teachers digs

your house is public now
and visitors can see the scratched table
where you wrote your proscriptions
for country graveyards

the town made you a fine afternoon
for your centennial did you know that
the school band in the gymnasium
played vaguely through several
variations and there were
pretty good speeches
and a commemorative stamp

4
this is a late winter river
a dangerous sangamon
with a jerry-built dam

the awkward angle rebuffs the current
it backs in an eddy
below the west bank
and small whirlpools
surface and disappear in it
like mouths in a pit
an insidious babble
whispering in a sick mans soul

it was the weekend after taxes
as people remember
when kevin washington
lost his life here with the child
he tried to save lifted on his arm
so it was mid april
all in a swollen spring

the whole town knows
the sangamon is a living current
that does not abide still water

so some here will tell you
the river sucked him down
and evened a score with his grandfather
who snatched so many from the river

confluence

the suns eye gleams on the burnt black prairie
the winter blackened moraines of all conclusions
and the white egret
ascetic alone with his promise
knowing where the river is
threads a fiery needle

it was always more than dawn
that we looked for
something that we had not seen
as we watched here
gathered from the ashes of our vision

may new prayers and new fires
the beloved pleiades
welcome the kickapoo home
star daughters in their hoods of light
dancing at their zenith while the sun
burns down the horizon

this world in peace
this laced temple of darkening colors
it could not have been made for shambles
this green twilight of echoing voices
as the sun hurls its fireball
down the other side of the world

it is long miles through marshgrass
the sangamon sifting to its ending
and beyond us the illinois
intensifies south
beneath the eagles at grafton
our ancient mississippi
its wide slow waters

bath

and when lincoln came here
that was august 16th 1858
he felt like his age was something
hanging on him he remembered
surveying the town 22 years earlier
in deep wilderness then and river timber
how he staked out the first plat
with his own hands he said

and these old men around him
they were as young as himself
27 years ago in 1831
messmates in the black hawk war

the crowd heard him with respect
tell all of them why slavery
was an evil thing

bath is trailers and shacks
and make-do livings anyway you can
full of particular folk

who like pink flamingos in driveways
and peonies on the lawns
cradled in used tractor tires
things good for looking at
they tell you if you want to know

lincoln had six years
beyond his stump speech at bath
six years for the history of the world

this year in late spring
the children will go down the river bank
midmorning on memorial day

as they have since the civil war
and set their little boats
drifting on the illinois
with cargoes of flowers

dark spaces: thoughts on all souls day

someone might live
even beyond one self and come
dreaming into the evening of his dream

entering his garden
without a thought in mind
much as a dancer spins with his eyes
focused on a point out there

does not see
stage prop or conductors baton
or the uncurtained
dark eyes of the audience

there are no surprises
yesterday in his garden
there were spring beauties

this is his freedom
the joy of the aged
the solemn moment before
everything goes down

it has to be that day
the stars do fall
and they will fall
so that we may grieve their passing

and perhaps
grow older than any flowering

LISEL MUELLER

Alive Together

Speaking of marvels, I am alive
together with you, when I might have been
alive with anyone under the sun,
when I might have been Abélard's woman
or the whore of a Renaissance pope
or a peasant wife with not enough food
and not enough love, with my children
dead of the plague. I might have slept
in an alcove next to the man
with the golden nose, who poked it
into the business of stars,
or sewn a starry flag
for a general with wooden teeth.
I might have been the exemplary Pocahontas
or a woman without a name
weeping in Master's bed
for my husband, exchanged for a mule,
my daughter, lost in a drunken bet.
I might have been stretched on a totem pole
to appease a vindictive god
or left, a useless girl-child,
to die on a cliff. I like to think
I might have been Mary Shelley
in love with a wrong-headed angel,
or Mary's friend. I might have been you.
This poem is endless, the odds against us are endless,
our chances of being alive together
statistically nonexistent;
still we have made it, alive in a time
when rationalists in square hats
and hatless Jehovah's Witnesses
agree it is almost over,

alive with our lively children
who—but for endless ifs—
might have missed out on being alive
together with marvels and follies
and longings and lies and wishes
and error and humor and mercy
and journeys and voices and faces
and colors and summers and mornings
and knowledge and tears and chance.

Highway Poems

For Lucy and Jenny

We keep coming back and coming back
To the real: to the hotel instead of the hymns
That fall upon it out of the wind.
    —Wallace Stevens, "An Ordinary Evening in New Haven"

1

The narrow black veins on the map
will get you there, but the fat
red arteries get you there quicker
and without pain:
you can go from the head
to the toes of America
without seeing
a hospital or a jail
without ever coming on tears
              toys
              wrinkles
              scars
              fists
              guns
              crossed fingers
              broken teeth

2

Between the roof of the Howard Johnson
and the star of the Holiday Inn
falls the shadow
which is myself.

Question: am I real
when I exist only
inside a hot steel body
at 70 miles per hour
and when I'm freed, become
a certain car-door slam,
a brief pattern of footsteps
outside a numbered door?

3

Hardly anyone takes
the old state road anymore.
The town is dying.
Its blood being pumped
into the new expressway
five miles east of here.
Sad and miraculous now,
transfigured by extinction,
are the ones who stay
to go down with the town:
the proprietor of the General Store
and the Restwell Cabins (vacancy always)
and the postmistress, his wife,
angel of government checks
and news from a world with receding walls.

4

Camping, you learn people
by their shoes in the toilet stalls.
The brown loafers support
white legs and a silver trailer;
the navy tennis shoes go
with Pepsodent and a black wig;
the tiny saddle shoes match a voice

that talks about being three;
and I must be a pair
of yellow sneakers, blue-patched at the toes,
although, being filled with my life,
I don't believe it.

5
    Illinois, Indiana, Iowa
Austrian food is not served in Vienna,
and people in Paris drink Coke, not wine.
Lebanon has its Little League
and Warsaw its Civil War cannon.
Carthage is full of blondes,
and Cairo divides, American-style,
into white and black, money and rage.
Gnawbone keeps teasing, a tricky riddle,
and What Cheer defies punctuation,
but Stony Lonesome is all that it says.
I have seen Hindustan—Hoosier twang,
no belly dancing allowed—
and I have been in Arcadia:
one street by a railroad track,
blue chicory, goldenrod.

    O telltale country, fact and mirage,
    coat of many colors
    stitched in homesickness, threaded with dreams,
    land of the seven fat cows,
    is it finished, your poem?

6
We keep coming back to the old hotel,
to the old Main Street, in the old part of town,
to the tottering giant, the elephant
sagging on concrete feet.

We keep coming back to the white-railed porch,
the geraniums and the wicker chairs,
the glass doors and the Persian carpet,
the banquet hall with the chandeliers

where the Chamber of Commerce meets and talks
about pride and achievement, while the stores
on the block are vacant, their windows blind,
their clerks gone to the big new mall
outside of town, where the chain stores are
with check-out lanes and shopping carts,
where shoplifting is a crime.

We keep coming back to the corpses of elms,
imagining shade, umbrellas of peace,
imagining grandparents, newspapers, cups,
people out walking, the ticket booth
of the movie theater occupied—
were times really better when the hotel
served the best Sunday dinner around
and the bridal suite was booked solid,
when the governor campaigned on the steps,
promising dollars for votes?

We keep coming back to what we gave up;
remember, we never wanted to live here
in the days of parades and the Firemen's Ball
and the high school musical once a year.
No, these are deathbed visits: regrets,
surprising grief and sudden love,
terror of loss, the need to lay
hands on the past before it is gone,
hold on to the knowledge at least, if not
the stairs and walls of our history,
walk away weeping at least, assured
that sometime, a long time ago,
we came from somewhere, that we are real.

Another Version

Our trees are aspens, but people
mistake them for birches;
they think of us as characters

in a Russian novel, Kitty and Levin
living contentedly in the country.
Our friends from the city watch the birds
and rabbits feeding together
on top of the deep, white snow.
(We have Russian winters in Illinois,
but no sleigh bells, possums instead of wolves,
no trusted servants to do our work.)
As in a Russian play, an old man
lives in our house, he is my father;
he lets go of life in such slow motion,
year after year, that the grief
is stuck inside me, a poisoned apple
that won't go up or down.
But like the three sisters, we rarely speak
of what keeps us awake at night;
like them, we complain about things
that don't really matter and talk
of our pleasures and of the future:
we tell each other the willows
are early this year, hazy with green.

Naming the Animals

Until he named the horse
               horse,
hoofs left no print on the earth,
manes had not been invented,
swiftness and grace were not married.

Until he named the cow
               cow,
no one slept standing up,
no one saw through opaque eyes,
food was chewed only once.

Only after he named the fish
               fish,

did the light put on skins
of yellow and silver oil,
revealing itself as a dancer
and high-jump champion of the world,

just as later
he had to name the woman
                            love
before he could put on the knowledge
of who she was, with her small hands.

Monet Refuses the Operation

Doctor, you say there are no haloes
around the streetlights in Paris
and what I see is an aberration
caused by old age, an affliction.
I tell you it has taken me all my life
to arrive at the vision of gas lamps as angels,
to soften and blur and finally banish
the edges you regret I don't see,
to learn that the line I called the horizon
does not exist and sky and water,
so long apart, are the same state of being.
Fifty-four years before I could see
Rouen cathedral is built
of parallel shafts of sun,
and now you want to restore
my youthful errors: fixed
notions of top and bottom,
the illusion of three-dimensional space,
wisteria separate
from the bridge it covers.
What can I say to convince you
the Houses of Parliament dissolve
night after night to become
the fluid dream of the Thames?
I will not return to a universe

of objects that don't know each other,
as if islands were not the lost children
of one great continent. The world
is flux, and light becomes what it touches,
becomes water, lilies on water,
above and below water,
becomes lilac and mauve and yellow
and white and cerulean lamps,
small fists passing sunlight
so quickly to one another
that it would take long, streaming hair
inside my brush to catch it.
To paint the speed of light!
Our weighted shapes, these verticals,
burn to mix with air
and change our bones, skin, clothes
to gases. Doctor,
if only you could see
how heaven pulls earth into its arms
and how infinitely the heart expands
to claim this world, blue vapor without end.

Triage

Bertolt Brecht lamented that he lived in an age when it was almost a crime to talk about trees, because that meant being silent about so much evil. Walking past a stand of tall, still healthy elms along Chicago's lakefront, I think of what Brecht said. I want to celebrate these elms which have been spared by the plague, these survivors of a once flourishing tribe commemorated by all the Elm Streets in America. But to celebrate them is to be silent about the people who sit and sleep underneath them, the homeless poor who are hauled away by the city like trash, except it has no place to dump them. To speak of one thing is to suppress another. When I talk about myself, I cannot talk about you. You know this as you listen to me, disappointment settling in your face.

Curriculum Vitae

1992

1) I was born in a Free City, near the North Sea.

2) In the year of my birth, money was shredded into confetti. A loaf of bread cost a million marks. Of course I do not remember this.

3) Parents and grandparents hovered around me. The world I lived in had a soft voice and no claws.

4) A cornucopia filled with treats took me into a building with bells. A wide-bosomed teacher took me in.

5) At home the bookshelves connected heaven and earth.

6) On Sundays the city child waded through pinecones and primrose marshes, a short train ride away.

7) My country was struck by history more deadly than earthquakes or hurricanes.

8) My father was busy eluding the monsters. My mother told me the walls had ears. I learned the burden of secrets.

9) I moved into the too bright days, the too dark nights of adolescence.

10) Two parents, two daughters, we followed the sun and the moon across the ocean. My grandparents stayed behind in darkness.

11) In the new language everyone spoke too fast. Eventually I caught up with them.

12) When I met you, the new language became the language of love.

13) The death of the mother hurt the daughter into poetry. The daughter became a mother of daughters.

14) Ordinary life: the plenty and thick of it. Knots tying threads to everywhere. The past pushed away, the future left unimagined for the sake of the glorious, difficult, passionate present.

15) Years and years of this.

16) The children no longer children. An old man's pain, an old man's loneliness.

17) And then my father too disappeared.

18) I tried to go home again. I stood at the door to my childhood, but it was closed to the public.

19) One day, on a crowded elevator, everyone's face was younger than mine.

20) So far, so good. The brilliant days and nights are breathless in their hurry. We follow, you and I.

LUCIEN STRYK

Oeuvre

Will it ever be finished, this house
    Of paper
I began to raise when I was seventeen?

Others scramble from foundations far less firm.
    Seasons of
Pondering, name by name, the past's magnificent,

A squandering. Surely I might have lived.
    Spitefully
Watching as rivals stole the girls, got the jobs,

Won the laurels, the misery seeped in,
    Tinting the
Windows, darkening the fairest day.
But how should I have known, a house to please
    Need not be
Outlandish? And that searching everywhere

The fresh, the rare, prowling the gaudier
    Capitals,
Something of each would rub off, deface.

Well, we build where and as we can. There are
    Days when I
Am troubled by an image of the house,

Laden, rootless, like a tinseled tree,
    Suddenly
Torn to a thousand scribbled leaves and borne off

By the wind, then to be gathered and patched
  Whole again,
Or of the thing going up in smoke

And I, the paper dreamer, wide awake.

Return to DeKalb

Expecting no miracle, we found none:
One retarred blacktop, another supermart,
  The sum of change—

Apart from the waiting neighbors, in which
Plentiful loss of hair and swollen girth,
  Those additions

To a catalogue of woes, came as small
Surprise. We were the lucky travelers
  Come back to plan

A further flight, happy to learn that none
Remembered an earthquake in Persia or
  Rioting in Greece.

Suddenly sick of so much reality,
We climbed the long-worn staircase to the
  Bedroom, and found

What each had thought was shaken off—Time
Rose stinking from the mattress, perched, a
  Raven, on the sill.

Cormorant

Men speak lightly of frustration,
As if they'd invented it.

As if like the cormorant
Of Gifu, thick leg roped, a ring

Cutting into the neck, they dived
All night to the fish-swelled water

And flapped up with the catch lodged
In the throat, only to have

The fisher yank it out and toss
It gasping on a breathless heap.

Then to dive again, hunger
Churning in the craw, air just

Slipping by the throat-ring
To spray against the lungs.

And once more to be jerked back in
And have the fisher grab the spoil.

Men speak lightly of frustration,
And dim in the lantern light

The cormorant makes out the flash
Of fins and, just beyond,

The streamered boats of tourists
Rocking under *saké* fumes.

From *Issa: A Suite of Haiku*

Song of skylark—
night falls
from my face.

> After night in
> the dog's bowl,
> butterfly scoots off.

Cherry blossoms
everywhere: this
undeserving world.

> Frog and I,
> eyeball
> to eyeball.

Winter moon—
outer moat
cracks with cold.

> Woodpecker on
> the temple pillar—
> die! die! die!

What a moon—
if only she were here,
my bitter wife.

> My thinning hair,
> eulalia grass,
> rustling together.

Plum in bloom—
the Gates of Hell
stay shut.

> Charcoal fire—
> spark by spark,
> we fade too.

Morning glory—
whose face
is without fault?

Wonderful—
under cherry blossoms,
this gift of life.

New Year's Day—
blizzard of
plum blossoms.

Snail—baring
shoulders
to the moon.

My empty face,
betrayed
by lightning.

Into the house
before me,
fly on my hat.

Paul Carroll

Ode on a Bicycle on Halsted Street in a Sudden Summer Thunderstorm

It feels so neat to be a fish again.

In the Shakespeare Garden at Northwestern University

Your mother, tall as a flower
        if you and I were bees, Luke,
  her complexion complex in its lucidity
           here in the half-light of this late June
             afternoon
        as the idea of eternity
entertained by men inside of dying bodies, brings
              a bunch of purple flowers, lays
        them next to us
entwined on this wood bench
             beneath the bust of Shakespeare. Old
           devil
      with flowers in his mouth
              is enjoying carnal knowledge of a
          woman
who wears the mask of harvest moons amid
             foliated ornamentation on the wall
      of the 10th century temple of Angkor Wat.
The limestone townhouse in which we live, Luke,
                   wears its summer suit of ivy;
       has stood on Mohawk Street
    since 1890. You're almost three months old.

Ode to the Angels Who Move Perpetually toward the Dayspring of Their Youth

To James Dickey, John Logan and James Wright; and to the
young poets in the Writers' Workshop at the University of Iowa

I

All over Chicago, Jim, the angels are making love.

Over there on Lakeview Avenue nearby the Zoo the psychiatrist
Caressing,   coming,   makes
Sunday-morning love inside his delighted wife.

                                                        Beneath this bone-
Chipping,   bone-dry Brueghelean sky
Mobs of kids   careen on Christmas sleds   down
The highest hill in Lincoln Park,   their cries
The sounds of the original animals;   their faces
Barbaric bright ski masks   flash
By,   like, abruptly,   in the middle of a confusing dream
A hand in traffic cop's big orange glove
                                          begins to write a poem.

Remember, Jim, that winter noon we goofed around this Zoo?
That grey timber wolf   moving with rage   and
The cold dignity of an old devil   around
Its cage of tiny concrete hills   moved you to wonder:
"Isn't it marvellous we're allowed to live
In the same universe with such a splendid beast?" You made
A feast of words.   But I was fascinated by
How the grated shadows of the wolf   created   artificial
Night in the middle of the raw abundant haze of light.

                                                        Now I know
How durable the roots of joy   nothing can destroy.

II
                        Except the shadows
of the angels, John.

That other park I rushed
past Grant Wood frame homes and corner grocery stores
to find, frantic
                    in the chill spring of 1953,
a few months before we met by accident
                    one midnight in South Bend—
two poets in their 20s dazzled by
                    the skeletons of words.
Web
of evening delicate-
ly spread-
ing among birch branch and benches
half concealed the body of the park. Shellacked by oil
and scum from the Chrysler factory the river
carried last of the light along it
and away.
                    (I'd tasted the blood of a god
          in a dream)

                    O the angel
          singing (bird spread hard wings
                    inside the bright nimbus)
          of the humiliation
          of encroaching bone

And in the alley
behind the Portuguese fisherman's saloon
that Labor Day night in Provincetown, my mouth
of bits of broken glass, I stumbled
closer to the roots: The devil is incandescent with desire.
He is beautiful. Shadow cuts where glass can't.

                    But you taught me
                    what's harder to endure, John:
to find what exists behind the faces of the angels, bearing
witness to the old reality:
                    disjecta membra poetae
                    embody the business
          of the heart
          of men and women anywhere. The angels are within us.

III

My big body feels filled with poems today.
Long shadows of the Chicago afternoon
Are the silos
Of tomorrow.
I want to live as if each day were
The final poem
I'll have the luck to write, Jim—like
That homely kid, trapped behind bifocals, sewn
Into a blue snowsuit,
Talking to a naked walnut tree.
The tree
Is why we write.

IV

    I feel so goddamn good today I try
the old corkscrew windup of Leroy (Tarzan) Parmalee
        pitching a snowball at a tree.
   When I meet the young poets
out at the University of Iowa next month
       I want to rush into the class
    like Groucho Marx, his crouching zany zip
(like Yogi Berra roller skating into New Years Eve)
      as he puffs on outsized stogie, circling
   ritzy Margaret Dumont in *A Day at the Races*, saying,
So you want to learn about poems, eh? Well,
      a poem can wear galoshes too.
      Or sit doing the crossword puzzle on the bus.
      A poem can be
      the melancholy hard-on
      of an angel.

    Or be a way to box
    desire in;
    or shut it out for good.

   Or exorcise the bees
   that crowd
   about the mouth.

A poem can be (circle one of the following three)
(1) The girdle of the grandmother of Hugh Hefner

(2) The surprisingly low fares on the meters of the cabs of
purgatory

(3) The chameleons of our feelings (they seldom sleep)

(4) None of the above

A poem can turn nasty too—
like truth, the tractor of the psychoanalyst.
Yet there's no delight
like the trip which is the writing of it:

"As I came home through the woods with my string of fish, trailing my pole, it now being quite dark, I caught a glimpse of a woodchuck stealing across my path, and I felt a thrill of savage delight, and was sorely tempted to seize and devour him raw; not that I was hungry then except for the wildness which he represented."

Or if you're lucky the trip may begin and end with Heidegger's "Why are there things that *are*—things which exist at all—rather than nothing whatsoever?"

Or even this:

"The intricacy and subtleties of Donne's imagination are the length and depths of the furrow made by his passion. Donne's pedantry and obscenity—the rock and loam of his Eden—but make me the more certain that one who is but a man like all of us has seen God."

Best of all,
each poem wears its own skin,
the bones of style being
(like any successful marriage)
only ½ of what it's all about.

DAVE ETTER

Andy Hasselgard
Gone with the Grain

Wind whines the wine-colored telephone lines.

Girls who hang around grain elevators here
are always tucking in faded blue shirts,
two buttons unbuttoned from the top.

There are questions that will be asked:
"Who wrote my middle name on the water tank?"
"How many funny farmers in Farmer City?"

I don't care a whit what you say,
this is where I want to hang my hat.
Sure beats the park and the county courthouse.

The voices in the grand and grainy noon:
"Now I prefer an older-type woman myself."
"I used to had me a dog like him."

The girls slide around like lovely lizards,
moving in and out of the dusty shadows.
I say howdy and then my tongue turns husk.

Wind whines the wine-colored telephone lines.

Roma Higgins
Cricket

For a whole week
there was a cricket

in the cellar,
somewhere between
the furnace
and the croquet set.
I would go down
every evening
to hear him chirp.
He would note my steps
and break off
his magic music.
Then he would begin
to sing again.
It got so
I would talk to him
and call him friend.
But tonight
in the cellar
I found nothing
but cold silence
and a spider
working on a shroud
by the window.

Elwood Collins: Summer of 1932

On sticky summer Sunday afternoons
there would be lots of people
standing around in the yard,
mostly relatives and neighbors
in cotton dresses and white shirts.
They would come and go until dusk,
talking, talking, talking, talking
about jobs, bread lines, foreclosures,
about Hoover and Roosevelt,
about the latest layoff or suicide.
Someone, usually my father
or one of my unemployed uncles,
would be scratching in the dirt

with half a hoe or ragged rake,
not to plant, not to cultivate,
but to do something, to be busy,
as if idleness was some kind of dark shame
or red pimple of embarrassment.
I was there, too, a silent child
with my blue wagon and blue spade,
making little mountains of dirt
and patting them down with my fist.
When the lemonade ran out,
my mother or a maiden aunt
would bring out a pitcher of water
and someone would always say,
"You can't beat good old water
when you have a terrible thirst."
The Ford in the driveway was ours.
It was leaking oil, drop by drop,
and the battery was dead.
We were obviously going nowhere.

Drink and Agriculture

. . . to die of drink and agriculture.
  —Dylan Thomas, *Under Milk Wood*

Not to die, as in cold-hands dead,
but to die slowly, a slow death,
farming being an old way to die.

Fighting the weeds, cursing the stones.
No cash in pocket, none in bank.
Only pennies turning dark in a jar.

The wife is mostly sick now.
She can hardly wash dirty dishes,
can barely tend the garden plot.

My credit stretched to the last notch.
Stuck with balky tractor, shaky combine,
a barn with a leaky roof.

Booze in the car, booze in the icebox,
booze in the sideboard, booze on the shelf,
booze in the cellar, booze in town.

Lost pigs, sick cows, dead chickens.
Our gray horse won't eat, won't stand up.
The dog has gone, has hit the road.

There's six townships in this poor man's county,
six cracked slabs of flat prairie
under a farmer-breaking sun.

Erosion gives us the nightmares,
the good black loam all washed away,
the land scarred, gullied, turned ugly.

You have a good year, prices go down.
Have a bad year, no one knows your face.
Feast or famine, it hurts the same.

The wife is after me to sell the farm,
to get what we can and get out.
But what's so hot somewhere else?

Sometimes I refuse to sweat this life,
just let my mind drift off like seed
and reach for a bottle of wine.

Dirt farming is for fools like me.
So fool I am, fated to fumble
with a place I can't, won't let go of.

Singing in the Toyota

I've been booed in the shower,
put down on the patio,
ridiculed at the beach,
but when I sing in the car
I get nothing but approval:
big smiles from the dashboard,
handclaps from the windshield wipers,
rousing cheers from the steering wheel.
Even though I'm no Tony Bennett,
no Nat King Cole of the tollways,
I can croon along on every song
the Delco radio serves up,
and when I get going good
on some old favorite,
like perhaps "Rags to Riches"
or maybe "Answer Me, My Love,"
I start to see my name in lights.
The face in the mirror is mine.
I have a captive audience.
And I can do me better than me.

Ralph J. Mills Jr.

For Lorine Niedecker in Heaven

Lorine, Lorine,
the catch is
in—

    fish scales
crystal en-
crusted among the
wet grasses

House roof's
new-shingled
now, the walls
done all in
white—
        Nothing for
you but to
drift the river:
"a silent boat"
in this hollow of
green, leaf-shady
& still

But see, a visitor,
the sun has
come, dropping through
birches & firs—
           its light
spreads a band
on your hair,
        Lorine
the catch is in

Water Lilies
For Helen

    sky on this mountain
pond's glaze
                —murk, waving weeds,
shadow of pads below
its silver—
          high cirrus seem
even farther riding there
              where water
lilies
open over them
          in slow, un-
watched explosion
            : star petals :
pale
suns

Evening Song

late day flames
orange
      birds call
far off in dropping
wind
    on the lake
waves phosphoresce
          sun's
gone
the other way
        voices on a
bus or
up this street
        motes &
bits
    spun in cold air

falling where
feet scrape concrete
                    names
thin syllables
break loose
                    shadows fill
one shadow
beneath a tree
                    overhead
clouds billow
                    shred to
take new
shapes
            faces forms
dislocate
            yellowy
leaf dust
            circles
circling down

                    (up too soon)
in the least flare
of sun
                    —& friends
dead this
winter,
            two strange, lovely
ones,
                    the air's come
together after them, tight &
excluding,
                    making a glossy
blur where each
                    moved, spoke
or once
stood

James Ballowe

Starved Rock

We are the children and the epigone
Of the Illini, the vanished nation.
    —Edgar Lee Masters

They expired of starvation
with true Indian fortitude.
    —The State of Illinois

Pontiac, dressed in his French officer's uniform,
died from a blow to the head. He had been drinking
and had gone to the woods to sing and sleep it off.
His assassin: an Illini of the Kaskaskia or perhaps the Peoria.
The place: Cahokia, across the Mississippi from St. Louis.
The time: 1769.   April.
    (—enough remains to tell us that over the grave
    of Pontiac more blood was poured out in atonement
    than flowed from the hecatombs of slaughtered heroes
                                 on the corpse
    of Patroclus; and the remnant of the Illinois who
                                survived the carnage
    remained for ever after sunk in utter insignificance—)
The Pottawatomie and the Sauk set the matter straight.

    Spring moseys up the Illinois in April. Warm air
    dampens the prairie. The clefts of a prominent sand-rock
    formation two hundred miles from the mouth of the River
    show life for the first time in five months.
    Natives of this place sniff the breeze
    as though it carries the scent of lotus blossoms.

The LaSalle County Banker's Group holds
its annual dinner dance at the lodge adjacent
to the Rock. They are all fifty years old,
including the couple begging Johnny Kaye
to play some rock. They pledge themselves to an evening
of joy, food, and drink

                             a madness they feel
in being in a foreign place. From their vantage
the River here resembles the Rhine, industrialized,
inhabited, between clouds of trees at a distance
darkly medieval.

                    "Wouldn't you like this
in your backyard?" a banker's wife sighs,
sipping her old-fashioned.
                         Across the River
to the North   LaSalle's first fort   a steeple
rises above a village. The dance lasts
two hours, punctual. In spite of spring   or
because of it   there's work to be done. It's
Wednesday night. Banker's hours to keep.
Spring ends as it began, a waft of air.

Fort St. Louis was here a full century
before April's winds brought death's stench
up the River.
             No longer French.
                       Not St. Louis
now but an erection from which to survey grounds
plentiful with game. The British owned the land.
The Illini,
          subservient,
               held the gun and axe,
relaxed through yet another winter's boredom.

That spring as always the rock thawed,
                              the canyons
came awash with the sperm of the earth,
                              the Indians
danced, made love, and waited for the appointed time
when they would set to work, trapping and killing
the issue let loose from winter's icy womb.

     This ancient signal
                    (—*starved scarp of stone/*
          inverted cup of our insatiable thirst—)
rises serene from what we've done to the River.
Children on holiday arrive in yellow buses
slip and fall somewhere beneath the water.
A dishwasher murders women who come for bridge.

To Starved Rock, hunted, a band retreated.
Their options: be massacred   or dress in motley and slip
to the Wabash, near Terre Haute, forever cursed.
Better this high earth, a source of pride.
Their native land.

               The bountiful river valley
stretched below.
               They must have known.
                              Ropes
let down were cut. Game fed at the River.
Day settled into night into day.
                    They starved
and savored their Indian martyrdom for a hideous act.

Were their women with them? Or did they that spring
scent the sickness on the land and leave
                              one
by one
     their men hungering for the next day only?

The Coal Miners

For My Grandfathers

The holes you made
like yourselves
are collapsing
inward. Whole towns
rest within
the graves you dug.

This is your legacy.
Not Lawrence's togetherness
even then prompted you
to consume the blackness
that became your soul.
It was coal. It was coal.

Drugged by the dark,
you imagined light
shining from Christ
and crucifixions
indistinguishable
in the dust that turned
you into dust.

You were the miner
deep in the pit
whom no one knew.
You a shade
in a blackened world
I see too. I see too.

LAURENCE LIEBERMAN

God's Measurements

(Todaiji Temple, Nara)

The statue weighs 452 tons, measures 53.5 ft. in height, and has a face 16 ft. long by 9.5 ft. wide, eyes 3.9 ft. wide, a nose 1.6 ft. high, a mouth 3.7 ft. wide, ears 8.5 ft. long, hands 6.8 ft. long, and thumbs 4.8 ft. long. The materials employed are estimated as follows: 437 tons of bronze; 165 lbs. of mercury; 288 lbs. of pure gold; 7 tons of vegetable wax; and an amazing amount of charcoal and other materials.
  —*Japan: The Official Guide*

As incense smoke thins, a stupendous,
        wide, brooding face emerges above us. The long ribbon-looped
ears, ending in weighty teardrop-
        fat lobes, slowly unravel from the wrappings of smoke trails
    as we advance, the whole bronze olive-green head
        mushrooming from its mask
            of mist. It floats, hovers—balloonlike, isolate—
        over the befogged shoulders. A cosmos
            of global body,
                seated cross-legged on a great lotus-
                blossom bronze pedestal, ascends

into the clearing before us,
        the pedestal in turn installed on a broader stone base
which knows touch of our hastily donned
        slippers, blocking our passage. Not one forward step possible,
    we backstep twice to see the more clearly
        over the jutting head-
            high edge of stone, the full figure now vivid
        and preternaturally clear before us,
            body draped in swirls
                of cloud, itself cloud-shaped, cloud-alloyed,
                growing into a mass, a solid—

if wavery—form. Still, it is the head,
      so distant, holds us. Why do we so thrill at eye-guessed
estimates of measurements, measurements!
    The eyes and mouth, wide as you are long, my son; the length
    of ears makes two of you, the height of lofty face
        three of me, and, yes,
            you could ride lying on the thumb, your near mate
        for length and width, the two of you nestled
            together mimicking
                a God's freakish double thumb! But, no, I
                will not lift you to the stone ledge,

launching your unstoppable climb
      to test my twin-thumbs caprice, despite your scandalous wails
reverberating in the temple
    upper chambers, strident in my ears; nor shall I scold
    or muzzle you, but hoist you to my shoulders
        where, first clasping hands
            for lift and support as you unfold to your full
        height above my head, I clench your ankles,
            as much to steady
                and balance you as to prevent surprise
                leaps. Together, of a tallness

to match, or exceed, the whole hand's length,
      let us promenade around His Excellency's right flank.
Now, wobblingly, we stalk: you, stiltjack,
    in love with instant towers sprung from the idiot body's
    endlessly stretchable elastic of flesh, I
        half scaffold, half anchor,
            the two of us a father-son hobbling hinge—
        telescope of our bones, joined end to end,
            not doubled up
                in laughter or loss of balance but bending
                and unbending into beatitudes . . .

We look up, to scrutinize the God, stilt-
      walking our charmed gavotte. Then, looking into each other's eyes—
I staring up, you staring down—
    we both shudder, communing between your flexed legs, spread

the width of my two shoulders: our four eyes,
        riveted in silence,
                agree! We have seen the bronze head nod. The eyelids
        flutter. The bronze bosom draw breath. The tarnished skins
                of metal wrinkling
                        into folds over charcoal hid ribs. Organs—
                        heart and lungs—of vegetable wax, waxen

liver, waxen pancreas. All glands,
        mercury, but in pure form, not poisons fed upon by dying
fish hordes. Our eyes swear we both saw
        bronze flesh breathe, bronze knees shift for comfort under all
        that obese weight (no gold in the fat buttocks, fat
                hips, we agree to that!),
                        grand flab he can never jog off in throes
        of deep meditation. Does he diet, or fast?
                Does he shed bronze, gold,
                        or weightless, sad wax only? We crane our necks
                        to see how he leans and sways, as we wend

our wide, counterclockwise, happy circle
        around him, counting splendid curled petals of the great lotus-
blossom seat, the petals alternately
        pointing upward and curving downward, the puffed whirlwinds
        of incense smoke eddying up, thinning out,
                in sudden gusts and lulls,
                        as if the blossom itself exhaled the perfume
        clouds submerging all but the Ancient's head, breath
                after vaporous breath . . .
                        We revolve, degree by slow degree, circling
                        the statue's base, half again wider

than the vast lotus throne half again
        the diameter of the bloated God's girth, and we behold
the thousand views of the Buddha's
        changing postures, the torso's bulk crafted by an army
        of master sculptors. *Eight near-perfect castings*
                in three years. Aborted casts,
                        unnumbered. No *surmising how many dozens*

of failed castings, cracked one-hundred-foot-wide
           molds, collapsed scaffolds,
                      casters of irreplaceable genius crushed
                      in falling debris . . . Sudden glare!

We squint, sun cascading into the hall
           from hidden windows high in the temple cupola—thousands
of sparkly points on the statue's
      coruscating skull flare on, off, on, off, and I can see
      great circles connecting all dots of light
           on meticulously shaped
                      rondures of annealed jaw plates, shoulder plates, breast
           plates, my sight traveling in arcs and swirls, curved
                      lines running in a mesh
                                 of intersecting spirals dense as cross-
                                 hatching in the divinely crafted

anatomies of Hieronymus Bosch
           or the woodcut body dissections of Vesalius: God's
or human's, all the light-lines engraved
      on the celestial body's grandly continuous surface
      intersect. *Our body, a wing shining*
           in the happy, happy
                      light of its wholeness. A moonlit angel's wing
           in flight. Or underwater devil ray's
                      wing torchlit
                                 by diver's forehead searchlight beam . . .
                                 High throne-back behind the Buddha's

head usurps our view while we wind
           around his back side, topped not by headrest or flat cushion,
as it had appeared to us wrongly
      in profile, but a goldleaf-covered broad wooden halo
      decorated with portraits of sixteen Bosatsu,
           by our ambulatory
                      count, a troop of gilt sub-deities, satellites
           in orbit perpetually—each a mirror,
                      or reflecting moon,
                                 to the one Daibutsu . . . *Oh, look! The whole halo*
                                 is shimmering, dancing before our eyes!

Lobsters in the Brain Coral

Freediving thirty to forty feet, only a few seconds to spare
at the bottom of each dive before the death
　　of my wind, I catch sight of an antenna or front leg-pincer
waving listlessly into the light like a weed-stalk:

　　the only visible appendage of a tough old bull langouste,
his spiny-thorned carapace of back wedged deep
　　into a crevice in steep flat near-vertical planes of rock.
His trench lightless, I can only guess his position—

　　impossible to snare him with a gig-noose, I aim the Hawai-
ian sling spear, stretched taut on the bow of my forearm.
　　The spear connects, freezes. I hustle to the surface for air,
hyperventilate, and dive again; hanging upside-down,

　　my legs dangling over my head, I peer deeply into the cleft.
No sign of life. Hah!—he's braced for the fight.
　　Tugging and tugging at the spear, I yank out his twenty-
pound impaled barrel-shell, his crotchety long legs

　　wriggling—he looks like a Gargantuan subaqueous spider!
He contracts his muscular powerful tail,
　　discharging high-pitched cries that seem to emit
from a sphere of sound surrounding him, a queer

　　distancing remove between the creature and its shrieks.
I compress the tail. He silences. The spear
　　runs deep into his back, diagonally. I force the point,
flared-open within him, through to the other side.

　　and unscrew the spearhead, his great armored body-vault
shuddering quietly. Astonished by his suffering,
　　his austere beauty, I relax my grip—he jerks loose,
scraping his backspikes across my bare wrist,

three streaks inscribing my skin. *The red ink smears,*
runs, thinning off into swirls, a spreading
    stain. Slow leaks—painless—from my punctured inner tubes,
I deflate. Oh stop, precious flow. A blow-out,

    I may go flat, caving-in on my bones. The lobster zooms
backwards, his tail flapping—violent, noiseless—
    his body a single bony claw swiftly clenching, unclenching,
his whines a siren wailing softer in the distance.

    In pursuit, I chase him below a massive brain coral. I swim
under a grayish bulge and drift into the interior,
    my hand gripping the rim. Am I staring inside somebody's
dream? In five or six rooms of his skull—

    sockets like sinuses, honeycombing the coralhead—stand
lobsters of all sizes: some upside-down,
    others on the walls, the floor; always in the dark
corners, favoring the shadows, leaning away

    from the light, antennae waving. I move my glove
to the nearest cubicle, and tap a pincer.
    It falls from the body. The lobster drops out of sight
into a hidden channel. Then, the whole colony

    move in unison: bodies uplifted, legs stretched taut,
unbending, all begin sidling in a slow trot
    around the linings of the caverns, a dance of skinless
bones, creakless many-jointed rickety stilts

    dragging the glossy-plated bodies this way and that,
somersaulting over and over, sagging
    without letting go, until I forget if my feet are under
or over my head. Let me out of your brain,

    I command the dreamer. I suffocate in this airless hive
where I lose my mass in your sleep. Awake!
    My weight drifts, fades to a gas in your mind.
Do I decompose? *You become an enamelled box*

on spindly crutches. Lay out your fingerprints lengthwise
and braid them into two feelers—antennae.
Fly backwards, snapping your whip of tail; your tail
the one muscle, the one hatchery, the one edible.

Wail, if attacked. When cornered, back to a wall,
drop off your legs, twiggy stick by stick,
flop in the gravelly bottom-muck, a glum squat egg,
quadruple amputee. A basket case. Give me back

to my jails of skin, to my soaps of blood-suds, to my glands,
lungs and lymphs, to all those emerald birds—
heart, liver, gall bladder and balls. Oh spheres and cubes
of my body, multiply strangely into diamonds

whose many shining stars are eyes, eyes that glow,
eyes that radiate light but admit no spark—
eyes luminous, eyes opaque—a universe of eyes sparkling
in another's dream. Eyes of my flesh, restored!

Compass of the Dying

That hoop-back man,
      in wide brim straw hat,
            clomps past on a donkey. Franz calls
            a halt: Pa Guillermo
revolves on his bareback mule perch to greet us.
Himself a first generation son of slaves, now in his mid-
            eighties, Guillermo's voice
            rumbles and hisses like a rusty antique
      Ford radiator
            boiling over. His voice waves—
                  in presence of witnesses—have blown
                  that three ton volcanic rock across the grassy
flat-topped mesa . . .

He *sounds out* family earth plots
with divining rods,
his guttural hum snorting as he measures and sighs
and inches his way
toward the best place, the perfect
site, to build a house. Tapping the ground, his touch

shivers: he traces
minute pulls, or infinites-
imal repulsings; he feels their sucks,
or rebuffs, on the pads
of bare toes. *Magnets underground,* he lovingly names
that occult force: tap, tap—he listens for echoes, and fathoms
the hidden palpitant life
of terrestrial currents. And when he knows,
he knows in gulfs
of his bone marrow. *Build here.*
Lay the cornerstone there, not yonder.
Make your house foundations radiate to northwest,
not southeast; yessir,

there can be no mistake about it . . .
And long-lived
though he be, his health on an even keel, he knows
the secrets of dying.
They rush him to bedside vigils
to chant and hum and teach the breather of last breaths

how to expire.
And if time permits,
Guillermo leads him to the right place
to lay his head. Where
to die, how to embrace death—he is the best guide
for dying. More and more, he says, he turns to the animals
for answers to those last
questions. He shepherds us afoot, yet never
leaving his donkey
roost, to a secret place
beside high pileup of lava boulders,
a perennial graveyard of the animals. He pokes

with his gnarled stick,
                pushes aside a weedy furze patch
                loosely braided
over a shallow pit: brimful of rain-polished bones,
                bones of all shapes
and sizes—no solitary animal
      species claims this dying zone. All land-rover denizens

of Bonaire—*save men*—
      though natural enemies
           they may be in life, share this common
           grave site. If we pick
through the bone pile, we find the brittle vertebrae
of lizard, iguana, nestled beside goat skull, donkey leg bone,
                sheep hip shank, wild turkey
                or duck breastbones—which bespeak a commonality
      in the dying
           breaths . . . The animals gather,
           punctually, often three or four in tandem,
           at the death pits. They may wander miles, or a mere
one hundred meters,
           perhaps, to the nearest mass grave.
           Consult Guillermo,
      at any hour, at any far reach of this small country's
                outsweep: he'll escort you,
forthwith, to the closest death plot.
      There are many such, scattered about the cunucu desert.

He finds them, always,
      with unerring surety
           of gauge—as if some internal death
           compass pointed its dial.
Does scent of the dying carcass linger in the air,
long after the flesh has rotted away, the bones scoured clean?
                How do those animals,
                shambling and dragging crushed limbs, near-lame
      with fatal wounds
           and gasping last breaths, find
                their way? *The hidden magnets draw them,*
           he intones. *It's nothing you can hear or see or smell,*

no senses touch it,
        our instruments can't measure it,
            but earth's pull
    on the dying beast is great—he can't resist its tugs.
                I, too, feel pulsings
below, though I'm not ailing yet.
        The animals know pain, pain—O how they are hurting! Here

come they, when death
    throes be upon them, to die
        quicker, they come to die more easily,
            to welcome the last stirrings
of life and greet death's snaggle-toothed clean bite . . .
So it is, great heaps of bones collect there. Pa Guillermo, still
                propped on his mule, now circles
            the volcanic rock pile and stops at a dung heap,
    where the layers
        upon layers of poop beyond
            reckoning have been strewn by a wide range
                of sick or bruised creatures, fresh manures splashed,
daily, into the ever-
    dank and fetid compost. Hereupon,
        the wounded beasts,
    not dying, not dying, come to heal themselves, and here
            they find rich poultice
or succor for their hurts, whereby
    they recover their strength, and revive their lost powers.

The healing grounds,
    like those mass grave sites,
        are scattered, randomly, over the desert.
        Survivors, of whatever species,
may crawl, limp, creep, or shuffle to the nearest. *And how*
do the hurt animals know, I ask, if it's a time to die, or a time
                to be healed? . . . They're not humans,
            he replies. *It is never in doubt. They must know!*
    It is one time
        or the other. Confusion, doubt,
        that is our invention. Always, a hurt critter
        knows which time it is—whether time to finish, or time
to begin again.

Daryl Hine

Man's Country

For Joseph Parisi
Inde datum molitur iter.
AEN. VI

So this is what the afterlife is like!
Pallid in perpetual twilight
The perambulating spectres seldom speak
Unless to ask the time of day
Or for all they know or care of night.
The acrobatics of their blue ballet
Suggest Euhemerus was right:
Eternity is here to stay.

In that hole-and-corner hide-and-seek
Fortunate who finds a face he knows,
Or, short of a pictorial physique,
Improvises an arresting pose.
Heroes armed and frivolous and weak,
Some defeated briefly doze
While others keep it up all night
Excited even in repose.

How vapid and dissatisfied they seem
After the act, discrete on asphodel,
Dejected members of a beaten team,
Dispirited bodies sensual as hell,
Silent partners of each others' dream,
Condemned to the grosser senses, touch and smell,
Writhing prettily amid the steam
In ecstasy or torment, hard to tell.

Lines on a Platonic Friendship

Virtue was the sunset creeping in the grass
Or fireworks supplied with paradise;
But surely the day has come and gone—
The regal chestnuts burning in the ice—
When you could hold my face in the burning-glass
And flash a hole to China through my flesh.

You will search the skies to bring me down
Because I shall escape to other suns
Reflected in the geographic calm.
It seems to me your love was like a gun
That could break into the blind, myself,
With a racket like a hunter falling down,
Showing us how to capture through the trees
Palaces to house the widowed fox
And Captain Courage dead among the phlox.

Whenever I wished we used to talk of vice
Holding his chessmen balanced in the glass
Or suddenly illuminating flesh;
While a bee for beauty boomed behind the grove
Exploding comments on the world of love
Above a hill that shone like bone;
Not as you would think, white and smooth,
But a mangled affair of feathers guts and blood
In the wide and waveless waters of the wood.

The sun will set among these sacred pits
Filled with gillyflowers and cats
Rephrasing silence till the silence fits
Sleepers will wake upon the precipice,
Their beardless faces sunburnt by the glass;
Guides or strangers in my place.
And you, whom virtue beautifies no more,
Where the print ends like a wave upon the page
Indicate a comment in the margin:
'Love's a shadow like a current in the garden.'

EUGENE REDMOND

River of Bones and Flesh and Blood
(Mississippi)

For Doris Cason

River of Time:
Vibrant vein,
Bent, crooked,
Older than the Red Men
Who named you;
Ancient as the winds
That break on your
Serene and shining face;
One time western boundary of America
From whose center
Your broad shoulders now reach
To touch sisters
On the flanks

River of Truth: Mornings
You leap, yawn 2000 miles,
And shed a giant joyous tear
Over sprouting, straggling
Hives of humanity;
Nights you weep
As the moon, tiptoeing
Across your silent silky
Face, hears you praying
Over the broken backs
Of black slaves who rode,
Crouched and huddled,
At your heart in the bellies
Of steamships.

River of Memory:
Laboratory for Civil War
Boat builders
Who left huge eyes of steel
Staring from your sullen depths;
Reluctant partner to crimes
Of Ku Klux Klansmen;
River moved to waves
Of ecstasy
By the venerable trumpet
Of Louis Armstrong.

River of Bones:
River of bones and flesh—
Bones and flesh and blood;
The nation's largest
Intestine
And longest conveyor belt;

River MISSISSIPPI:
River of little rivers;
River of rises,
Sometimes subdued
By a roof of ice, descending finally
On your Southward course
To spit
Into the Gulf
And join the wrath
Of larger bodies.

Dennis Schmitz

Climbing Sears Tower

Stuntman Daniel Goodman, dressed in a Spiderman outfit, climbs the west face of
the building, using suction cups and metal devices, in 7½ hours . . . is arrested after
ascending the 1,454 foot building.
    —*New York Times*, 5/26/81

4 hours into the climb,
you're still in a reflected Chicago,
against the reflected downtown
grid of older buildings, hardly discernible

humans mirrored close
to your cheek on the breath-wet glass.
Or maybe you imagine humans,
imagine their small concerns

after some time trying.
The sky comes
onto the glass some floors later;
it includes a TV copter

you don't turn to see
examining you, wanting the arachnid
change TV will show as pathos.
You sweat across a divided sun

into the out-focus
western neighborhoods where I imagine
the Douglas el rattling
past my window on Leavitt, sucking

curtain against the rusted screen—
instead, the copter camera
shows fatigue-points a wiseass announcer
superimposes on your back

as though you're holding Humboldt Park
like a bandage over racial turmoil.
He looks for human
failure, for regret not exhaustion—

as the bartender switches to the Cubs
& miming a spider scurry,
clears lunch glasses, olives & chorizo

scraps into a basin.

Making Chicago

We cannot take a single step toward heaven. It is not in our power to travel in a vertical
direction. If however we look heavenward for a long time, God comes and takes us up.
He raises us easily.
   —Simone Weil

let it end here where the blueprint
shows a doorway,
where it shows all of Chicago
reduced to a hundred prestressed floors,
fifty miles of conduit and ductwork

the nerve-impulse climbs to know God.
every floor we go up is one more down
for the flashy suicide, for *blessed man who*
by thought might lift himself

to angel. how slowly we become only men!
I lift the torch away, push up the opaque
welder's lens to listen for the thud
& grind as they pour aggregate,

extrapolating the scarred forms resisting
all that weight & think
the years I gave away to reflexive anger,

to bad jobs, do not count
for the steps the suicide
divides & subdivides in order not to reach

the roof's edge. I count the family years
I didn't grow older with the stunted
locust trees in Columbus Park,
the ragweed an indifferent ground crew
couldn't kill, no matter the poison.
now I want to take up death more often
& taste it a little—
by this change I know I am not what I was:
the voice is the voice of Jacob
but the hands are the hands of Esau—
god & antigod mold what I say,

make me sweat inside the welding gloves,
make what I thought true turn heavy.
but there must be names
in its many names the concrete can't take.
what future race in the ruins
will trace out our shape from the bent

template of the soul,
find its orbit in the clouded atmosphere
of the alloy walls we used as a likeness

for the sky? the workmen stagger
under the weight of the window's nuptial
sheet—in its white reflected clouds
the sun leaves a virgin spot

of joy.

MICHAEL VAN WALLEGHEN

In the Chariot Drawn by Dragons

Such a chariot has Helios, my father's father, Given me to defend me from my enemies.
   —Medea

Fascinating the way our dreams
accommodate the muddled here

and now—the phone we answer
in our sleep for instance
before it startles us awake

or just this morning, the cat
killing something in the yard—

a baby rabbit it turns out
squealing that one high note
only nightmares comprehend . . .

the one where real children
lie dismembered in their beds—

as, indeed, I heard it spoken
on the evening news . . . Medea
of course, was never mentioned

although I understood at once
the way we often do in dreams

that it was she again—disguised
in this last, horrific incarnation
to look like almost anyone . . .

a forgotten second cousin say
whose husband studied neutron

stars, black holes . . . matters
so quantum mechanically intense
so distant, it would take her

nearly fifteen billion years
of living practically abandoned

in married student housing
with two frenetic, infant sons
and no help at all from anyone

before she understood at last
that everything was hopeless—

that nothing, not even light
not the merest glimmer of it
could ever escape such gravity—

a force so crushing in the end
she could barely lift the knife

and wake us up again, heart
pounding, to some poor rabbit
screaming as the sun comes up

or Medea in her bloody bathrobe
and the chariot drawn by dragons.

The Age of Reason

Once, my father got invited
by an almost perfect stranger

a four hundred pound alcoholic
who bought the drinks all day

to go really flying sometime
sightseeing in his Piper Cub

and my father said *Perfect!*
Tomorrow was my birthday

I'd be seven years old, a chip
off the old daredevil himself

and we'd love to go flying.
We'd even bring a case of beer.

My father weighed two fifty
two seventy-five in those days

the beer weighed something
the ice, the cooler. I weighed

practically nothing: forty-five
maybe fifty pounds at the most—

just enough to make me nervous.
Where were the parachutes? Who

was this guy? Then suddenly
there we were, lumbering

down a bumpy, too short runway
and headed for a fence . . .

Holy Shit! my father shouts
and that's it, all we need

by way of the miraculous
to lift us in a twinkling

over everything—fence, trees
and powerline. What a birthday!

We were really flying now . . .
We were probably high enough

to have another beer in fact,
high enough to see Belle Isle

the Waterworks, Packard's
and the Chrysler plant.

We could even see our own
bug-sized house down there

our own backyard, smaller
than a chewed-down thumbnail.

We wondered if my mother
was taking down the laundry

and if she'd wave . . . Lightning
trembled in the thunderheads

above Belle Isle. Altitude:
2,500; air speed: one twenty

but the fuel gauge I noticed
quivered right on empty . . .

I'd reached the age of reason.
Our pilot lit a big cigar.

More Trouble with the Obvious

A baby bird has fallen from its tree and lies feebly peeping
dead center of the bright circle under our streetlight.
What is there to do but bring it in? We dutifully prepare a
shoebox, then mix up the baby food and hamburger of an
old routine we know by heart, the ritual we've learned as
children—but the truth is, in all the years since child-

hood, neither my wife nor I can remember having saved a single bird. We won't save this one either, trembling weakly now on the kitchen table, refusing to do so much as open its beak for our ridiculous food.

It lives with us two days, then dies suddenly in my hand—of "heart attack" my neighbor says. "Young birds like that almost always die of heart attack." He says this pounding nails in his porch and I believe him. In fact, I feel stupid for having mentioned it at all. A heart attack. Of course. The best thing would have been not to touch it. Perhaps it would have found a place to hide; and then, in the morning, its mother might have flown down to feed it. In any case, it's dead now and buried in the garden. The same garden, by the way, from which my neighbor's cat wrestled a live snake once into the hubbub of our barbecue.

But then I seem to have always had trouble with the obvious. Once, when a friend died, and after my parents had told me he had died, I came around the next morning anyway to call him out for school. His mother came to the door weeping and told me Orville couldn't go to school that day. I felt as if I had been walking in my sleep. I knew my parents hadn't lied, and I certainly knew what death meant; but somehow, until that moment, I must have thought it was just a dream I'd had. At school, another friend said he thought Orville died from eating donuts every night for supper. I had no trouble at all be-lieving that. By then, donuts made about as much sense as anything.

A baby bird has fallen from its tree . . . someone you love perhaps is dying in another city. There must be some-thing we can do. I remember one Sunday Orville and I got down on our knees in an alley and asked the Blessed Mother for a kite. When we found a rolled-up kite in the next ashcan with the rubber bands still on it, we *knew* it was a miracle. And we were glad, of course; but neither one of us, I think, was overwhelmed. We just believed in miracles and thought they happened all the time. We thought the birds we found needed milk and bread. We thought when they got big they would be our friends, do us wonderful favors, and keep us company forever.

Crabapples

Somewhere in the Midwest
crabapples are falling

on a new Buick; crabapples
are littering the sidewalk

and a man is muttering darkly
to himself. It's not pleasant

to contemplate these crabapples.
Ordinarily he'd be having fun

oiling the doors of his Buick
in perfect silence. But not today.

No sir. Not with these crabapples
falling. Not with the driveway

looking like this. He oils up
and slams both Buick doors

then opens up his trunk
and removes a brand-new yellow

plastic garbage can. Perfect.
It's the perfect thing. Now

he must carefully cut up
his old plastic garbage can

and toss it piece by piece
into his new one. It's important

not to hurry and that each piece
be exactly four inches square.

It's important to do things right.
After all, he's got himself

a nice place there. Occasionally
a crabapple hits the roof

trunk or hood of his Buick
or bounces on the driveway

but basically it's a nice place
a good life. Crabapples, insomnia

tumors the size of someone's
little finger? That's nothing.

That's why he stays up past midnight
raking the driveway.

Walking the Baby to the Liquor Store

It's nearly ten o'clock in the morning and I have work to do. I have to write a novel and a book of criticism. I have also a book of Mongolian double sestinas to translate, a verse play that needs a final act, and a movie script that's hardly off the ground. Besides that, I haven't published a book of my own poetry in weeks, so it's absolutely imperative that I get busy. But first, first I have to take the baby to the liquor store. A brilliant career is one thing—but being a good father, that's what *really* counts.

The baby adores going to the liquor store. In her infant mind there is, perhaps, nothing so beautiful or significant in this world as sitting up in her yellow stroller and rolling bravely west toward some exotically remote BUNNY'S—or, on Sundays, a place as unimaginably far away as KIRBY'S LIQUOR. Such, at least, is the radiant dignity of her expression. And when that snarling German Pinscher throws himself, all teeth and slather, against the pigeon lady's fence on Maple Street, she doesn't turn a hair. Why should she? This morning she's Cleopatra and the liquor store is Rome.

Believe me, I wouldn't miss these excursions for the world. I wouldn't miss them even if it meant giving up the National Book Award. How much trouble is it, after all, to go out walking with the baby? How much work could one possibly do in that brief half-hour? And measured against such joy, such pure infant bliss (which may well indeed anticipate a lifetime's happiness), how important is it that I go to work at all? Sometimes, when we get home from the liquor store, the baby and I are so happy we even do the dishes and have a drink, by God, right there in the kitchen.

The baby knows four words: mommy, daddy, banana and doggy. Could anyone write a novel more interesting than that? It's something I think about often in the glittering fluorescent kitchen after the baby's gone to sleep. And who knows what she'll come up with next? Luckily enough for me, the rigorous disciplines of my craft have trained me in patience. I can probably wait until tomorrow before going to the liquor store again. I can probably fall asleep on the porch tonight like any tired father in mid-career—watching the fireflies coming on and going out again in the long grass like so many sparks flying off the anvil of the world.

MICHAEL ANANIA

The Fall

I
Sunday in the snow
moving like an old man
I corner, slip and fall
with my hands out
twist my head to meet
the world I fall into—
present, precise to the moment
concrete, stinging, exact.
     The snow trees
feathered out with wind
across the damaged road
way, Route 20, through
township, east and west:
points of my life drawn
out along the thin, bending
highway—dead dog in Iowa,
the bridge at Clinton
arched like a scimitar
across the brown dream river;
Mississippi, Mohawk,
Niagara, Missouri,
did I dream you into
the world, as far off
as you now seem,
beaded out, lost to distance
by the fractured road.

II

The snow trees are luminous,
the frosted globes, archaic
by the neon signs, come on
like a flash. Mid-fall,
the fountain fills with snow;
I beat my arms in the air
like a cartoon cat finding
that my ladder is gone,
or do I remember, falling,
the girl in green
nightclothes lost on the highway,
the girl with the red eyes,
brown hair, green nylon
forced between her legs
by the base December wind,
screaming, help, screaming
with her fingers, red-tipped
in her blowing, brown hair,
or an unhinged door on the prairie,
or old newspapers across a lot
fluttering, tearing on a cyclone
fence. The lights go on and I
fall hands first in the snow.

III

My world goes out,
dream, distance, picture
ice on the river, I know,
gone to distance, broken
in the inevitable present.
I am incapable of the present
fall, while at koolade
cocktail parties no one
gasps, stops for a moment.
It must be reconstructed;
I can not find the beauty,
can not stop it at the
point of impact, can not
make the vision, what I see,

go on from beginning to end,
can not keep it going:
the clouds move, grey,
around the blurred moon,
the snow fills the streetlights,
the highway breaks to pieces
like Mr. Ripley's glass snake
because I touch it;
it will not rearrange itself.
In the lighted window worsted,
in the sky the red neon scrawl,
Pepsi Cola—Drink Light,
I drink light, bathe in light,
fall into my broken world.
It is the inevitable order
that destroys, the necessity
of falling, river to river
shore to shore,
instinctively outstretched
hands to the waiting ground.
Those are my hands breaking.
Dream of my hand moving
with my eye, eye following
my hand from the word to the place.
Seeing breaks the storewindows;
the streetlights and neon are
falling together in the snow.

The Judy Travaillo Variations

For Eugene Wildman

*Of course the other one looks just like her, but if you really know her,
you can tell the difference even at a distance.*

I

There is always the other one
pushing a cart in the supermarket
or standing on a corner waiting

for you to make the obvious mistake,
begin, that is, a smile and catch
yourself halfway, leaving your face
just that much in disorder, no chance
to recover yourself or turn away.

The problem and the test, knowing her
enough—the eyes, perhaps, certainly
not just the hair which shifts and tangles
or the posture that is put on and primpt;
that dress she wore once, the other might
take by stealth or even bargain for,
the one making the other herself briefly
in exchange for certain favors, anonymity,
of course, and possibly her own confusion
somehow relieved, the other wearing it.

And no one, knowing the facts of the case,
would blame you, knowing the disorder
she settles in upon you, the choice
you sometimes make, wanting only choice,
and after all the retreat is expected—
who wouldn't, knowing what you know—
and is judged only when she, the other,
takes your absence as her success.

II
For three weeks
among high lucerne,
saw them grazing like
cattle in familiar meadows,
birds bobbing their heads,
prized mostly for their feathers.

Lunch at the Royal Albertinia,
the consommé springing to the spoon,
the tea thick with mint leaves.
On the veranda talk of a trek
north along the coast.
The natives, they say, have

their women in common,
covering their bodies
with warm red clay,
all their wives becoming,
as the clay dries to powder,
the one wife they can share.

Whitney says this mission
requires more soap than sermons.

III
The arms and legs of Chicago—
fingers that push hair back
from the face, pick clothes
away from wet skin, the face
relaxing as the first air in hours
is drawn in between and expelled,
grit darkening the creases of the neck,
grinding like pumice behind the knees.

Her back to you, swaying with the train,
fine hair clotted with sweat, hand
passing, occasionally, under it.

IV
A cut-out Eskimo in cardboard
spells it out in frost, COOL INSIDE,
icicles hanging from every letter.
In the darkness the chill settles
down on your neck like a wet cloth.

If he had an airplane or a car,
could trail white vapor into ice
clouds above the tangled streets
or glide like a landlord through
the city toward country-club cocktails
and summer evenings with Lizabeth Scott;
if he had not begun so badly, desiring
so much, not taking it all with boredom,
tossing his cufflinks onto the dresser

from a bedroom chair, dinner jacket
sprawled across the carpeted floor.

It is hot tonight, she says, turning,
offering her zipper to his hands.

V
Lost again, strayed from the picnic grounds,
they should have tied him to a tree.
Alone, his Indian companion or the dark-
eyed lady from the grocery store
gone back for supplies or help,
breechcloth or lace panties drift
down the sluggish stream; he fishes
it out with a branch, remembering
his devotion and her eyes when they parted.

Interstate 80

The detail, of course
it quavers in our view,
like the verge we press

the highway toward,
edge of an expected
season, implied greenery,

water shimmering always
at the same distance,
ever retreating spring.

O my America! moist
hand at the wheel,
the present moment

flattened like an insect
on the windshield, traces
of color, bits of wing,

reminders of an ulterior
delicacy, the wind itself,
a quiet air transgressed.

On the Conditions of Place

Loitered, you might say,
at the edges of the ceremony,
the golden colonnade, red
streaked yellow marble, cattle
so real they seemed to graze
upon the stone, the god
himself, flowing robes,
and Augustus talking again
of Actium, the honorable dead.

Love, things weigh on us,
certain occasions, the gods
in their auspicious moments,
men of state. Think of the crowd,
sun on the sun's bright
counterfeit, woe and wonder
shifting from point to point
like a flight of birds unfurling,
turning shut, then opening again.

I saw you once at the window,
twisting a strand of hair
around your finger, sunlight
curling inward to your touch,
poplars in the wind, white
underleaves like sea flowers,
lines of foam, bright wings
or sails in rough weather.
"Bid them all fly. Be gone."

Sometimes it seems that more
has been lost than ever remains,
that we live in a slow passing
among indecipherable signs.
Strangeness and charm, the numbered
particles of weight and light
spin out the patterns matter takes.
All that we know is consequence—
hand, hair, moist skin, leaf curl, the day.

As indistinct as water is in water,
places dissolve into places, words
among words, what is carried along,
names whose sense shapes our memory,
all that is said or might be said,
Palatine or Platte, a leaf, a stem,
a proper noun, a spit-curl of scum
that draws along a moving stream
the probable line of what is seen.

STERLING PLUMPP

Billie Holiday

Feel and hear.
Her insistence on in
side lore. Personal in
jury. Subpoenaed
by tears dripping in silence.
After each throb

surrenders
to epochs of stillness.
She
rises from impulses of
hurt/to sing fine
print on the pain.
Employs
a microscope in her ears.
Crawls a
round in silence.
Finds
diurnal slaps side TJ's head.
Immersed
in knocks on
her back. Feels deep,
his screams stick in
her fingers. After
digging/she hears
Lottie Jean's mis
carriages groan
in her lungs. She

hums history
when she opens
her mouth

in silence.
Her night
quilts stories from depths
in her touch.
I can
not let
go and I
can
not keep the music.
She feels with
in flesh of tones.
I
believe/I'll
go back
to college and
major in kneeling
with my ears.

Saturday Night Decades

For Langston Hughes, Originator

I dug your bull
dozing a
round in my weariness.
Your fingers
tickling lead
belly keys in doom.
To pry
the New Negro
from plantations.
I
got my first season
inked by hurt Simple's feet
moaned
over tenderness of
my river of longings.
Hey now:
daddy

young griot of dawn.
Hip
linguist of Harlem
Diaspora. With centuries
bleeding culture
from your tongue.
Sundiata of Harlem,
shoving a porch of opening
from stereotypes.
Hey now:
quilter of folk
lored patches/black
folk stitched from spirits.
Singer of steps I must
take on nameless streets
in my lonely hours.

Hey now:
sundiata of Harlem,
Original legender of my time.

Hey now:

Susan Hahn

Nijinsky's Dog

Nijinsky danced his last dance, "World War I," in January of 1919. He then suffered an irreparable breakdown.

Nijinsky's dog, if he had one, died last August.

She was a beautiful animal
with all that was rational
beaten out of her strong
cleanly chiseled head.
We'd circle each other,
lonely, in the heat
of the late summer nights,
both of us waiting for you—
for some crumb of attention.
When I didn't finish the dinner
you'd sometimes offer,
you'd slip it into her bowl
and she'd spring toward you,
more starved for love than food.
I'd watch her from my chair,
passing the time until you'd turn yourself
toward me—remember (O please)
I was there. Out on the ledge

she'd sit, elegant and damaged—
her scars buried in her dense gnarled
fur. Since I've come up here I twist
my hair so hard it snaps
and now I have a bald spot
that my barrettes can barely cover. You

almost seemed to cry
when you told me that she died.
But as I came closer I saw
your eyes completely
dry. You left her
on that hot August roof—

the tar blistering
her dog feet. She couldn't stand
to touch the surface
so she sat and sat
on that asphalt edge,
her mind on fire with memory
of how you once took care
with her, gave her a yard
to play in, rolled with her
in cool green grass.
She'd dream of that
and want it back—before
the war that destroyed her world:
your wife's shrieks *take the goddamn*
dog if you leave

me. And the dog
in her dog mind thought and thought
it was all her fault.
I wish I'd been there
when she took her leap
into the too blue, parched
air, over the anchored
oak tree and the naive lilies
reaching toward the idle sky,
to see her resolve—the pause,
then the quick

amazing move—the elevation, the gift
of rising, her thick mane ablaze
against the dazed noonday sun.
How she broke
free in that *grand jeté,*

sailing in holy
madness past her dog life,
her soul bounding out
of her sad dog eyes
while her ragged body hit
a barren patch of earth.

Perennial

So what if next year the deep pink burst
will not appear outside my door.
What if, after all the tending,

the IV's filled with said miracles—droplets
from the blood bags that reawaken your body,
ignite your mind—your face,
a blossom, will not appear outside my door?
Today, June peonies lighten my path—so what

if next year they do not come back? If
they do and you do not,
I'll hack them down with an ax—
that they dare reappear,
their spread petals wild tongues
screaming SO WHAT?

Confession

ADMISSION
In the cabinet with the lattice
opening, I confess to all
the calls and hang ups—obsessions
with the glands and muscles
of the hair: follicle, papilla, blood vessel—
the soft bulb at root's bottom that I love
to pull out and suck. I knew

Krishna, Lucifer and Zeus,
phoned them late at night
but would not speak.
When we'd meet at all the seedy strips
of airport motels, my heart
would swell and beat my body
wild until I'd heat into high
fever I thought would last forever.
I stalked their wives and lovers, had license
numbers, kept records of their busy
tones—who was talking
to whom. Adonai in the temple
said a silent prayer over
my bald spot and wept.

INTERROGATION

Do you swear to tell the whole truth . . . ?
No, Sir, the truth hemorrhages in my pen,
but lies clotted on my tongue.

Do you want a lawyer?
No, Sir, I like the unprotected exposure.

Are you a Confessional Poet?
No, Sir, they all committed suicide
in the 60s and 70s.

How many lovers?
Once I thought there was one, Sir,
but in fact I have to answer "none."

Any rapes?
Including you, Sir, four,
but no one got firmly in.
The last served me
a quarter of a chicken
and while I was delicately
trying to separate the meat
from the bone, yanked me
from my chair to his futon

on the soiled hardwood floor.
His child had napped there
earlier. I could smell
the urine. I know it's sick
to say it, but his
desire made me feel young.

Have you considered plastic surgery?
Yes, Sir, but just in places no one can see.
I keep looking for the soul—that pure egg
inside the body. How I long to hatch it.
I'd let my doctor-lover keep sucking
out the fat and grow so light—
translucent in the sun—
I'd find the perfect shape,
intercept it with my pen-
knife. Then, I'd sit on it like a hen.

Did you make all those calls?
Yes, Sir, but just in June
when the hot pink peonies exploded
inside my head—thromboses of love.
My blood gushed like a bride's
bouquet, then dried and left me empty.

Do you really have a bald spot?
O Yes, Sir, a perfect circle
of "Yes's." I look at it with awe.
It is my flawless flaw.

ARE YOU A CONFESSIONAL POET?
NO, SIR, I ALREADY SAID THEY ARE ALL DEAD.

When do you die?
Sir, every morning when the world wakes
new I go to sleep naked and wrapped
in a simple white sheet.
Unembalmed as an Orthodox Jew,
I watch my body disintegrate.

PUNISHMENT
All agreed to leave her
disconnected—cut any pulse
of light that might travel
from her. Jailed, without
a mouthpiece—diaphragm
and carbon chamber—
it was believed
she could not call, never answer.

TRUTH
I love this claustrophobic box,
the formality of its walls,
the hidden arrangement,
the simple judgement chair.
I do not need another's ear,
just a pen and some paper.

Incontinence

When love gushed out
of me too cloudy—
not the amber
it should be—
and I couldn't control
my permeability or the journey

of my capillaries,
I grew heavy
with liquid, gravid
with disease of the nut-
shaped gland lodged within
my twists of brain.
I wanted to run

backwards through ontogeny,
far from dry
land, for I couldn't
concentrate or conserve
my wits or salts.
The sea seemed
the only safe place
to let go
and live again—
a return to where
it all began, before
the urgency and burn
of anything human.

STUART DYBEK

Sleepwalking Solo

Where did your underwear wander
while your spirit unraveled from sheets,
floating off, earphones trailing their cord?
The hallways descend as quiet as an unplugged escalator . . .

Where are you going? I am going
to throw out the garbage. I am going
to put a nickel in the meter,

I am going to grandmother's cellar,
I am going to visit my old grade school,
I am going to the playground to run the bases,

I am going to row across the pond in the moonlight,
I am going to walk on the water, to levitate
just above clover-leafed highways, through graveyards
in billowing nightclothes, I am coming

to fuck you Sally Kunkelevski,
while protoplasm glides through the zodiac
between eyelids and eyes. Red lights

flash green as I step into expressways,
a breeze ripples pajama legs as I turn
like a remote-controlled robot at the edges of roofs,
I can stand for hours with one foot poised

over cataract oceans at the end of the dock.
You're running naked among allies,
you shuffle unnoticed through crowds of insomniacs
faces pale under streetlights, someone buys you a beer,

but nobody wakes you. Wake a somnambulist
and he loses his soul, his body
lies helpless, like an epileptic gagging on his tongue,
you have to care for him like a baby

Windy City

The garments worn in flying dreams
were fashioned there—
overcoats that swooped like kites,
scarves streaming like vapor trails,
gowns ballooning into spinnakers.

In a city like that one might sail
through life lead by a runaway hat.
The young scattered in whatever directions
their wild hair pointed, and gusting
into one another, they fell in love.

At night, wind rippled the saxophones
that hung like windchimes
in pawnshop windows, hooting through
each horn so that the streets seemed haunted
not by nighthawks, but by doves.

Pinwheels whirred from steeples
in place of crosses. At the pinnacles
of public buildings, snagged underclothes—
the only flag—flapped majestically.
And when it came time to disappear

one simply chose a thoroughfare
devoid of memories, raised a collar,
and turned one's back on the wind.
I remember closing my eyes as I stepped
into a swirl of scuttling leaves.

Haki R. Madhubuti

Killing Memory
For Nelson and Winnie Mandela

the soul and fire of windsongs must not be neutral
cannot be void of birth and dying
wasted life
locked
in the path of vicious horrors
masquerading
as progress and spheres of influence

what of mothers
without milk of willing love,
of fathers
whose eyes and vision
have been separated from feelings of earth and growth,
of children
whose thoughts dwell
on rest and food and
human kindness?

Tomorrow's future rains in
atrocious mediocrity and suffering deaths.

in america's america the excitement is over
a rock singer's glove and burning hair
as serious combat rages over
prayer in schools,
the best diet plan,
and women
learning how to lift weights
to the rhythms of
"what's love got to do with it?"

ask the children,
always the children caught in the
absent spaces of adult juvenility
all
breakdancing and singing to
"everything is everything" while
noise occupies the mind as
garbage feeds the brain.

in el salvador mothers search for their sons
and teach their daughters the way of the knife.

in south afrika mothers bury hearts without bodies
while pursuing the secrets of forgotten foreparents.

in afghanistan mothers claim bones and teeth from
mass graves and curse the silent world.

in lebanon the sons and daughters receive horror hourly
sacrificing childhood for the promise of land.

in ethiopia mothers separate wheat from the desert's dust
while the bones of their children cut through dried skin.

tomorrow's future
may not belong to the people,
may not belong to dance or music
where
getting physical is not an exercise but
simply translates into people working,
people fighting,
people enduring insults and smiles,
enduring crippling histories and black pocket politics
wrapped in diseased blankets
bearing AIDS markings in white,
destined for victims that do not question
gifts from strangers
do not question
love of enemy.
who owns the earth?

most certainly not the people,
not the hands that work the waterways,
nor the backs bending in the sun,
nor the boned fingers soldering transistors,
not the legs walking the massive fields,
nor the knees glued to pews of storefront or granite churches
nor the eyes blinded by computer terminals,
not the bloated bellies on toothpick legs
all victims of decisions
made at the washington monument and lenin's tomb
by aged actors viewing
red dawn and the return of rambo part IX.

tomorrow
may not belong to the
women and men laboring,
hustling,
determined to avoid contributing
to the wealth
of gravediggers from foreign soil
& soul.
determined to stop the erosion
of indigenous music
of building values
of traditions.

memory is only precious if
you have it.

memory is only functional
if it works for you.
people
of colors and voices
are locked in multibasement state buildings
stealing memories
more efficient
than vultures tearing flesh
from
decaying bodies.

the order is that the people are to
believe and believe
questioning or contemplating
the direction of the weather is
unpatriotic.

it is not that we distrust poets and politicians.

we fear the disintegration of thought,
we fear the cheapening of language,
we fear the history of victims and the loss of vision,
we fear writers whose answer to
maggots drinking from the open
wounds of babies
is
to cry genocide while demanding
ten cents per word and
university chairs.
we fear politicians
that sell coffins at a discount
and consider ideas blasphemy
as young people world over bleed from the teeth while
aligning themselves with whoever
brings the food.
whoever brings love.

who speaks the language of
bright memory?

who speaks the language of
necessary memory?

the face of poetry must be fire erupting volcanoes,
hot silk forging new histories,
poetry delivering light greater than barricades of silence,
poetry dancing, preparing seers, warriors, healers
and parents beyond the age of babies,
poetry delivering melodies that cure dumbness & stupidity
yes, poets uttering to the intellect and spirit,
screaming to the genes and environments

revitalizing the primacy of the word and world.
poets must speak the language of the rain,

      decipher the message of the sun,
      play the rhythms of the earth,
      demand the cleaning of the atmosphere,
      carry the will and way of the word,
      feel the heart and questions of the people
      and be conditioned and ready
      to move.

to come
at midnight or noon

to run
against the monied hurricane in this
the hour of forgotten selves,
forgiven promises
and
frightening whispers
of rulers in heat.

The B Network

brothers bop & pop and be-bop in cities locked up
and chained insane by crack and other acts
of desperation computerized in pentagon cellars producing
boppin brothers boastin of being better, best & beautiful.

if the boppin brothers are beautiful where are the sisters
who seek brotherman with a drugless head unbossed or beaten
by the bodacious West?

in a time of big wind being blown by boastful brothers,
will other brothers beat back backwardness to better & best
without braggart bosses beatin butts,
takin names and diggin graves?

beatin badness into bad may be urban but is it beautiful & serious?
or is it betrayal in an era of prepared easy death hangin on
corners trappin young brothers before they know the
difference between big death and big life?

brothers bop & pop and be-bop in cities locked up
and chained insane by crack and other acts
of desperation computerized in pentagon cellars producing
boppin brothers boastin of being better, best, beautiful
and definitely not Black.

the critical best is that
brothers better be the best if they are to avoid backwardness
brothers better be the best if they are to conquer beautiful bigness
Comprehend that bad is only *bad* if it's big, Black and better
than boastful braggarts belittling our best and brightest
with bosses seeking inches when miles are better.

brothers need to bop to being Black & bright & above board
the black train of beautiful wisdom that is bending this bind
toward a new & knowledgeable beginning that is
bountiful & bountiful & beautiful

While be-boppin to be
better than the test,
brotherman.

better yet write the exam.

CAROLYN M. RODGERS

The Black Heart as Ever Green

My heart is
ever green, green
  like a season of emeralds
    green as in tender & like buds or shoots,
          determined to grow
          determined to be
        warmed by summer, winter or any seasons
        sunlight
      green
          like a light
        in the world, for freedom,
              for
          what is to come
          what we must know
          what we must be

              for freedom
          for the harvest

            my heart is
                      ever green.

•

LUCIA CORDELL GETSI

Woman Hanging from Lightpole, Illinois Route 136

Hitchcock would have loved 136,
straight furrow plowed toward winter
horizons, emptiness sweeping
into you for miles. Not like western
terrain that yawns away, these midwestern
landscapes unsettle even as they flatten
the dips near the rivers, erase
the farmsteads barricaded by trees
against winds hostile to balance
and staying put. People here
have stood straight in the winds
so long they can't easily bend or open
eyes squinted at winters dissolving
into themselves repeatedly. Strangers'
eyes are marked by their wide search
for some anchor, some mid-point
to make the repetitions cease,
they wonder how artists here can find
a frame. Their bodies freeze
in the elemental dread of open
space non-herding creatures have. They huddle
in buildings while natives move hard
and stiff into the winds to secure
possessions with strong rope.
                           Anonymous
sister, one printed New York card
marks you stranger or prodigal child
alien in this home. No one claims you.
To travel 136 in winter you have to know
where you're going to arrive there.
Was this your destination or
did you climb the pole to see

how far you'd come, where you needed
to go?—instead merely flooding with light
your body shaken with cold
and wind in this open, open
place endlessly repeating. You hang
illumined in my dream of cutting
loose, weathercock turning
hopeless as your sense
of direction in winds that never seem
to stop. Somewhere, despite the tall
protection of skyscrapers (or mountains)
you learned what these farmers know.
To stay here you've got to be tied
to something.

Washing Your Hair

Too much is made of choice.
   —Eleanor Wilner

I want to tell what happens
when a life slips into its cells,
when a whole body is transformed
into a laboring love that bends,
twists, stoops, gives to, takes from,
re-positions, straightens up, and wipes,
like a body sliding sideways
from the boat into water
and treading, going
nowhere because there's nowhere
to go, it being night.
Even the boat has floated off
and I've got to keep my head
in the air.

          Your eyes close
under my stroking, your rich golden
hair fans in the pouring

water that runs soapy into plastic
pails. The nurse and I work
in tandem, she pours, I lather
and condition, she empties
the pails. I towel dry, she holds
the hairdryer, I brush, supporting
your heavy head on its weak
neck carefully as a baby's
until the sheen casts a light
about your face.

            The comfort of caring,
the routine of chores, the leading
out of the stable the playful horses
who walk at your pace beside you
in such trust they will surrender
utterly to grass while you muck
the stalls, empty the steaming
wheelbarrow, spread the deep fluff
of straw, fill with water the dry
pails. One by one, you brush
them sleek, pick out their hooves
and send them back delighted
to the hanging baskets of alfalfa,
the feeders of oats. The hall fills
with snorts and munching, a wheaty
smell and the peace of knowing
you could do this forever and be
happy, letting the thoughts slip
in sideways and slow down
to the rhythm of work.

            Washing
your hair is ritual, our turning
your body from one side to the other
to allow your lungs to drain,
your skin to breathe, your view
to change from window to door
and back every two hours, over
and over as if there is something

to learn from this, the way
a child of difficult delivery,
just learning to crawl, repeats
the trauma of her birth, bellies
up your seated trunk like a snake,
slides across your shoulders and down
headfirst through the hole
your two legs make, then pulls
back up again, as though practice
can render innocuous the crush
of skull that forced the door
to the world.

          It's possible
with only normal adult strength
to tread water almost forever
without tiring, the lateral current
like wet Christmas ribbon tying
and untying your arms and legs
builds the shelf you seem
to stand on.

Bruce Guernsey

Maps

Those who've been to war love maps.
They keep them everywhere: in pockets, drawers,
the glovebox of cars and stacked by the toilet.
Maps are what they read, these poems for soldiers
who hear in the lines the whir of blades,
who smell in the colors the char of smoke.

They know the hidden meaning of rivers,
the true symbol of water, how dry a last breath—
that here, spread flat on the kitchen table,
are really mountains, the strategic home of gods.
For those such as these, myth is truth,
and this paper you touch, a metaphor for earth.

The Apple

So this is the fruit that made us all human.
So this is the fruit we reached for and got.
So this is the fruit that ripens in autumn.

—◊◊◊—

Cezanne,
I envy your eye.
Knowing roundness,
you put an apple in a bowl,
curve into curve
like lovers.

Mother,
you sliced the green ones for pie,
steaming like morning on the sill.

Doctor,
the apple I eat to keep you away
is the shape, the weight of a heart.

—⁓—

Long before the child, reaching up to pick,
before the ladder in the branches,
long before the tree, full in our yard,
a farmer rests
in the shade of his team.

Their dark sides shine.
In summer's last heat,
in the field's long work,
the apple he's saved
is cold on his teeth.

—⁓—

Shine an apple on your pants.
Make the apple genie dance.

Rub him, rub him, into life.
Ask him for a pretty wife.

And for children I'd ask next,
talismans for the witch's hex.

One more wish is all that's left.
Beg him for eternal breath.

—✺—

Quartered,
a seed rocks
in each tiny cradle.

Like blood,
in the air an apple
rusts.

DAN GUILLORY

From *Snowpoems*

NOV. 2
Retinal burn of warm November light:
Afterimages,
Windmills, wires, hawks and barns—
Trees smoky in the distance,
Hillsides and ridges pucker
Into focus,
And all the souls are saved.
Ghost flakes assemble in the air,
The white choir humming.
Suddenly, the raggedy V
Of southbound geese breaks down,
Re-forms in perfect symmetry
And disappears.

DEC. 22
Birch come down to bones—
Last night's snow hardened
On the leaves like a white tarp,
The red plastic bird-feeder
Dependent on a dying branch.
Old, flatulent and arthritic
The black cat studies the scene:
Purple-crowned finches twittering,
Black-capped chickadees pecking
Ice and feed, the glazed window
He generously shares
On this shortest day of ordinary time.

JAN. 6
Trying to say *I love you*, the wind
Shakes the snowtrees,

Breaking the small, gloved hands
Of sycamore and spruce.
Ice bells ping and tinkle. Snow blows
Into dust   shattering
The choreography of dove and squirrel.
Like all loving, this is clumsy
But sincere: a mouth that will
Not stop, a howling in the ears—
Hair flying everywhere.

JAN. 25
Lutheran spire rising on the hill:
The dead tucked into the earth like poems
Or any other unread things.

FEB. 20
Mama likes it hard
Mama wants to know
On blizzardy days
Where do friends go, where
The hilltop roads
All smother in snow?

MARCH 11
Hitting the updrafts
The red-tailed hawk
(*Buteo jamaicensis*)
Sails into the valley
Photographing white
On white, only the verticals—
Telephone poles windmills
High voltage pylons, red
Smudged barns
Stand clear, pure staves
Humming on the page, he's dying.

MARY KINZIE

Summers of Vietnam

Rising toward New England along the throughway,
The car I drove in alone shot forward
Beneath me, sighing in the echoing return
Of the engine, banked repeating precipice,
Blue mounds of country that made me sigh to see them,
And the thought, which was several thoughts at once:
Again I am alone in the heavy growing
Of the huge, harmless American trees with hands
For leaves. Summer must be hurried to
But disappears before I can arrive.
I have been here before. I have been sent away.
Everything has always shot out from view
Beneath the wheel, my gaze.
                               Into the towns
Whose stop signs stall me on each hot blue hill,
Baking incline, monastery view,
I stutter through the shining afternoon.
Lives I look at going by, go on
To the end of the thirty-mile-an-hour zone
Where that last filling station has always gone to seed.
Farms start up again, in moons and arrows of field,
Then resume their sweep over quilts of beet, corn, clover,
And, gaining speed, past each clear square field,
The seats melt in the slant of the sun, tar
Wavers to nonsense with its childish patches
Across the pale magma that the road runs to
Through air growing colder by the clock,
Condensing the tarmac, the fields, my face, in fever.

I cannot memorize my license tags.
Each of the visiting days in the "facility"
That looks like a movie lot, placeless, fictitious—

Streets of metal crossed with trolley grooves,
The docks and hangars of heavy masonry,
No trees to speak of, in the air the layers
Of diesel, aftershave, ironed uniforms—
I wait in the sentry room with the other women,
None over thirty, who have come to see the men,
None over thirty, who have killed their commanders
In the loud, unmanning, placeless, fictitious jungle—
The man I come to see refused to go;
They keep him in solitary, the one officer here,
Whom even the guards would like to have extinguished—
And I always have to go outside again
To read the forgotten but over-familiar license
That, like their industry at spreading war
(As if ingrained too deeply in the body
To be summonable by the mind),
Still means nothing, although I recognize it.

As I am cleared, I map in thought the dead
Journey on service roads to tall gates
That will keep me straining to the posted speed;
Reach the rooms with peeling walls and spotless floors
That mirror forward the chairless latitudes
Through which I will halt to see you, under guard;
And I know that such foreboding has never mattered
Less than in these naval yards like cities,
Where those on the ground look the same as seen from the air,
From the deep, from the white cloud on a radar screen,
As everything that does not number, fades.

They bring you in. In pairs, they watch us meet,
Twin Molechs burning everywhere you pass
Lest someone see the hell from which you enter.
One's by the door on his feet. One's in the air,
It seems, lowering. He gets two chairs.
The place is filled by something horrible
Talking cannot dispel, the *tink* of metal.
What you are like is still beyond description.
I don't mean your thin arms, I mean your eyes.
You hum into my hair. I kiss your collar.

They break it up.
                    You say that you are happy
For this test. You say you're teaching grammar
To psychotics and the lesser dead.
You have discovered that Defending Counsel . . .
Your father's death when you were ten . . . your mother's
Operation . . . you've written it all down,
What you learned, what you must now renew.
They break it up again *(What a conversation!)*
Until tomorrow,
                    when two different demons,
Who will do their job, at barely twenty,
Much better than they need, won't see us weep
When we join what is not parted for another week.

As they take you out, I map in thought
Your hours of solitude, what you won't eat
And will not see, in that half-assembled
Country of the past where I don't travel.
For myself, the real reduces to
The pads of explanations you write in code
And the line from Portsmouth to Baltimore,
Which I think of in the small, seen from a distance—
How close my going puts me to coming back—
Until I am nothing unless I am in motion
Across a land that has no time for me.
You float above lost time, I race against it,
Until we are like those places seen only from the air
At high speed, without transition from street
To field, from fiat and thrift to the aimless fears—
Non sequiturs—imbedded in the given,
Which deepen long after we have passed them by.

Lunar Frost

For my father

The night of the day
That broke up at sunset in a beadwork

Of islands, my head
On the hot window glass, which gave
Back to me over the highway a face on an angle,
Tinted green over white like a lily
Or angel leaning down against the car—
It was then night drew apart
Like a planet the frost had raked level,
Cold, scored, abandoned.

        Ghastly,
The stars as we drove
Chattered with fear from their stations
Far above, unable
To warm us, or each other.

Night journey. The only warmth, from the dashboard
Far ahead where the announcer
Talks low with my father. They say
Nothing that I can hear. In the dark, my mother
Quiet beside him with the youngest,
My father has told me to sleep
So he can take his comfort from
The warm controls, hearing a neutral voice.
I am for him another sleepy child
Whom he can see, but doesn't, in his mirror,
Awake alone.

        Yet I have done
What he said to, been kind, been of use,
Learned to iron, and save.
And thought. He has told me to think.
So, when the lesson strums forward at school
With a dull breath like telephone poles going by,
I try to expand till my mind fills my body,
Even my ankles, even my eyes;
And as I fill with more than I can know—
The thought of number and the abstract term,
Collective noun, the beings that were once—
I start to shrink down to the facts,
I tear back all I know till I don't know it,

And I can see the jagged
Flicker at the core
Prior to understanding,
Tearing thought down into pieces
That sit about oddly under a different light,
Strange, hard, anonymous.

                                     I question
Everything, break the world down
By questions again
Into incompletion, as it was
In the beginning:

Why isn't shadow
Beside you, your size,
Not loose as a stain
That sinks over what's in the way
(These clots of weed and stuttering
Of rock along the highway)? Does the soul
Of someone who is falling out of life
Fall among such things?

                                Will water
In the desert also stagger
In the light that mimics it, until,
Risen from the shelf of thirst
Like Indians wavering in a last gauze
Of sunstroke, the fainting rivulets
Boil off to sand?

What is the sin for which
These lifeless places are the punishment?—
Laziness? impatience?—when one sinks
Into sleep in the garden (where Christ
Watches the hour)? What is it seeps
Away in the disciple's heart?

Would it be sin to eat His fish
(Even *His*), once you see how they are
Hauled in, hooked—all the quick

Darters, sunfish, bass, rainbow—
Through their rough inhuman mail
And hollow stare?

                    And then,
Huddled together at the final hour
As we are here, eyes on the dark
Where all the warmth dissolves
And every shape is hooded,
When would the narrow soldiers
Realize they will not leave
The garrison? that Santa Anna
Must lay his curving sabre
Even into the living chamber
Of the breast? Does the mind widen
With a wail
For the cold through-coursing
Of the gouts of dying?

With these last words,
Hooked at the end by my question,
I open to my fear. It is here,
Trying to outrun routine in the ever
Fainter countries of the lesson,
That I stumble into my smoky blank,
My center: Knowing of dying
A thought I see ahead with a rough
Porous rind like a column, abraded and hollow,
That can't even stand in its shadow,
All thinking broken, then worn down to this:
Do you know when you're dying?
When you lie, one night in the cold,
Does the ceiling glide open, like an eye
Into whose emptiness you start to fall
(Though you fall up)? Are you extinguished
Like a fleck of burning paper
Sucked out the chimney
Into a broad lake of cold, where there is
No more fire and the fish
Move endlessly away on all sides?

Here is no fire.
Here is a wound
Made in me by the smiling metal
Which as I think about it
Starts to pour.

        In the distance
My father cannot find another station
(I think, the radio, he means gasoline).
We slow through a dead town, the motor breathing;
Pull into unmanned places bathed in neon
That purples our mouths
And turns the rusted drums and glass moon-green.
Mother turns to me her brown eyes
And loosened kerchief, but her longed-for nearness
Comes like a sharpened stone:
She will die before me;
There is a moment, to come,
When a worse solitude than this
Would drift across the acres
Where Mother, Father will be forced in fact
To disappear, and I to sink into
Mere sleep, though I tremble, weep,
And watch the rigid hour
Like an iron lung
Press shining, around me, their deaths,
Which I will see, where I lie frozen,
In the sparkling rearview mirror above my head.

CALVIN FORBES

Killer Blues

Blackbird, blackbird, where's
Your nest now that Mister Rat ate

Your family and made a widower
Out of you? Hide higher than the sky

Next time. I'm housing one
Broken baby sucking milk from pieces

Of bread; but it won't live long.
Two bitten wings, and wet bread isn't

His mother. Mister Rat feasted,
He found you out in the red barn eaves;

And now blackbird you pick up
Feathers, a new nest, a dumb blackbride.

Some men will say it was his
Last supper and conscience his cross.

Who gave him a soul, why are you
Flying in circles as if you were a hawk?

G. E. MURRAY

The Rounds

For My Father (1917–81)

The dark changes guard
With the Swiss-blue hardware of morning.
So the world and its debts are spitshined once more.

But nothing so alive and loyal
As the single light kept lit all night in the pantry—
Our best provisions slightly out of reach.

Nothing so killing
As the sudden parentheses of your years
As I sprawl here mourning,
A fast-moving idea, finally, come home.

It is Fourth of July and the music's
Strummed down and up my spine,
Long-playing tunes of a burial time.

It's the rounds again, so cheers—
Your prizefights, secret whiskies, the blood-love
I learned like a hardwood burn.

Only your favorite god knows
I buy no news about you,
Save the practical
Demonstration of your death.

My brother, my mother told me so, told true:
Death on the holiday, death at noon.

With the last of your peach brandy,
I salute us and the icy light in the pantry.
And already I learn to settle for more.

—⧫—

No dawn ever comes back.
No others need apply.
No more the irrigated life.
No final instructions.

I huddle here colder and clear,
Reinventing everyone
In first sunlight's streaming dust,
Remembering things whole

And unbloodied, in chiaroscuro.
Thus, I hardly know where to begin
This hemorrhaging, this life
As gorgeous as your heart.

Your absence floods. Being solitary
Becomes the matter and the affirmation
Of good gray soul in turnabout.
But we both knew we knew that:

One man's shining idol, another's
Spittoon. Also, the first ending: you
Dying in the middle of a sneeze,
Slumping back to a black fuss,

Shot through like a fuse
Exploded in its socket, a pain
Now made precisely important
And perfect as a child's love.

In those sold, latter days,
What was in us still turned lyrical.
Yet our stories altered by the month;
Each utterance, a suction

Of solitude and foul weather,
Even now new proving grounds.
Keep the weep out of the voice.
Nay-say the night, its aspirations.

Ah, but we traveled mostly at night,
Lucky to be so lost
To our gigantic businesses,
None of which will ever miss us.

I aped the traveling man,
Loved this and that, surely,
Chasing after rounds of your life.
Now I no longer make them.

—⁂—

Let me get this right
Or let me be wrong again and again and again
With my dry reachings, resolute,
Determined as mahogany not to splinter.
I come this far on sincere condolences:
No rescue there, no outstanding issues.
Simply the necessary languages of the dead.
Simply time given over to time;
One more lasting, invisible snow.
It only returns to this: a stammering
That's the east wind; a harsher wind
That's love in its outwash. Funny how it works
On the bullet-proof, those of us
Certified as anvils.
One time late in the pressing twilight
Of hardball times,
You half-berserk on work's edge,
And me stuck with more stories of my near-drowning,
You went hot-eyed, tear-drunk
For your far-gone father, still psychedelic
Against mill flame, mule-backed, forever stoking
Furnace and the beauty of the literal.
You were chasing his light.

You were becoming it.
You knew then that last fierce
Loving touch we Irish reserve for the dead,
Long before that Swiss-blue morning
I changed guard with your darks.

On Being Disabled by Light at Dawn in the Wilderness

For Joanne

Boulder Junction, Wisconsin

Sight seems colored by the hour,
Sucked up through the trees' capillary fans,
Streaking out to sunlight well-kept: marsh-red morning,
Pale blue at noon, the connubial warmth
Of lemon with a late sun and, later, always
Black disapproving black, there in the middle of love.

Yet how beautiful when submitted fully to hungers
Of time breaking into you, as if sitting alone
In a room when glass cracks, necessarily unexplained.
First sight again, light's dispensations
At dawn, segue to all you volunteer
And preserve of the uninvestigated dream.

Forget remembering what fear has loved.
I wake to you and the morning that has come up
Crystal, its facets endlessly reflective, nearly
Deathless, but dying nonetheless, and so,
Undefinable as luck, which cautions:
Do not harden in light; occur only in ecstasy.

American Cheese

She was made from scratch in Wisconsin,
Slowly at first, given to disguises

As a child, a figure swept
By sunshine toward the free fall
Terror in her heart. A declension of circles,
She grew round and firm and ready,
A processed miracle,
Sealed in wax of nervous gestures,
Exported to Chicago as a necessary foodstuff—
Old prairie fiction.
When she turned the wind's
Hard corner, aging decades in days,
She announced, during a daylight attack
Of logic, straight up and down
Like an exclamation point, she was her own
Worst obsession, the failed product
Of a putty knife. Years later,
Crazy on Clark Street, her one stocking
Rolled below the snow line
Of an ankle swollen with city winters,
She becomes available
As litter, blown around the trainless
Midnight of Union Station, talking
A blue streak to the terminal darkness.
In the midlands, there is no telling
The stories of the dead.

Art of a Cold Sun

I realize the horse seen from an airplane looks like a violin,
though it is more and otherwise . . . knowing
gives a shape to jealousy,
to make-believe sins or off-key laughter,
as if hiding a mouse
in my vest pocket . . . all of a piece
from the sun's rude nightly defection.

One must judge much junk before it becomes
someone's art.
Ever consider the heretical impulse

as prologue to new familiars,
somewhat baffling at first glance,
initial shock or stench.

How plausible an eye that could herd scorpions?
In feral ways, marble-mouthed,
you come to think of it,
art's enlightenments
and the sting of its tail.

What's this strange, febrile lyricism
to an otherwise cooling composition? Ah, so,

Time won't lie, but it'll wink.

PAULETTE ROESKE

Preparing the Dead

Saint Anthony's Hospital Geriatric Ward

After high school Latin class,
I put on the yellow pinafore
of the employee-of-least-consequence
and drove to Mrs. Goetzman,
paralyzed for forty years,
who taught me how to turn
her body and arrange the feather
pillows along her spine,
and to Bud, blind from birth,
who translated my features,
his tentative fingers on my eyelids and lips
etching out another me,
and who, brushing back my hair
he said felt black,
concluded, "You are beautiful."

In the broom closet at break time,
Virginia and Lucille, others of my caste,
black women double and triple my age,
joked about the dim logic
and lapsed etiquette of the lifers
on the ward. Virginia handed out
Lucky Strikes all around.
Among the mops and wringer pails,
eye-smarting antiseptics,
and in a space so small
we stood hip to hip,
we smoked ourselves blue.
It was Lucille, swaybacked,
gap-toothed, who schooled me
in the preparation of the dead.

Sanctioned to open the door
posted KEEP OUT, she ushered
me into a scene larger than conjugations
or textbook formulas.
We would work our inexact science
in eerie half-light, the late
afternoon sun through the gauze curtains
washing ceiling, floor, walls,
the draped figure, everything
the same hospital green.
Whipping back the sheet
like a magician uncovering a prop,
Lucille uncovered Bud, blind eyes
unweighted, naked as birth.
The green light settled on his body,
plump as a lapdog's. His bald head
shone like a third eye.

We took our positions,
one on each side, like angels
conspiring at the gate.
From the hospital-issue death kit,
Lucille removed a roll of cotton wadding.
Crossing herself before she crossed Bud's legs,
one well-placed push flipped him
on his side. I held his wrists
while Lucille packed his rectum.

In silence we washed his face,
neck, arms, chest. The only sound,
ordinary tap water sloshing
in the porcelain basin.
Over his round stomach,
down toward the frazzled white hair
fringing his abdomen, it was there
I hesitated. With thumb and forefinger
Lucille lifted his penis
onto her palm. She kneaded
it slowly, deliberately, her private test
for some last vital sign. Admitting

the doctors were right, she sucked
her teeth then added men were maddened
by that little animal. She told me
I was getting old enough
to know the calming trick with spoons
(silver is best) and what code
to tap against its head. Thighs,
calves, ankles, feet, we rolled
him over and began again.

Lucille assured me his soul
was loose in the room, one among legions
come to lead Bud to the next world.
"Girl," she said, "they all around us.
Keep your arms close at your sides.
Don't crowd." I searched the air
for something elusive as smoke or feathers,
as fingers brushing back my hair
but returned to the irrefutable iron bed,
the starched sheets, to one hand
capable of holding the other.

In indelible ink I printed
Bud's name on a luggage tag
and looped the thread three times
around his toe. We eased the crinkly paper bag
down past his bald head, blind eyes,
past every newly washed part of him,
then Lucille pulled the drawstring tight,
and tied a double bow.

Martha Vertreace

Caged Stone

My mother asks if I read about the sculptor
who raised a bell garden for his wife,

each bell a thousand prayers,
how the gentian breeze keened

through holes he chipped in stone walls,
how he stacked them, one atop the other,

as if Jacob dreamed a carillon reached heaven
as angels rose and fell, striking into speech

the tongueless bowls—then offers me

her Christmas box of chocolate bells
so I can eat the bits she leaves

biting each, looking for cherries or nuts,
but finding only cream, abandons the rest

to fluted cups, unwilling to waste.

If I keep faith she will give me
the pendant she lets me wear,

blue agate sheathed in silver mesh
dangling from a leather thong—

blue to honor a woman's moons, she says—
pressing it in my hand like the secret

I've grown old enough to know. We both

know the outcome, a loan, she claims,
swearing I must leave it when I leave—

I, her middle-aged daughter; she, my mother
giving me everything she owns

piece by piece.

Black Tulips

Winter is the snow with black silhouettes.
   —Vincent van Gogh

I spent the afternoon rummaging through
old photos, solemn black-and-whites
like stills from a forties' newsreel
trimmed with pinking shears. My brother
and I squinted as sun bounced off mica
flecks in old cement. Shadows of our
father who took the snapshot, and mother
who waited, covered our feet, climbed
our skinny legs to the knees. In tan
and yellow sunsuits, we sucked our penny
licorice sticks which melted like oil
slicks in our palms—a posed picture; he
never liked them, holding his like dried
fish or a garter snake which blood
warms. When the shutter blinked, wind
sprinkled crows like pepper from aspens.
Almost a lie, this scene. Van Gogh
wrote Theo that no true black exists,
never thinking that where air thickens
with the brown smell of cow, Dutch
biologists would separate the last
intrusive purple from the marriage
of Queen of Night and Vienerwald. My
aunt would say we stood like flowers,
black tulips, she called us.

PAUL HOOVER

Family Romance

You like
showing photos

blind as
light, decades

ripped to
shreds and

littered in
an album.

The future
is present

in history's
window, where

the brief
green world

observes its
turning. An

apple is
yellow at

the edge
of red.

In the
pallor of

the storm,
someone is

rouged in
distance. Your

mother and
father just

after marriage
smile at

the light,
their eyes

dark as
a harvest.

Form is
deep in

portions your
whole life

long—no
winter shadow

thin as
sin, just

broken stones,
a tottering

ghost. Ragged
as pleasure,

rain stabs
water. A

lighthouse on
the prairie

does no
less. What

is life,
what world

born five
miles back?

The *this*,
the whole

boat. When
your heart

is beating
and the

porch is
soaked, you're

drowning in
arousal and

always in
the frame.

Theoretical People
For Maxine

Pervasive and
strange, love's

singular language
has ten

tongues. The
actual present

is blessed
with traffic,

intense bits
of emotional

baggage constant
as genres.

In memory's
rite, *I*

love, you
love is

all love's
yielding, to

cast our
shadows, cold

to cold,
on this

bright bed.
All our

histories fly
over a

white horizon
into a

patch of
park where

swell turns
dark. The

mind's ripe
distance is

transparent as
an edge.

We come
from afar.

That's that
then. The

map maker's
colors denote

no place
where the

sting of
love isn't.

Beyond all
resemblance, be

for me
the question.

Letter to Einstein Beginning Dear Albert

On the shores of my animal there was a zoo,
thick hair a field of swaying bars,
the chromed machine of a flea
cruising like a Mafia don,
collecting what is owed it.
Half raccoon, half basket,

my animal slipped down the hallway
as if across a keyboard, in heat,
brimming with apples.
My animal was nice in bed with me.
Now I have forgotten it.
Instead, these overlapping versions
of "Pennies from Heaven,"
one so different from the other
it's like writing Donald Duck
on top of your pretty signature,
the one unraveling in darkness
as soon as the letters are mailed.
But excuse me, today's omens have just come in:
a tuning fork garden,
the E sharp of underground water,
the fact of finding Indifference Lounge
in the phonebook just now
while searching for Orphic Grill.
These are of course "mere facts."
I must no longer dignify them.
Yet I still wish someday
a conversation with Doppler
if only to hand him the moebius
that blew up the street to me
with its endless poem
near the Rue Gravity.
You'll remember the park there,
thousands of wind-up squirrels
run down and rusted due to
factions in the city council.
I recall equally your amazement
at a violin we found,
so soft you draped it over a shoulder
like a towel from the Palace Hotel.
Do you still have it, I wonder,
and are you always dripping wet,
wanting a chance to play it?
Then one night, alone on the train,
you thought you felt a feather sprout
under your clothes and it had.

The sheer speed of your panic
enlarged every teacup in the diner,
a fact so measurable
the bureau of statistics denied it
for fear of material inflation
whenever a genius gets scared.
After a while, even your microbes had hat sizes
while I prepared an infinite homburg,
a hatband its horizon,
snow the paralyzed feather.
Once, you see, I begged to be dreamed
in one less dimension
("he keeps the third for vacations")
or I had dreamed myself in *only* one,
a stick figure seeing in the alphabet
merely an interesting skyline
or a series of "ethnic types."
Miracles, after all, are simply
a matter of good concentration.
My tooth a refrigerator
humming in the ideal desert,
that little room on the bed
where the head is stored at night,
money borrowed from the Entropic Trust
for one second only, just before closing time.

MAURA STANTON

A Few Picnics in Illinois

Sometimes I hear haunted mouths
tearing at leaves or thistles
in the woods. At Starved Rock
the Indians entered their bodies
like caves, delving for rain
in the green spaces between bones.
I saw bones, later, at Dixon Mounds
where families like mine
gaped at skeletons
excavated scientifically from farmland.
At Jubilee Park, a soft fungus
licked pews in the stone church.
I couldn't grasp "a hundred years old"
& ran from a face in the wavy
glass that was me, distorted—
Once I tossed a Lincoln penny
over the tourist guardrail at a bed
in Lincoln's house, wondering
if he slept like me, legs curled
against the danger of wolves.
Oh yes I see Lincoln's ghost
down on his hands and knees
after that coin. Touching the head
like braille, he shrieks—
A Chicago woman drowned
at Starved Rock one summer:
For two weeks she made history,
the spot on the bank marked X
for children like me who imagined
her white neckbone in the weeds.
As her eye glazed, she saw
something new in the water, her body
floating away from her . . .

Sorrow and Rapture

The April sun burned through the dirty glass.
My eyes burned. My wool skirt burned my knees.
Beyond the window of the city bus
As it turned up Forrest Hill, I couldn't see
Red brick, and frame, and budding maple trees,
But only the dark theater, where all alone
I'd watched "La Traviata" on the screen,
Surrounded by two hundred empty seats.
I'd bought the ticket from a nun at school
For two dollars, and a written promise
Not to go home, or shopping, or idling.
I'd sunk back in the tattered velvet seat,
Glad to be out of Civics and History,
Breathing the odor of popcorn and licorice.
I wondered if they'd show the film for me,
Just me. I sat in the exact middle.
I was sleepy and warm. I hoped for color.
And then the sound track blared and leveled off.
The black and white singers floated far above me,
Magnified. Their singing made me dizzy.
The voices drew me forward on my seat,
And my face prickled with heat, my chest hurt.
I was more Violetta than I was myself.
I wore her satin gown. I loved Alfredo.
I raised her handkerchief to my own mouth.
The subtitles that flickered underneath
A passionate embrace, or stricken look,
Seemed more foreign to me than the music.

Then the bus stopped on top of the hill.
I looked over the rooftops of Peoria
Shaken with rapture. What town was this?
I saw the brewery, my high school, a steeple,
Slate-colored shingles, the glimmer of river,
And beyond, smokestacks of Caterpillar
Where the wire mesh gates had just opened on thousands
Of laborers with their metal lunch pails.
Still dazzled, I got off at my stop.

At home our maple almost cast a shadow
With its early buds, and I threw myself down.
No ants were stirring in the pale, cold grass
But here and there, in thick, green clumps,
Violets had bloomed, not yet choked by weeds,
Purple petals the size of fingernails.
I stroked the violets' heart-shaped leaves.
I looked at my hands. I stretched them in the sun.
I could remember the face of Alfredo,
Violetta's room, the view of Paris,
But not a single tune. I was tone deaf.
Still, I rolled over and over in the grass
Unable to speak, burning and longing,
As cars from the factories arrived on our street
And the smell of supper drifted out of doors.

Little Ode for X

Sometimes I call X nostalgia.
My mother telephones her fear of snow
caving the roof in; she hired a man
who rakes it off every time, but today
he's sick & so my mother paces room
after room, watching the ceiling . . .
When she hangs up, I imagine
her face resembling the crisp fly wing
stuck on the storm window, or her raisins
heated in pans until they dry out,
although their bitterness ruins cakes.
Last night a child threw a stone
hard against my front door. That's X, too,
for I've no father to chase him away.
Now I find the stone on the step,
milk crystal so strange I wash
my hands over & over in the kitchen sink,
afraid the child soaked it for hours
in poison from his Christmas chemistry set.
X is the fifth time a friend says no

to dinner, preferring to polish heirloom
silverware until the garland handles gleam,
or my brother's letter from Florida
describing a fight with his third wife.
That feeling of ants in my father's chest,
red fighters circling his heart that night
he sat up in bed, sure of death;
that's X, the specific hum of blood
beating against a clot in my mother's leg.
I hold a mirror behind my own knees,
touching the blue tubes running like roots
into my body, finally an equation for X,
as it, too, now grows by subtraction.

Reginald Gibbons

Sparrow

In the town streets
pieces of the perishing world
Pieces of the world coming into being

The peculiar angle at which a failing gutter descends
from a house-eave; a squirrel's surviving tattered nest of leaves
woven into a high bare crook of an elm tree
    (the last one alive on this street);

the small bright green leafing out of that elm;
a man shaking coins in a dry Coke-cup and saying
Small change, brother? Small change?;
                          a woman
in scuffed white running shoes and a fine suit hurrying
down the street with a baggy briefcase that must have
papers and her purse and her good shoes inside it
Perhaps a small pistol

Gusts rattle the half-closed upstairs window
    in the old office building that's going to be torn down

Skittering across the sidewalk, a scrap of paper
    with someone's handwriting on it, in pencil
A message that will arrive

Things in themselves

A few minutes of seeing
An exalting

Or a few minutes of complete shelter
A protectedness, a brief rest from the changes

Sparrow moments

But this emblem I take from the world—
able, fussing, competing
at the feeder, waiting on a branch,
sudden in flight, looping and rushing, to another branch,
quick to fight over mating and quick at mating,
surviving winter on dry dead seed-heads of weeds
and around stables and garbage and park benches,
near farms and in deep woods,
brooding in summer-hidden nests—house sparrow,

song sparrow, fox sparrow, swamp sparrow,
field sparrow, lark sparrow, tree sparrow, sage sparrow,
white-throated sparrow of the falling whistled song
that I hear as a small reassurance—

Would my happiness be that the sparrow not be emblem—
that it be in my mind only as it is outside of my mind, itself,
that my mind not remove it from itself
into realms of forms and symbolic thinking?

My happiness, that is, my best being

Words like branches and leaves,
or words like the birds among
the branches and leaves?

They take wing all at once
The way they flee makes flight look like exuberance not fear
They veer away around a house-corner

"Luckies"

A loop of rusty cable incises
its shadow on the stucco wall.
My father smiles shyly and takes
one of my cigarettes, holding it

awkwardly at first, as if it were
a dart, while the yard slowly
swings across the wide sill of daylight.
Then it is a young man's quick hand

that rises to his lips, he leans against the wall,
his white shirt open at the throat,
where the skin is weathered, and he chats
and daydreams, something he never does.

Smoking his cigarette, he is even
younger than I am, a brother who
begins to guess, amazed, that what
he will do will turn out to be this.

He recalls the house he had
when I was born, leaning against it
now after work, the pale stucco
of memory, 1947.

Baby bottles stand near the sink inside.
The new wire of the telephone, dozing
in a coil, waits for the first call.
The years are smoke.

Maureen Seaton

Nostradamus Predicts the Destruction of Chicago

Radiation bubbles beneath the skin.
I'm sick with indeterminacy, the way
light seeps in, thickens the blood with neon.

Strontium in my breast milk, that onion-
skin glint on the freshest salami.
Radiation bubbles beneath the skin

of five-legged calves, poor sucking orphans
of cold war. What did Nostradamus say,
scary sights filled to the brim with neon,

about the balding spot of the man
upstairs, a whirling insomniac? *Hey,*
radiation bubbles beneath the skin

in Batavia, top quarks and a boson
so wraithlike and belligerent they claim
a small bang might sicken the earth with neon.

When the God Particle collides with its twin,
the Anti-God, I'd rather leap away
where bubbles flit, bereft of radiation,
and light, neon god of gases, thickens.

Ice

We were driving down the Kennedy having a great time guessing old groups
   Spinners
Commodores La Belle maybe I was driving fast we'd been cold for a month
   not regular cold

scary the kind that wears you down twenty forty below dark so cold you
   know hell
is scratchy wool and miles of hard ice forget heat and everything suddenly
   stopped the Lincoln

which was not our Lincoln but my sister's boyfriend's Lincoln not even his
   but the leased
whim of a fired employee crashed into the back of a steel-gray Mercedes
   Benz you could feel

the ice eat your bones your bumpers the plastic grill curling up the back of
   the Mercedes Jesus
that Lincoln imploded *good old American* the Mercedes owner said as we
   shook in the

ridiculous cold cars whizzing down the frozen highway and Lori's arm shot
   across my chest
like a mother's we'd been spoons sleeping on the sunny couch earlier while
   the temperature

reached a record low in Chicago my ex-husband used to say stop breathing
   on my back
Maureen the only thing I remember about the crash is the way Lori's left arm
   reached out and

saved me from ice crystals on the windshield she said whenever I breathe on
   her back she
melts.

Tagging

There's something we call a game show with all kinds of dings and glitches
going on in the next room, and outside the Queen of Angels points her
    steeple

at something we call heaven. We say Chicago's more polite than New York.
Driving around, you sometimes find a person who will give you a break.

He or she will signal for you to pull out in front, and if you're from New York,
you will wave and wave until he or she is lost in your rear-view mirror. We say

we're safer here. Lately I've been reading something called the *new* physics,
the kind where nothing's sure and that's just fine with us: Dissipative
    structures,

inconclusive theories, discontinuous motion—one big *huh?* at time and
    space,
one small question leading to others we ask and ask until we're giddy, all
    those

unexpected foldings into a seamless universe. We say brazen electrons
    leaping
into invisible orbits. We say blood invisible as Jesus. I was star dust

when the first atom exploded on Chicago's South Side. Now
our children discover ways to kill each other without metal—they scoot

through detectors like excited hydrogen armed with plastic guns they call
    gats.
They scatter down Clark and land beneath a sheet outside our front doors.

Their wars are small, American. They name themselves *the people* and *the
    folks,*
tag the land as if there is anything left that's free. Nothing in the universe

exists separately, we say—us, our kids, fear, blood, grief. First,
a man and a woman spin a wheel and then they try to guess a phrase, and if

they're lucky they win a car or money. We call this *The Wheel of Fortune*.
I'm holding my breath as an architect from Los Angeles uncovers a sudden
rush

of vowels. I love the vowel *a*. It's round or flat and beautiful and free.
In New York we say cat, hat, tobacco. In Chicago we say cat, hat, tobacco.

We say we are dissolving into sky, our breath is piquant with rumors,
our whole body frantic for the leap and the sweet light that follows.

ALBERT GOLDBARTH

Letter to Friends East and West

What's new? I'm still in Illinois,
and the pamphlet says I can find white squirrels
in Olney if I wait long enough. They're rare
you know, and a dung-daubed boy from Kinderhook
swears how their whiskers are each attuned to one
of the four Primeval Whites: snow,
milk, sperm, moonlight, but that's just a rumor;
the squirrels are fact. And there's a gorge "nearly
200 feet deep" near Starved Rock; if it's no
Grand Canyon, Diane, if cracks don't zag here
quite like they do near the nation's extremes,
your awesome schisms, still even *my* disappointments
won't fill 200 feet though I chunk them like stones
all day at the face in the crick at bottom. All night
a wind howls through, and scours out Skeleton
Cave, The Giant's Bath Tub, Well-In-The-Wall
and hones the Illinois rock: Twin Sisters, cradled,
Needle's Eye, pierced, The Devil's Smokestack, pared and polished,
you'd have to see such wind to understand
what shaped the raking hands
above my sleep, you'd have to let it
sodomize you too or hear it lap once
at your mattress. It's not easy here, white squirrels
are never easy. I wouldn't lie to you. But
Abraham Lincoln christened the town of Lincoln,
Illinois by squeezing a watermelon onto the dust
and it's hard, as you could intuit, to run from a state with stains
like that; and even you, as far as Maine or Florida, will think
of that story the next time a sweet rivulet of any kind
froths, rich, across your lips. And didn't you write me,
Ron, to say how deer in California print the Silverado Trail right up
to your sill, you parse out apples, four deer legs are dark

bars squares of sunlight cool in. Well in Illinois we've sows
like troughs of oleo, we've rat-packs in Chicago
till our sewerpipes shake with all the will
of epileptic nerves, and a broom-handle
chopped across the gnawing snout-bones sometimes
does no good. But, though there's nothing so far north
in my life as the bear, so thinking
as the porpoise, here in Illinois is dark
the thickest filament from a sweet corn
couldn't glow through, here's a dark in the field just made
for our own mammalian radiation and, though it's low,
it's light, this star in the Illinois night,
this udder. All I need to do is bide my time:
no kidding, Olney hosts white squirrels
"unique in all the world" and I adopted the stance
of a beech last week to coax them,
wish me luck. The search is difficult, yes, and nothing
even so small as a white incision tooth or whitish pap
as yet rewards my diligence. But, honestly, a plaque
outside of Byron commemorates soldiers under Major Isaiah
Stillman who shot point-blank at a band of Black Hawk Injuns
approaching with the truce flag; you can't just high-tail out
of a land like that, it deserves a certain observation
or, perhaps from the damp underside of the brain,
one root. In any case, Ron, when you visit
bring Cheri, tell me what a twin bed's like, here
"once each year the town of Nauvoo celebrates The Wedding
of Wine and Cheese Festival"; it's true, I'll show you.
I'm in Illinois. I know: a statue of William Jennings Bryan
"created by Gutzon Borglum," I have: trilobites
in the Jersey County quarries, shell bracelets, chert blades
and stemmed stone hoes from the giant Cahokia mounds.
When you were in last May you'd say the ocean
defines *expanse*, report how you chugged up from New Haven, Conn.
to the Cape, there are stories of coeds and jellyfish, Michael,
I believe them all. Now
you must believe me: I'm still here, remember,
Illinois? A man could kneel to Apple River to drink
and let the touch of his tongue go
mainlining, quick, a fix, through the evening prairie;

maybe my mouth gone silver in the rush of the Kaskaskia,
the Sangamon, the Sinnissippi, Big Slough, Vermilion River,
or the Kankakee, is even now a shine at the lip
of far-off faucets, intimacy with me will not sustain
and still: I'm here, I'm pouring, I know, if one is patient
there are white squirrels. I wouldn't bullshit you,
my friends. I'm stuck, half-chance, half-choice, and some
left over to weep in the stand of virgin white pine
along Rock River. Really. Can you imagine? I'm
still in Illinois, I've waited long enough
for anyone else to meet and mate
and raise a whole teat-dangled brood, and still
the Olney Woods has not released its secret beasts
for my catching. Someone . . . Can't you see him,
year after year, running for squirrels like these with the taste
of Devil's Kitchen Lake in his cheeks,
sun on his scalp and dust up his breathing,
screaming through Geneseo
and Bald Knob and Burnt Prairie and Peoria
and Kickapoo "I'm here
I'm here in Illinois with the nation's
oldest evaporated milk plant!"
How could it *not* be true?

The Talk Show

. . . in 1930, The Bell Telephone Company commissioned one of their employees, Karl
Jansky, to find out why the new car radios suffered from static. Jansky set up radio an-
tennae, and heard a steady hiss coming from the direction of the Milky Way. Radio
astronomy was born thirty years later.
    —James Burke

A woman "heard angels." The paper says angels
sussurra'd her body, rang their praises daylong
through its reedy places, stirred her
smallest water. And elsewhere, Larry
"Dude Man" Chavez raises his #2 wrench
indifferently overhead on the C-track tightening line,

and feels something like lightning—only
there isn't lightning—beam to the wrench head,
branch down his arm, make all of his muscles
electric feathers, then exit his other arm out
its guttering candelabrum fingers and into
the frame of the Ford. It's stored

there. It happens. We all know it happens.
The cops and the hospital nightshift crew know
what a full moon means, and
if their decades of statistics don't cut diddlysquat
with you, here's someone being wheeled in
from a 3–car smashup while the universe hums
its lunar kazoo, and adrenalin everywhere dervishes.
And statistics on sunspots, and suicides.
And statistics on lines of magnetic pull,
and conception. We're the few but beautiful
units of the first day of the cosmos
densed-up over time; when the lady I love

flaps suddenly in sleep like a wire discharging, it
makes sense as much as anything—bad dreams,
zinged nerves—to simply say *we're* where
the Big Bang ripples to the limits of a continuous medium,
flickers a little, kicks. I've disappointed her
sometimes; and so, myself. I've left the house then,
while she slept, and while my neighbors slept, as if
I could walk noise out of myself
through darkness, finally dialing-in
the talk show where the blood calls with its question,
and the "sky," whatever that is, whatever portion we are
of it or once were, answers. And

I've walked past where the university's planetarium
dish-ear swivels hugely for the far
starcrackle Karl Jansky more primitively
dowsed. It happens any size; that woman? picked up
cop calls on her IUD, the paper adds, in bubble-bursting
glee. Although if angels are voices beyond us
in us, everyone's umbles are singing hosannahs

under their everyday wamble and gab. I've
slipped back into bed some nights and clasped her
till I slept, then woke to her heart
in my ear, that mysterious sound,
on earth as it is in heaven.

Meop

1

The scenario is: I'm six, and an invincible Venusian army of robots
swarms the city, easily conquering its human defenders with (guess what)
death rays shooting like 1954 home-move-projector lightbeams
out of their boxy heads, in *Target Earth.* In *Devil Girl from Mars,*
the eponymous leather-fetishy siren of outer space attacks
accompanied by Chani, stomping hunk-o'-hardware robot
extraordinaire, whose particular laserlike sizzle disintegrates
a tree, a barn, a village truck, and a villager. No oratory
dissuades these invaders, no pitiable stare. And if this
somehow all sounds comic in my cavalier retelling, I
assure you it wasn't, then—no, it was set to exactly
my level of terror then: we're born instinctively knowing
an enemy awaits us, and the world provides it a series of faces
keyed to match our aging understandings. Though there's also Tobor (robot

backwards), he of 1954's *Tobor the Great:* playpal of the movie's
plucky eleven-year-old kid-star "Gadge," and rescuer of the boy
from threatened tortures at the hands of foreign spies
(of the kind who speak like ziss, and hiss and glower).
The lesson is: of every order of being, there must be
nemesis and hero, in a tug-of-warring balance. Satan
predicates St. Michael, and vice versa: they
require one another. Yes, but how to tell? The neighbor-lady
led away one afternoon by a county official
for holding her daughter's open palm against the flat of an iron
"so she'd listen good . . ." spoke not one hokey ziss or zat to flag
her culpability. I knew about the moon's dark side:
aliens' secret bases were there. But what about people?
—what about *in*side? what about simple earthly night?

2

The fabled Kansas flatness seems to go so far, we *couldn't*
be the same "us" by the time we've finally exited its distance.
When I drive this wheaten vastity, I see how life is space
enough for each of us to segue through a programmed range
of consecutive selves, some less than what we'd wish for, some
so seemingly "other" we shiver in our passage. And that Shiva
the Destroyer, and Shiva the Dancer of Life, are one—is just
a mythic hyperstatement of whatever robot/tobor me-*du-jour* we
carry confusingly into the lives of those we love (see
Paramount's 1958 *I Married a Monster from Outer Space*).
My wife's in bed tonight with a novel in which one brother becomes
a ruthless mafioso, one a priest. And then she sleeps,
whoever she is in her recombinant life, while I'm up
writing, whoever I am. Sometimes I think of Skyler

and myself: a car is driving through the lengthways Kansas landscape
like some blip on an ongoing medical readout, everyone hoping
it stays within the central "steady-state" for soma
and psyche, but sometimes it peaks off toward the edges.
Then, whatever (even ordinary) patience we can summon
is required; or it thins into ire; or infrastructures itself
into something amazingly like forgiveness. Just last night
I turned in bed to see us both awash in moonlight
made so jittered by the stir of nearby trees, it looked
as if we gave off semaphore—although the message
might have come from Alpha Centauri, for all I understood it.
Her face went visible, then guarded; clear, then variegated
weirdly. All night, both of us: a flickered glimpse of beings
from the lunar dark side. Trebla. Relyks.

DAVID HERNANDEZ

Rooftop Piper

To Ken Serritos, from a Friend and Admirer

When the city snores in blood-shot eyes
her dress is rumpled and perfume stale
the Marlboro man flew home real tight
Kenny's on the rooftop
with a midnight wail.

> His saxophone is playing
> in the dry clear blue-steel moon
> a satin city lullaby
> a silhouette in swoon.
> And it seeps right through the buildings
> the bus stop and the bars
> Kenny is the Piper
> he leads the sleeping hearts.

When the city is high-heeling
through echoing alley stairs
to visit night life ladies
and tease their neon hair
Sharing secret wishes
Read each other's mail
Kenny's on the rooftop
with a drifting midnight wail.

> His saxophone is playing
> reflecting streets below
> where the Old Champ shadowboxes
> so he won't feel the blows.
> And the music soothes his memory
> with all the punch-drunk scars
> Kenny is the Piper
> He patches Beat-up hearts.

When the city reads the menu
in all-night restaurants

her head is undecided
between her needs and wants
The El train slowly snaking
a rattle on her tail
the stars hang out on rooftops
to hear the midnight wail.
        It hits the 1st shift workers
        and calmly wakes them up
        and it starts the coffee perking
        and rattles all the cups.
        The saxophone is playing
        a morning virgin note
        Kenny's on the rooftop
        He leads the heart to hope.

Workers

Papi worked the factory
for 25 years he worked
leaving his drop of sweat
deeper than the ocean.
He would replenish his dream
wipe off the sense of not belonging
and think of mami
on the other side of town
working in the hospital
cleaning bedpans with full-strength
  ammonia and Ajax for institutional use only
   and made the beds with fresh sheets
    while the old/sick people saw her
     as an angel of mercy who understood their pain
     and she would smile a soothing smile
      that word got around that she was a real soft touch
      because she shed real tears when anyone
       left the hospital dead or alive
       and they loved her mucho because
       she would talk about her oldest son
       who woke up at 5 in the morning

before going to Waller High School
 and sweep and mop floors for a company
 around Fullerton and Sheffield
 and how he would give her 10 dollars-
   a-week to help out with the groceries
    and keep enough for the movies on Saturday
     him and Manuel Perez who also worked hard
      but they were bold and dared to ask
      /is this the way forever?
      Something better got to give/
     as they watched all the upheaval and drama
    on the screen but the movie was way deep
   inside their hearts specially the ending
  where all the badness got blown apart
 and they left the theater
real happy and full of hope
that cold day of 1959
                    was never the same again
                    was never the same again.

Georg Nikolic

Under the Ninth Sky

Without a single sun
Under the ninth sky

I am without care
Not afraid of anything

I cannot move from here
Why try to go on

With bones only
Among men

Key to Dreams

The gate closed
The dark child
Of the lock

Still lost

BARRY SILESKY

The Kingdom

Gold and whores a thousand years announced that
heaven: another feast, wine, music. So the Pope
slept with the daughter, who slept with her brothers.
So the king beheaded another wife. Let's torture
the infidel, march to the next border.

But that was another century. Everyone says
this Cardinal's "a regular guy." His house has more rooms
than we can guess, old, square chimneys on top,
a Mercedes in the drive. It's the only yard
at the end of the block. Blood and gold

leaves stir the sky, the park across the street,
the museum of history on the corner. There's no sound
inside the house, then muffled chimes, and the back door
opens. Plain as her white habit, the nun takes
my letter: his message reaches us all: I'm a Jew,

I want to tell his story. They say he'll write back
thanks, but there's no time to talk, nothing
new to say. The child walking to school
is shot in the back, a car wraps the bridge's frame,
the father is gone. Face twisted with the loss, the throat

shuts, but we can't look away. Every day there's more
pain. Don't we love this death, the wild blue water,
the trees' fire? Hold this hand. We're alive.
So the Indians watched the geese circle these banks
as the buffalo swept the prairie, huddled

for the invaders' guns, dove off cliffs. So the priest
drinks with the mayor as they toast the re-election.
Steel and glass blink in the sun, and it's Halloween, winter,
spring again. But the basement of this house has a hole
I've got to fix, an upstairs window that needs a new frame.

The Cardinal leads another prayer. Everyone knows
he's dying, and we can't resist the details:
he's thanking the priests, blessing the schools,
writing to the Supreme Court. He's trying to breathe.
The river that emptied into the lake flows the other way.

His letter never comes. Now, he says, he's free.

Screens

They were supposed to be fixed by today, now that they're hardly needed—
though they will be again. Keep the dust down, the bugs out. Of course no
screen will stop the ones there are. He'd describe them if he knew. How they slip
in after the children are sleeping, sink into the nerves and send him after the
gun. The brain's still clear: the taste is lousy, the barrel stiff, uncomfortable in
the mouth. He knows there must be other positions just as certain, where the
feel's cleaner, the weapon simply a tool, apart from the mess of flesh. And he
doesn't want any accidents. The angle's the least of the problem. Sorry, my son,
my wife, he writes, really you're better off. Last week someone brought pills for
the monthly pain, spermicide, a fuse. Was it burned out, or the replacement?
So it's another story about sex, and what comes next. The gods were supposed
to teach us a lesson, and he was home, waiting. This time, the repairman finally
came, he knew how to fix the machine, but though they both looked hard, they
couldn't see a problem. The beautiful women get further and further away. The
snow coming and going belongs to the neighborhood. There must be a way to
avoid it, he thinks. Then he doesn't.

JIM ELLEDGE

The Man I Love and I Shop at Jewel

Untouched, the door swings open before us, and—*voilà!*—we're in the produce section. We pass up the bananas and zucchini, but can't resist squeezing hot-house tomatoes, knock-knock joking with the cantaloupe. He breaks a bulb of garlic into cloves, then snaps one clove open and rubs it behind his ear. I grow dizzy, lay my head on the produce scale, and growl.

We ignore the stares of the biker chicks and the grandmas pushing carts, the retired high-school coaches and fundamentalist preachers lugging baskets.

Aisle 2: Cellophane crackles as we pass. Aisle 3: Pop tops snap open, spew. Down the paper products aisle, boxes of Reynolds Wrap and packages of Charmin split open, unroll, festoon themselves across the ceiling.

"Stay close," I say.
He says, "StaSof."
"Huggies," he says.
I say, "Depends."

Theft detection cameras spin planet-like on their pivots.
"Fluorescence," I say.
He says, "Flower essence."

For hours we plunder the shelves and, aisles later, change our minds and return some of the loot. Our peg legs tap 50s lyrics in Morse Code on the glistening tiles, counterpoint the piped-in Muzak, our vision narrowed string-straight by patched eyes, our hooks perfectly adapt at snagging our hearts' tamper-proof treasures.

Then, as we pull into the 10–items-or-less check-out bay, I lose control, climb onto the conveyor belt, hang ten to Don Ho's greatest hit past the *Enquirer* and *Weekly World Report,* pipe-line through the miseries of talk-show hosts and soap-opera stars, of Liz and Magic, of Di and the Kennedys as crowds form: the

Morton Salt girl hand-to-fin with Charlie the Tuna; Aunt Jemima, Sara Lee, and Mrs. Butterworth closely flanking a blushing Oscar Mayer, their hands moving unfettered, wildly, and out of sight—and that cereal's toucan.

Blowing kisses to my fans, I squeal, *This is life,* in my best Richard Simmons, as the man I love pays the cashier what the cash register says we owe and snags the "Paper-or-plastic?" the bagger offers. Waving bye-bye to the crowds, *This is what it's all about,* I grunt in my best Steve Reeves.

Then, as the door opens all by itself again and we return into the arms of the universe, I belt out "I feel pretty, oh, so pretty" in the best Ethel Merman I can muster.

14 Reasons Why I Mention Mario Lanza to the Man I Love Every Chance I Get Tonight

Because they're both Italian, and I prefer sneakers to boots, sneakers to wing tips. Because their voices run deep, and nighttime—blue-black, silver-sleek, and full of Roman-named planets dizzy in their orbits—runs in them. Because in his apartment above a deli on Federal Hill, a violinist, his heart set on a Stradivarius someday, tunes up and the scales set his room aflame. In the distance, robed and crowned, enthroned among Cardinals, Urban VIII demands Galileo recant the solar system, beads of star-bright sweat in ellipses speckling his lips.

Because wind rustles leaves in cornfields and olive groves alike—its sigh, Dante blowing dry each word of his tercets. Because today, during our cappuccino break, he covered my eyes with his hand then, giggling, gave me a bouquet, no scent but, better, each bud a condom. Because, in the distance, Michelangelo polishes *Il David* one last time, and in the recent distance, those marble veins and strained muscles made my flesh tense, my blood drum. In the distance, a soprano crosses himself, kneels, and studies his hands, imagining the gelding knife's glint, then shudders—not from the chapel's chill but because he hears, approaching, footsteps.

In the distance, a body dangles above a mob, the piano-wire noose a taut cinch. Because our parrots woke us this morning chortling "Vissi d'arte, vissi d'amore" backed-up by our finches' tinny chirp. Because Domenico Modugno, not Al Martino, croons "Volare" over the CD player: "Nel blu dipinto di blu."

In the distance, a lion laps puddles of blood, another gnaws slivers of bone and strips of flesh, and above, even the vultures circling the Colosseum, a circle, wince. In the distance, twin boys nuzzle against a she-wolf: gurgle and howl, growl and burp. Because candles stand at attention, the sauce simmers, the pasta boils, the Chianti breathes—and the man I love and I do too.

Triptych

PANEL 1: ELBOW-DEEP IN DISHWATER, I TELL THE MAN I LOVE A SECRET

The tree of nothing matters grew red leaves then dropped them confetti-like. The brook of let's forget iced to a mirror. The stars of probably tomorrow clamped their eyes shut. Meteors of regret nothing festooned the noonday sun. The wind of it feels good beat its snare drum as the wind of that feels even better whirled. The brook of let's forget iced to a mirror. Waves of now what folded into themselves once, twice, again. The forest of shhhh rose on its haunches and brayed sunward. The wind of it feels good beat its snare drum as the wind of that feels even better whirled. Thunderstorms of just this once blew the sun out. The quail of ohhhh pecked blue grapes that grew by the rose trellis. The forest of shhhh rose on its haunches and brayed sunward. Vines of why long for yesterday wound up oak bark. The quartz of take a deep breath buzzed then folded its wings. The quail of ohhhh pecked blue grapes that grew by the rose trellis. Lizards of calm down sang hymn after hymn a cappella on the beach. The tree of nothing matters grew red leaves then dropped them confetti-like. The quartz of take a deep breath buzzed then folded its wings. The stars of probably tomorrow clamped their eyes shut.

PANEL 2: THE SECRET I TOLD THE MAN I LOVE TELLS ITSELF

The tree grew red leaves then dropped them confetti-like The brook iced to a mirror The stars clamped their eyes shut Meteors festooned the noonday sun The wind beat its snare drum as the wind whirled The brook iced to a mirror Waves folded into themselves once, twice, again The forest rose on its haunches and brayed sunward The wind beat its snare drum and the wind whirled Thunderstorms blew the sun out The quail pecked blue grapes that grew by the rose trellis The forest rose on its haunches and brayed sunward Vines wound up oak bark The quartz buzzed then folded its wings The quail pecked blue grapes that grew by the rose trellis Lizards sang hymn after hymn a capella on the beach The tree grew red leaves then dropped them confetti-like The quartz buzzed then folded its wings The stars clamped their eyes shut

PANEL 3: THE SECRET I TOLD THE MAN I LOVE TELLS ITSELF AGAIN
nothing matters . let's forget . probably tomorrow . regret nothing . it feels good / that feels even better . let's forget . now what . shhhh . it feels good / that feels even better . just this once . ohhhh . shhhh . why long for yesterday . take a deep breath . ohhhh . Calm down . nothing matters . take a deep breath . probably tomorrow.

Edward Hirsch

Husband and Wife

1

I woke up and found you above me—
your face peering down through shadows,
your hair sweeping slowly across my chest,
your voice crying out a name in the darkness,
my name, just once,
as if it had been pulled out of you
from a great distance, from oblivion itself,
as if a rib had been carved from my side
and given back in your shape,
as if we were two halves of one body—
a cell, an egg floating in water,
a new being gathering force like a storm
(wind tossed, tossing the wind)
until the rain seeding the clouds
and the thunder bloating the sky
could stand it no longer
and we burst forth in a wild flood.

2

Then we were falling away from each other,
breaking apart, tearing ourselves loose
from a cupped palm
and putting on our torsos, our limbs,
our separate distinguishable selves.
The ecstasy—the oneness—was unbearable
and so we expelled ourselves,
who had tasted the fruit,
who had discovered our nakedness . . .
I woke up and found you lying next to me,
already awake. How long did we stay there
like strangers, shoulder to shoulder,

scarcely touching, until you got up
and went to the window, and I followed?
Outside, the branches scraped in the garden.
The lightning splitting through the trees
was a sword over Eden's gate.

For the Sleepwalkers

Tonight I want to say something wonderful
for the sleepwalkers who have so much faith
in their legs, so much faith in the invisible

arrow carved into the carpet, the worn path
that leads to the stairs instead of the window,
the gaping doorway instead of the seamless mirror.

I love the way that sleepwalkers are willing
to step out of their bodies into the night,
to raise their arms and welcome the darkness,

palming the blank spaces, touching everything.
Always they return home safely, like blind men
who know it is morning by feeling shadows.

And always they wake up as themselves again.
That's why I want to say something astonishing
like: *Our hearts are leaving our bodies.*

Our hearts are thirsty black handkerchiefs
flying through the trees at night, soaking up
the darkest beams of moonlight, the music

of owls, the motion of wind-torn branches.
And now our hearts are thick black fists
flying back to the glove of our chests.

We have to learn to trust our hearts like that.
We have to learn the desperate faith of sleep-
walkers who rise out of their calm beds

and walk through the skin of another life.
We have to drink the stupefying cup of darkness
and wake up to ourselves, nourished and surprised.

American Apocalypse

(Chicago, 1871)

It was as if God had taken a pen of fire
        Into his flaming blue hand
And scrawled a chapter of horrors
        Across the city at night,
Burning the world in a day-and-a-half. . . .

It was as if, after 98 days of drought,
        The furious oranges and reds
Of the Last Judgment erupted
        In a barn on DeKoven Street:
God had burnished the Gem on the Prairie.

Fire seethed through the shams and shingles,
        Through the parched bodies
Of cottages and sheds, of cow-stables,
        Corn-cribs, and pigsties,
All the tinder-dry precincts of Garden City.

The raised sidewalks were piles of kindling-
        Sticks under pine and hemlock
Fences, the shanties were logs
        Lit by kerosene. The barns
Were giant ovens exploding in a lumbermill.

The heavens blazed and a husky southern wind
        Turned into a mass of devils
Whirling through the streets,
        Advancing in a column
Of smoke and a wall of flame, a steady torrent

Of sparks and a shuddering wave of lightning
		Crackling in the air.
	The fire bells clanged and the
			Steamers stood by helplessly.
Soon the fire swept across the sluggish river

That flared like gasoline and seemed to boil
		In the 3,000 degree heat.
	It burned on three sides of the water
			At once, eating bridges and ships,
The huge grain elevators stacked along the banks.

First, the Tar Works exploded and then came
		The Gas Works and the Armory,
	The police station and the fire house,
			Conley's Patch. There were
Explosions of oil, crashes of falling buildings,

And down came the Post Office and the Water Works,
		The impregnable Board of Trade,
	The Opera House and the Design Academy,
			The sturdy Chamber of Commerce.
Down came the banks, the hotels, the churches. . . .

The tornado of fire rolled toward the north
		And people jammed the streets
	With wagons and carts, with
			Wheelbarrows of belongings.
They came tumbling out of windows and doorways,

Shrieking in all directions. There were horses
		Breathing smoke in dead alleys
	And dogs racing like live torches
			Toward the burning water.
The noise was calamitous, torrential, deafening,

As the world staggered to a last fiery end.
		The firemen might as well
	Have tried to arrest the wind itself

Since the wind and the fire
Were a single fury hurtling through the night.

The dogs of Hell bounded over the rooftops
    And leaped from tree to tree.
  There were no stars and no clouds,
        There was nothing else
In the sky but the fierce vengeance of flames

Flattening the world into stones and ashes.
      This was the Great Catastrophe
And some responded to the terror
        By kneeling down in embers
And crying out for release from the prophecy:

For behold, the Lord will come in fire and
      His chariots like the stormwind
    To render his anger in fury
        And his rebuke with flames.
For by fire will the Lord execute judgment. . . .

But then the judgment was stayed, the rains
      Descended like manna,
  Like a fresh pardon from Heaven,
        And the winds calmed.
The fire devils died in the arms of the lake

And the wrath abated along the open ground
      At the edge of Lincoln Park.
  The Great Destruction was over
        For the city in ruins.
So this was the smouldering end of Time.

And this was the Lightning City after 36 hours—
      a muddy black settlement
  On the plains, a ditched fort
        After a quick massacre.
This was the Garden of Eden reduced into cinders.

The boom town had become an outpost again.
      Soon the army was called in
   To save the city from citizens
       Who plundered and looted,
And stormed through the rubble in despair.

There were those who set themselves on fire,
      Those who fled together
   On the first trains heading east,
       Those who cursed and wept
For the lost civilization on the prairie.

But there were also the unrepentant ones
      Who were young and free
   Of history at last. They moved
       Through the ruins alone
In a jubilant new world blazing under the sun.

They stood in the cooling ashes without grief
      And imagined their future
   Rising out of the blue lake as
       a man-made mountain range,
a city that aspired upward toward the sky.

Wild Gratitude

Tonight when I knelt down next to our cat, Zooey,
And put my fingers into her clean cat's mouth,
And rubbed her swollen belly that will never know kittens,
And watched her wriggle onto her side, pawing the air,
And listened to her solemn little squeals of delight,
I was thinking about the poet, Christopher Smart,
Who wanted to kneel down and pray without ceasing
In every one of the splintered London streets,

And was locked away in the madhouse at St. Luke's
With his sad religious mania, and his wild gratitude,
And his grave prayers for the other lunatics,

And his great love for his speckled cat, Jeoffry.
All day today—August 13, 1983—I remembered how
Christopher Smart blessed this same day in August, 1759,
For its calm bravery and ordinary good conscience.

This was the day that he blessed the Postmaster General
"And all conveyancers of letters" for their warm humanity,
And the gardeners for their private benevolence
And intricate knowledge of the language of flowers,
And the milkmen for their universal human kindness.
This morning I understood that he loved to hear—
As I have heard—the soft clink of milk bottles
On the rickety stairs in the early morning.

And how terrible it must have seemed
When even this small pleasure was denied him.
But it wasn't until tonight when I knelt down
And slipped my hand into Zooey's waggling mouth
That I remembered how he'd called Jeoffry "the servant
Of the Living God duly and daily serving Him,"
And for the first time understood what it meant.
Because it wasn't until I saw my own cat

Whine and roll over on her fluffy back
That I realized how gratefully he had watched
Jeoffry fetch and carry his wooden cork
Across the grass in the wet garden, patiently
Jumping over a high stick, calmly sharpening
His claws on the woodpile, rubbing his nose
Against the nose of another cat, stretching, or
Slowly stalking his traditional enemy, the mouse,
A rodent, "a creature of great personal valour,"
And then dallying so much that his enemy escaped.

And only then did I understand
It is Jeoffry—and every creature like him—
Who can teach us how to praise—purring
In their own language,
Wreathing themselves in the living fire.

RODNEY JONES

TV

All the preachers claimed it was Satan.
Now the first sets seem more venerable
Than Abraham or Williamsburg
Or the avant-garde. Back then nothing,

Not even the bomb, had ever looked so new.
It seemed almost heretical watching it
When we visited relatives in the city,
Secretly delighting, but saying later,

After church, probably it would not last,
It would destroy things: standards
And the sacredness of words in books.
It was well into the age of color,

Korea and Little Rock long past,
Before anyone got one. Suddenly some
Of them in the next valley had one.
You would know them by their lights

Burning late at night, and the recentness
And distance of events entering their talk,
But not one in our valley; for a long time
No one had one, so when the first one

Arrived in the van from the furniture store
And the men had set the box on the lawn,
At first we stood back from it, circling it
As they raised its antenna and staked in

The guy wires before taking it in the door,
And I seem to recall a kind of blue light
Flickering from inside and then a woman
Calling out that they had got it tuned in—

A little fuzzy, a ghost picture, but something
That would stay with us, the way we hurried
Down the dirt road, the stars, the silence,
Then everyone disappearing into the houses.

Mortal Sorrows

The tortures of lumbago consumed Aunt Madge,
And Leah Vest, once resigned from schoolmarming,
Could not be convinced to leave the house.
Mrs. Mary Hogan, after birthing her fifth son,

Lay bedfast for the last fifty-two years of her life,
Reporting shooting pains that would begin
High in her back and shear downward to her feet,
As though, she said, she had been glazed in lightning;

Also men, broken on bridges and mills,
Shell-shocked veterans, religious alcoholics—
Leldon Kilpatrick, Johnson Suggs, Whitey Carlyle:
They came and sat there too, leafing through

Yellowing *Pageants* and *Progressive Farmers;*
One by one, all entered in and talked,
While the good doctor gargled a dark chaff
In his pipe and took down symptoms,

Annotating them on his hidden chart—
Numbness, neuralgia, the knotted lymph,
The clammy palms—and then he'd scratch
His temple's meaningful patch of white

And scrawl out his unfailing barbiturate prescription
To be filled by his pharmacist brother-in-law
Until half the county had gathered as in a lap,
The quantum ache, the mutiny in every house.

How much pain, how many diseases
Consigned to the mythological, the dropped
Ovaries, the torn-up nerves, what women
Said, what men wanted to believe? Part of it

Laughable, I know. Still I want someone
To see, now that they lie safe in graves
Beyond the vacant stores, that someone
Listened and, hearing the wrong at the heart,

Named it something that sounded real, whatever
They lived through and died of. I remember
Mrs. Lyle, who called it a thorn in the flesh,
And Mr. Appleton, who had no roof in his mouth.

A Blasphemy

A girl attacked me once with a number 2 Eagle pencil
for a whiny lisping impression of a radio preacher
she must have loved more than sophistication or peace,
for she took the pencil in a whitened knuckle
and drove the point with all her weight behind it
through a thick pair of jeans, jogging it at the end
and twisting it, so the lead broke off under the skin,
an act undertaken so suddenly and dramatically
it was as though I had awakened in a strange hotel
with sirens going off and half-dressed women rushing
in every direction with kids tucked under their arms;
as though the Moslems had retaken Jerusalem for
the twelfth time, the crusaders were riding south,
and the Jews in Cadiz and Granada were packing
their bags, mapping the snowy ghettos of the north.
But where we were, it was still Tuscaloosa, late

summer, and the heat in her sparsely decorated room
we had come to together after work was so miserable
and intense the wallpaper was crimping at each seam,
the posters of daisies and horses she had pasted up
were fallen all over the floor. Whatever I thought
would happen was not going to happen. Nothing
was going to happen with any of the three billion women
of the world forever. The time it would take
for the first kindness was the wait for a Campbellite
to accept Darwin and Galileo or for all Arkansas
to embrace a black Messiah. The time it would take
for even a hand to shyly, unambiguously brush my own
was the years Bertrand Russell waited for humanism,
disarmament, and neutrality. And then she was
there, her cloth daubing at the darkly jellying wound.
In contrition, she bowed with tweezers to pick the grit.
With alcohol, she cleansed the rubbery petals.
She unspooled the white gauze and spread the balm of mercy.
Because she loved Christ, she forgave me. And what
was that all about? I wondered, walking home
through the familiar streets, the steeple of each church
raised like a beneficent weapon, the mark of the heretic
on my thigh, and mockery was still the unforgivable sin.

The End of Communism

Now I have Vallejo with me on the desk, his troubled words, and
    behind the words, his life tapped out
In Paris in 1938 while my grandparents shouldered one of the last
    springs of the Deep South depression.
Vallejo, who felt compassion for the travails of oppressed laborers,
    would not have imagined my grandparents,
Dirt farmers and slaves of nothing but survival, with no boss but
    cramping hunger and penury,
The work of a few mild days wedged between the cold spells and the rain.

They waged their revolution against clods, and when they'd dropped
    their seeds, the main battles were still to come.
The war against weeds yielded to the long August drought—
    stillbirths everywhere, cholera in the wells.
Maybe my grandparents would have had no compassion for the
    suffering of poets, who, even then,
Had time to dillydally over huge books and learn foreign languages and
    skedaddle halfway round the world and live
In impoverished splendor while they bent their youths against the
    cheating fields.

But when Bird Wilheit came starving and broke, they let him sleep in a
    room behind the house,
For which privilege he was given the field beside them to work, a place
    at their table
And the luxury of living fifty more years, a slave's son, and maybe a
    slave himself. My grandparents loved Bird Wilheit.
I do not know that they would have loved Vallejo for writing what they
    already knew, that the world was a thief,
That many murderers sat far away in the feathery chairs of heated parlors.

They knew that someone somewhere knew more than they knew,
    and that such knowledge,
Imperfect and querulous as it must have been, was more than tall
    cotton and no salvation.
They knew work started in the bitter dark and ended in the bitter dark.
They knew prices were fixed against them, and to hell with it
    as long as everything
They watered and pampered into life did not die of floods or droughts.

I have done a little work with my shoulders, back, legs, and arms. It
    has been a long time
Since I have done anything besides thinking, talking, and writing.
    What good is that
If it does not put a coat on someone's back. My grandfather, when he
    went into the nursing home,
Refused the government money. He was not rich, but neither was he
    broke. He worked.
Things came up. My grandmother moved beside him down the rows.

I do not know that anyone young will care what fomented the red dirt
     so I might fiddle with instruments
And read great books and mumble bad Spanish in my ripe Alabama
     drawl, but just because the shirt
On my back winds back to the drudgery of a field is no reason for guilt.
     I let the dead go on ahead of me:
My grandfather saying, "I reckon if you split up everything in equal
     parts, in five years the same folks would have it again";
And Vallejo reckoning "the enormous amount of money that it costs
     to be poor."

Nell

Not until my father had led her into the paddock
And driven her a month in circles and made
Her walk six weeks with the collar on her neck
And the bags of seeds on her back did he snap

The leather traces to the hames, for she was not
Green halter broke when he took her that way,
Rearing and shying at each birdcall of shadow.
It would be another year in blinders before she

Began seeing how it would go from then on,
Moving not as herself alone but as one of a pair,
With the sorrel gelding of the same general
Conformation and breed shuffling beside her,

And between them only the split tongue
Of the wagon. As is often the case with couples,
He the subdued, philosophical one, and she
With the great spirit and the preternatural knack

Of opening gates, they had barely become
A team when the beasts began vanishing from
The fields, and the fields, one by one, fell
Before the contagion of houses. Still, they

Were there for a long time after the first
Tractors and the testing of rockets, so you
Could see how it had been that way for years
With them, just the one motion again and again

Until at dusk when the harnesses were lifted,
The odor that rose seemed history itself,
And they bent to their feed in the light
That would be that way for the rest of their lives.

MICHAEL DAVID MADONICK

Settled In

My new neighbors keep asking, are you
settled in? And every time they ask,

in that moment before I answer, I think
of my lost possessions, the things

those frigging Mayflower people sent on
to someone else. I growl. I imagine

what a dirt farmer in Maroa
must be doing to my recording

of *The Tender Land,* and of how
my dog-eared copy of Kafka's

The Judgement is probably propping up
the tireless front end of his Ford.

But mostly when they ask me,
are you settled in, I move in my mind

to Rockaway, 25 years ago, and watch
my grandfather in the cane seat

of his ladder-backed chair shuffling
a pinochle deck while Bessie, my grandmother,

hunches, like Quasimodo, over the dog's
bowl that says ROXIE. She is breaking

Matzo into the dog's favorite, coffee
with cream, two sugars. They do not see me,

they do not see how real the arthritis is
in Roxie's bones, or that soon

some of the card players will be rising
like the smoke of their cigars,

their bets. The dog's tail is keeping
some ungodly rhythm, saying yes, saying

yes, and grandma goes back
to the kitchen. They do not see

the cane of the chairs giving way,
and a few of my grandfather's toes

going, in a year, to gangrene. They
play cards. Someone brings lunch. My new

neighbors come at me again. Are you
settled in? Are you settled in? And I want

to ask *them,* are *you* settled in? Do you
like the cards in your hand? Is that seat

safe? Will you sail the ship on that frigging
green truck and get my stuff back? Do you hear

the bells of sanctuary, of sanctuary, every time
I give you my answer, my yes, my yes, my

dog-tail yes?

ALANE ROLLINGS

In Your Own Sweet Time

For Imre and Maria Honrer

To bear your life you need accompaniment.
You apply for a license, buy crystals, and listen through the skip.
The world comes through in staccato bursts, bouncing
off the ionosphere. You can pick up Paris and WXRT,
Yo-Yo Ma and The Jefferson Starship.

In the soft light of an auditorium
beyond which it snows and grows dark,
the orchestra waits for the audience to stop arguing.
The audience waits for the music. A theme
of long separation begins. The audience makes up and holds hands.

In the Arctic Ocean, a humpback whale picks up a song
on the note he'd dropped it on a month ago.
In the auditorium, a thousand people
give themselves to symmetry. Scenarios of night and day
solemnly unroll. I hadn't heard that piece
since I had to listen to you play; I listened
the whole way through the way I never would to you,
slamming away at our piano on the sun porch
as though you were on stage. When you got stuck on the bells
the termites beat their heads on the floor,
flinging themselves into space.
A thousand people applaud. I put my heart
into the hand you hold. A Japanese woman
kisses her violoncello, a fish clicks his teeth
to the tympani of a school of mollusks, and a thrush
stops in mid-song and begins again, dissatisfied.
When I told you what I'd been supposing from your silences,
you told me I was wrong.

You need the charm of each C sharp
as China needs the secret music of growing rice.
Ideas with unreadable eyes hover over you in twos and threes,
choose you for their instrument, like Arab jinns
which perch on a man's shoulder and drive him till he drops.
They go to your head and feet; your hands beat like hearts.
 Then every night, as you lose count, you hear,
beneath the other sounds, continual music:
a nightingale sings his twenty-four separate songs,
a sea-man plays a bamboo flute, and a hundred women
chant to seed the clouds. They measure and remeasure
your happiness and sorrow. They quarrel like Mongolians
over where exactly in Mongolia
music was invented. They work out to the ends of dreams
which are that you can't have the dreams.
You aren't the theme of everything.

 I need your voice the way I need the temperate evenings
on the verandah, the weight and threat of happiness;
you'd rather not talk about loving each other.
You expect to overhear pedestrians say exquisite things.
 The Japanese government issues an edict of sorrow:
there will be no transformation of all matter.
You can count all your life, you'll never know
why notions of time involve weight and blood.
Five thousand marines sing "Row Your Boat."
Your life is in a minor key, more suspense than substance.
 I try with ten fingers to hear your heart, counting away
in your chest. When will you accustom yourself to night and day
and love them as they are, one after the other?
You'll never know how many songs you know:
songs that show you are still a novice at suffering
and can't be sung in public,
danceable music, the Ode to Joy,
songs that make you sing.

Dirty Dreams and God Smiling

Breath is warm.

Do people go to bed because they have the same ideals?
Absorbed into his atmosphere, I was unable to remain attached
to an abstraction. I was conscious only of the odd personal sounds,
of the pear taste of his lips, and of my most susceptible areas
and the imperative happiness to which I wanted them subjected.
Afterwards, "Love" claimed its place again.
    I said I loved his inside like his outside,
not thinking of his mind. He had somewhat blue eyes
and wonderful, huge feet. I loved the twists in his intestines,
the pain-bits sticking to the walls of all his corridors.
At every station of the body, he could tell me another way to die.

If He'd had the time, God would have taken great physical pleasure
in making a gesture another could understand: smiling;
blushing over an unexpected smell; arousing His own instincts
and sneaking into languorous, soft-porn dreams;
pushing Himself to the point of collapse.
Didn't He make us so that He could laugh, touch, ache?
Yes, we are alive.

Flesh can be played for music. The body hurts for pleasure
as dispassionately as a man taking off a shoe;
its dreams are dirty, pure, and primitive.
In the sector of the brain that makes obscenities,
there are smoke concerts where pleasure-blinded women
writhe and flaunt their nakedness. The female body,
an interior open on all sides
and perfumed with fish scales, flower sap, and seaweed,
is part seduction, part intractable pain of unknown origins,
part condescension, part sacrifice.

When he came flaunting his masculine charms,
all my breath entered him. I stretched my middle taut.
His hands as soft as the hooves of the dawn horse

left nineteen kinds of scratch marks on my body.
He shone with the irresistible sex of an angel,
and a bit of him entered me.

    The implacability of the body!
I've tried to domesticate this beast;
I've bathed it, fed it, tended to its indiscretions,
stroked it, clothed it, lived at its bidding, called it by my name.
But is it mine?
    I hate my leg for going to sleep, hate my head
for aching, hate being told all the time how I feel.
I don't mind shoulders, ankles, even breasts
with all the names they're given by the fearful and obsessed.
I can't explain nudity or the fault I find in secret with his neck hair;
I'm just his lover, tidied and meticulous.
    But how sweet that spot on his chest when he coughs, yawns, breathes.
When he parts his lips, how sweet the teeth!
Yes, we have got to know pain.

    And how to drink the air, its odors of dead saints fed to flames,
of lemon soap and dangerous atoms released in our breaths,
of the stamen of tulips, the reluctant coupling of snow leopards.
    "Am I naked enough?" I ask, plaiting my hair
to make his eyes grow bluer again. "Aren't I
a nice arrangement of bones, nerves, and muscles
luxuriating in itself, hiding in its hiding place—itself,
biting the heavy thread of pain embroidering its flesh,
and, even while sleeping, conscious of its existence?"
    Yes, and knowing whether,
just before our blood begins to evaporate
and our bones to take on their final, articulate white,
we'll be trying to remember how it felt to have a passion
or still be riding that wild horse down.

DEBRA BRUCE

Plunder

Now that your surgery's
savagery's smoothed over
and the calm you've put on is balm
for all, and in the interstices
between catastrophes you find yourself
enjoying joy;
now that your *why?*
is wisely subsiding, knowing no one
knows why one grows gold
slowly and one's bright green gets torched
overnight;

in this intensely present
tense, in its rush
of cherished perishables, you might splurge
skyward, spreading
your colors in a freefall
never dared before; or
with minimal fanfare slip
into the life you left, the least
predictable most delectable,
in whose midsummer noon you pop
a flip-top in thirst, and think . . .
And though you simply sip,
deeply drink.

Prognosis

I hold my breath and balance on a cliff,
instructed not to focus on the edge.
Instead of *when* my sentence starts with *if,*

though surreptitiously I spot a cleft
of rock and tiptoe toward the hope I can wedge
myself inside, be safe upon this cliff.

But what I'm searching for is what I've left
behind—the snug, sunlit privilege
of making plans with *when* instead of *if.*

Some climb the years, and in their sixty-fifth,
join Tuesday's book-club, take a course in French,
while others, younger, balance on a cliff,

listening for news whose wild relief
allows them one more step, one increment
of *now,* not *then.* My sentence starts with *if*

and plummets easily—if one streaked leaf
descends to circle at my feet, I clench—
hold my breath, balance on this cliff
where everything I think begins with *if.*

ANGELA JACKSON

Spinster Song: African-American Woman Guild
For Ginger

We'll all be Penelopes then.
Weaving by day, untying by night.
Deceiving the lovers who are not
quite right.

Waiting for heroes' arrival from fields
unraveling with bloody arts.
Throwing aside their cool shining shields
that cover their breakable hearts.

It's wasteful to be Penelope.
Spending days doing nothing
to undo nights.
Lying about loving
or knots.

I'd rather be in fields
Stripping away shields
Aiming needles at suitable
hearts.

Miz Rosa Rides the Bus

That day in December I sat down
by Miss Muffet of Montgomery.
I was myriad-weary. Feet swole
from sewing seams on a filthy fabric;
tired-sore a-pedalin' the rusty Singer;

dingy cotton thread jammed in the eye.
All lifelong I'd slide through century-reams
loathsome with tears. Dreaming my own
silk-self.

It was not like they all say. Miss Liberty Muffet
she didn't
jump at the sight of me.
Not exactly.
They hauled me
away—a thousand kicking legs pinned down.

The rest of me I tell you—a cloud
Beautiful trouble on the dead December
horizon. Come to sit in judgment.

How many miles as the Jim Crow flies?
Over oceans and some. I rumbled.
They couldn't hold me down. Long.
No.

My feet were tired. My eyes were
sore. My heart was raw from hemming
dirty edges of Miss L. Muffet's garment.
I rode again

A thousand bloody miles after the Crow flies
that day in December long remembered when I sat down
beside Miss Muffet of Montgomery.
I said—like the joke say—What's in the bowl, Thief?
I said—That's your curse.
I said—This my way.
She slipped her frock, disembarked,
settled in the suburbs, deaf, mute, lewd and blind.
The bowl she left behind. The empty bowl mine.
The spoiled dress.

Jim Crow dies and ravens come with crumbs.
They say—Eat and be satisfied.
I fast and pray and ride.

Transformable Prophecy

When the world ends
a great spider will rise like a gray cloud
above it.
She will rise and swell, rise and swell
until she covers green earth, brown rock,
and blue water.
She will seize Creation inside herself
when the world ends
in the last days between the fire and the cold
the ones left will gather tins to beat into shelter
and weeds to eat with decaying mouths
like women in South African bantustans.
They will love what they have gathered among ghosts
and heaped into a place.
The coffee can over smouldering ashes
will hold stone soup.
A thousand species of decay will be born
when the Great Spider squats Creation
back down. A thousand demispecies of spiders
will flourish like flowers walking through
the burning ash, the hot, hot dust.
Crickets will break out of their cages
and tremble down the sky like rain,
twitching on the ground, while the sky turns cold.
The ones left will gather sick skin around bones,
sit in fires that smolder in the earth.
Myriad-legged creatures will scramble through
scorching dust,
legs on fire writing writing prayers God knew
when earth first smoldered, squalled
and begged to be born.

BRIGIT PEGEEN KELLY

The Leaving

My father said I could not do it,
but all night I picked the peaches.
The orchard was still, the canals ran steadily.
I was a girl then, my chest its own walled garden.
How many ladders to gather an orchard?
I had only one and a long patience with lit hands
and the looking of the stars which moved right through me
the way the water moved through the canals with a voice
that seemed to speak of this moonless gathering
and those who had gathered before me.
I put the peaches in the pond's cold water,
all night up the ladder and down, all night my hands
twisting fruit as if I were entering a thousand doors,
all night my back a straight road to the sky.
And then out of its own goodness, out
of the far fields of the stars, the morning came,
and inside me was the stillness a bell possesses
just after it has been rung, before the metal
begins to long again for the clapper's stroke.
The light came over the orchard.
The canals were silver and then were not,
and the pond was—I could see as I laid
the last peach in the water—full of fish and eyes.

Young Wife's Lament

The mule that lived on the road
where I was married
would bray to wake the morning,
but could not wake me.

How many summers I slept
lost in my hair. How many
mules on how many hills singing.
Back of a deep ravine
he lived, above a small river
on a beaten patch of land.
I walked up in the day and walked down,
having been given nothing
else to do. The road grew no longer,
I grew no wiser, my husband
was away selling things to people who buy.
He went up the road, too, but
the road was full of doors for him,
the road was his belt and,
one notch at a time, he loosened it
on his way. I would sit
on the hill of stones and look down
on the trees, on the lake
far away with its boats and those
who ride in boats
and I could not pray. Some of us
have mule minds,
are foolish as sails whipping
in the wind, senseless
as sheets rolling through the fields,
some of us are not given
even a wheel of the tinker's cart
upon which to pray.
When I came back I pumped water
in the yard under the trees
by the fence where the cows came up,
but water is not wisdom
and change is not made by wishes.
Else I would have ridden something,
even a mule, over
those hills and away.

Song

Listen: there was a goat's head hanging by ropes in a tree.
All night it hung there and sang. And those who heard it
Felt a hurt in their hearts and thought they were hearing
The song of a night bird. They sat up in their beds, and then
They lay back down again. In the night wind, the goat's head
Swayed back and forth, and from far off it shone faintly
The way the moonlight shone on the train track miles away
Beside which the goat's headless body lay. Some boys
Had hacked its head off. It was harder work than they had imagined.
The goat cried like a man and struggled hard. But they
Finished the job. They hung the bleeding head by the school
And then ran off into the darkness that seems to hide everything.
The head hung in the tree. The body lay by the tracks.
The head called to the body. The body to the head.
They missed each other. The missing grew large between them,
Until it pulled the heart right out of the body, until
The drawn heart flew toward the head, flew as a bird flies
Back to its cage and the familiar perch from which it trills.
Then the heart sang in the head, softly at first and then louder,
Sang long and low until the morning light came up over
The school and over the tree, and then the singing stopped. . . .
The goat had belonged to a small girl. She named
The goat Broken Thorn Sweet Blackberry, named it after
The night's bush of stars, because the goat's silky hair
Was dark as well water, because it had eyes like wild fruit.
The girl lived near a high railroad track. At night
She heard the trains passing, the sweet sound of the train's horn
Pouring softly over her bed, and each morning she woke
To give the bleating goat his pail of warm milk. She sang
Him songs about girls with ropes and cooks in boats.
She brushed him with a stiff brush. She dreamed daily
That he grew bigger, and he did. She thought her dreaming
Made it so. But one night the girl didn't hear the train's horn,
And the next morning she woke to an empty yard. The goat
Was gone. Everything looked strange. It was as if a storm
Had passed through while she slept, wind and stones, rain
Stripping the branches of fruit. She knew that someone
Had stolen the goat and that he had come to harm. She called

To him. All morning and into the afternoon, she called
And called. She walked and walked. In her chest a bad feeling
Like the feeling of the stones gouging the soft undersides
Of her bare feet. Then somebody found the goat's body
By the high tracks, the flies already filling their soft bottles
At the goat's torn neck. Then somebody found the head
Hanging in a tree by the school. They hurried to take
These things away so that the girl would not see them.
They hurried to raise money to buy the girl another goat.
They hurried to find the boys who had done this, to hear
Them say it was a joke, a joke, it was nothing but a joke. . . .
But listen: here is the point. The boys thought to have
Their fun and be done with it. It was harder work than they
Had imagined, this silly sacrifice, but they finished the job,
Whistling as they washed their large hands in the dark.
What they didn't know was that the goat's head was already
Singing behind them in the tree. What they didn't know
Was that the goat's head would go on singing, just for them,
Long after the ropes were down, and that they would learn to listen,
Pail after pail, stroke after patient stroke. They would
Wake in the night thinking they heard the wind in the trees
Or a night bird, but their hearts beating harder. There
Would be a whistle, a hum, a high murmur, and, at last, a song.
The low song a lost boy sings remembering his mother's call.
Not a cruel song, no, no, not cruel at all. This song
Is sweet. It is sweet. The heart dies of this sweetness.

Wild Turkeys: The Dignity of the Damned

Because they are shame, and cannot flee from it,
And cannot hide it, they go slow,
One great variegated male and his harem of four wild hens

Halting our truck as they labor
To cross the road into the low fields they are indentured to.
They go slow, their hearts hardened to this;

Those laughingstock, shriveled, lipstick red hearts—
Swinging on throat and foreneck
Beneath the narrow heads that are the blue

Not of the sky but of convicts' shaved skulls—
Have been long indurated by rains and winds and filth
And the merciless exposures of the sun.

They do not look up, they do not fly—
Except at night when dark descends like shame,
When shame is lost to dark, and then,

Weak-winged, they heave themselves
Into the low tree roosts they drop from in the morning,
Crashing like swag-bellied bombers

Into the bare fields and stingy stands of trees
They peck their stones and seeds from.
Yesterday they were targets, but now they go slow,

As if this lacuna between winter and spring, still gray,
But full of the furred sumacs' pubescent probings,
And the faint oily scent of wild onion vials crushed open,

Gave hope to even them, or as if they knew
All seasons to be one, the going back,
The crossing over, the standing still, all the same,

When the state you defend is a lost state,
When lurching into an ungainly run
Only reminds you that there is nowhere to run to.

And this movement, this jerking
Of these heavy goffered carapaces forward,
This dumb parading that looks at first glance furtive,

Like skulking, the hunkered shoulders, the lowered heads,
Reveals, as we watch, the dignity that lines
Of pilgrim-sick possess as they halt toward some dark grotto—

A faith beyond the last desire to possess faith,
The soldier's resolve to march humpbacked straight into death
Until it breaks like oil over him

And over all that is lost.

Imagining Their Own Hymns

What fools they are to believe the angels
in this window are in ecstasy. They
do not smile. Their eyes are rolled back in annoyance
not in bliss, as my mother's eyes roll back
when she finds us in the dirt with the cider—
flies and juice blackening our faces and hands.
When the sun comes up behind the angels
then even in their dun robes they are beautiful,
with their girlish hair and their mean lit faces,
but they do not love the light. As I
do not love it when I am made clean
for the ladies who bring my family money.
They stroke my face and smooth my hair. So sweet,
they say, so good, but I am not sweet or good.
I would take one of the possums we kill
in the dump by the woods where the rats slide
like dark boats into the dark stream and leave it
on the heavy woman's porch just to think
of her on her knees scrubbing and scrubbing
at a stain that will never come out.
And these angels that the women turn to
are not good either. They are sick of Jesus,
who never stops dying, hanging there white
and large, his shadow blue as pitch, and blue
the bruise on his chest, with spread petals,
like the hydrangea blooms I tear from
Mrs. Macht's bush and smash on the sidewalk.
One night they will get out of here. One night
when the weather is turning cold and a few
candles burn, they will leave St. Blase standing

under his canopy of glass lettuce
and together, as in a wedding march,
their pockets full of money from the boxes
for the sick poor, they will walk down the aisle,
imagining their own hymns, past the pews
and the water fonts in which small things float,
down the streets of our narrow town, while
the bells ring and the birds fly up in the fields
beyond—and they will never come back.

James McManus

From *Who Needs Two*

Commercials exaggerate.

That Seinfeld, exemplar consumer, would recklessly debit his Amex
because two front-row Knicks tickets blew through the roof of his limo—
hyeah, right. It's about as believable as a rednecked turkey
successfully bribing its hungry ax-wielding hillbilly executioner
with a single cold Budweiser. Maybe such tactics would work
on a sweltering 4th of July afternoon, but on Thanksgiving morning?
Yet it makes perfect sense when a patient, etherized, comes to and grins
upon a table, a musclebound cop can't stop traffic or a gazillion-dollar deal
with Pacific Rim honchos is agreed to only when Bulls tickets are tendered.
The Bulls, after all, *represent.* Not only are they the best basketball team—
the most riveting team in any sport, probably—ever assembled
for our rowdy contemplation, they are also the most culturally intriguing.
A Croatian, an Australian, a Canadian; some middle-class black guys;
some young guys, some old guys, including for two years a dignified, dapper,
pot-smoking relic from the great short-pants-era, pre-free-agency Celtic
   teams.
Guys who pack heat, guys who surf. A coach who reads Homer. A whiz kid, a
   moron, a turd.
Straight guys, a bi-guy, a gay guy. Two guys whose fathers were murdered.
Witness the planet's most skilled, obsessed rebounder and its most oft-
   suspended;
the most libidinally peculiar, lewdly tattooed, bankably *outre* persona in
   sport
whipping outlet passes to sport's most bankably conservative spokesman.
Witness the end of the era of Jordan and Pippen and Jackson—unimaginable,
like having Davis and Coltrane and Evans in the same band for almost a
   decade.
We witness this thing, this unimaginable zero phenomenon—*Bulls!*—and are
   glad.

II

Who's the Man?

It depends, or it used to, on whether a white or black person is asking.

The term confers respect, even awe, on the best worker or athlete or leader,

or indicts the most viciously prejudiced banker or boss, policeman or
      politician.

As one politician, Bill Clinton, has told us, we need to keep bridging the
      chasm between parts of

white and black America. There are myriad reasons to be pessimistic,

but one ground for optimism is that here at the turn of the millennium, as
      racial loathing

and tribal slaughter remain the rule throughout much of the six inhabited
      continents,

a black man has become the role model for American males. Because of

his athletic excellence, force of character, physical beauty and sly sense of
      humor,

Michael Jordan is now the most admired and widely emulated man in
      America.

During this century, our principal male role models have been the likes of
      Babe Ruth,

Teddy Roosevelt, Lou Gehrig, Hemingway, DiMaggio, Bogart, Albert Einstein,

John Wayne, JFK, Walter Cronkite. Recent candidates include Bruce
      Springsteen,

Clint Eastwood, Cal Ripken Jr., Bill Gates, Jerry Seinfeld. But in 1997

none of these men begins to approach the scale of Jordan's pancultural
      presence.

How did this happen?

Joe Louis, Jackie Robinson, Duke Ellington, Jimi Hendrix and Muhammad Ali
      helped

lay the groundwork. Political leaders enlightened the public on issues of race,

and vice versa. Fair laws were passed and enforced. By the time

Jordan began to bloom in the mid-1980s, the country was comfortable

with non-white superstars in film, music, TV and sports. As playing and
      watching

basketball became the hippest forms of male entertainment, Jordan emerged

as that game's most spectacular player. Creative, unstoppable, gorgeous,

he epitomized grace under pressure. As the Cold War wound down

and religious fundamentalism flourished, team sports became an amalgam

of surrogate, symbolic warfare and liberal, secularized religion. Unfettered

capital was able to focus with laser precision and winner-take-all efficiency.

When the best and most charismatic player finally won, he took all.
The publicity machines of the NBA and a dozen immense corporations
advanced his persona in TV commercials of genius. The world's greatest
surrogate warrior became the ultimate avatar of free-market potency.
We may all be created equal and have the same rights, but some of our
    product
is valued more highly than others. The bottom line? *Swoosh*. . . .
When my 18–year-old son shaves his head, it has as much to do with
    Michael's
glinting dome as it does with Billy Corgan's lunar cranium or Tupac Shakur's
gangsta glare. When Steve Beal and Dee Hoover's four-year-old son David
watches the national anthem, he stands with his legs apart, hands clasped
    behind him,
like Mike; half an hour past his bedtime, he willfully insists that his dad
continue to play with him "the game of basketball." Even Jeff Hornacek's son
donned a black-and-red 23 jersey for Game 3 of the Finals in Utah.
Golf, Jordan's *other* other sport, became cool to non-country-club-types
years before Tiger Woods won his first U.S. Amateur. Men now preempt
receding hairlines by going clean instead of combing over. And the cut
of Karl Malone's purple and yellow game shorts, along with the shorts
of nearly every jock on the planet, derives from the real MVP's baggy
    jams. . . .

Jordan is not without flaws.
His notion of teammates as a "supporting cast" heads my own list of peeves.
He could do without hawking cologne, even if the commercials are
the smartest filmed narratives going. That he gambles, talks trash,
drives too fast, smokes cigars only gooses his stock with most men,
though he did come close to humiliating himself when hubris convinced
    him
to give our former national pastime a try during the '93, '94 and '95
basketball seasons. Fans of other NBA teams (especially those in Cleveland,
Orlando, New York, Utah, Miami, LA) can only grudgingly admire him
as franchises sink in his wake. They feel he gets preferential treatment
from referees, and they're darn sick and tired of him winning every year—
almost as tired of watching him pitch, however artfully, everything
from batteries to cereal, Bugs Bunny to cologne, burgers to Chevies.
He is also seen to lack an overt political dimension, to have more
solidarity with white corporations than with Asian seamstresses

or unemployed blacks. Yet his political reticence and corporate bankability
pay significant public dividends. Jordan may choose not to champion
populist social causes, but his philanthropy is copious and his impact
on the body politic pervasive. Perhaps even more than Martin Luther King Jr.,
more than LBJ and the Kennedys, more than Bill Cosby or Jesse Jackson or
Oprah Winfrey or Colin Powell, Michael Jordan has brought races closer
    together.
Americans of every stripe, color and level of affluence count on, admire
and love him, and some of this love becomes both transitive and associative.
The minds and hearts of Jordan's white fans are more open in the aggregate
to people of color, so we all feel less other, more one, than we did
before he arrived on the hardwood. And that above all is why 23 is the Man.

He's good and he's bad and he's *good*.

III

To see the Jordan-era Bulls play live is the moral equivalent
of having witnessed Sherman in Georgia, lions on the floor of the Colosseum,
Achilles and Hector beneath the walls of Troy, Odysseus inside the walls.
The mindbending horror of the *Iliad* is caused by King Agamemnon's refusal,
having been stripped of Chryseis, to equitably redivvy the spoils of war
with his most effective fighter, Achilles. In the *Odyssey* we learn how
    Odysseus
finally bailed out the Greeks with his Trojan Horse stratagem. The Greeks
then sack Troy, raping its women and boys and clubbing King Priam to death
with the head of his grandson. Agamemnon sails home with most of the
    booty,
only to be butchered by Clytemnestra, the mother of their daughter
    Iphigenia
whom Agamemnon had ritually sacrificed to help win the war.
Real war is funny like that. Similarly, Judas Iscariot betrayed Christ
to the Romans for thirty pieces of silver, condemning himself to be gnashed
by Lucifer's fangs for a gelid eternity. Hamlet's lustful uncle murdered
his own brother, destroying both Hamlet's sleep and the once-peaceful state
of Denmark. Macbeth knifed his king while he slept, blamed it on stableboys,
and never slept again. The South seceded from the Union over the right
to own slaves and was clumsily annihilated. The Germans lost World War II
because they sneakily violated their non-aggression pact with the Soviets.
And now Jerries Reinsdorf and Krause want to dismantle the Bulls. . . .

My brother Kevin, an almost maniacal Bulls fan, was a leukemia patient
in Washington, D.C., where he wrote for the *Post,* during the '97 playoffs.
One of the first things doctors will tell you in these situations is that
    optimism
and strength of will can be determining factors in overcoming disease.
Having a wife and two children to live for, plus six siblings and two perfect
    matches
for marrow and blood type helps too, since loyalty works at the cellular level
    as well.
Watching a pair of necessary Bulls road victories over Atlanta with his family
    helped Kevin
stay the vicious course of his chemotherapy, even though he didn't survive in
    the end . . .
He had confident, unalloyed joy all that weekend. "We're havin' some fun,"
    he would sing
as Steve Kerr, whom he somewhat resembled, buried a three from the
    corner . . .
What we all need in life is whatever will work. The Bulls and their fans need
    Michael and Scottie and Phil
and Randy and Toni and Jason, Jud, Luc, Steve, Harp . . . or BJ or Cartwright
    or Pax . . .
to help us to hammer death's ass a while longer, or at least make us feel like
    we can.

The Bulls (to repeat) represent. We identify. MJ is Achilles and then some, the
    greatest
surrogate warrior of all time, as Muhammad Ali still might put it. Pip is the
    loyal Patroclus,
the game's most tenacious defender, our Thelonious Monk of a swingman.
    (Rodman's just Rod-Man,
or Ringworm.) Phil is Odysseus, lighting out one more time for the edge of
    the cosmos
with a trusty crew of too-tall apostles, and all of us want to sail with them.

IV

Rumor has it Billy Corgan was approached about playing "The Star-Spangled
    Banner"
before one of the '97 playoff games. He declined. "Maybe next year," he said.
Well, so be it. An aggressively nasty rendition would probably feel more
    appropriate

if the Bulls were facing a team that the players and fans hated anyway—or,
what probably amounts to the same thing, a team that was likely to beat
    them—
when the enraged-elephant blare a la the solo guitarwork of "Bullet with
    Butterfly Wings"
or the trilling bagpipes of "Rocket" would make much more musical sense.
Whereas Poi Dog Pondering's soulful, glimmering a cappella rendition before
    Game 5
of the Miami series put us in mind of Marvin Gaye's rhythmically *dolce*
    rendition
before the 1984 All-Star Game at the Forum, a version unrivalled in the
    genre . . .
excepting, perhaps, for James Marshall Hendrix's visceral blaze of distortion,
    scattering
quarks and dislodged muoniums oscillating at zero-point energy toward 130
    Db,
red bandanna bisecting his by-then-barely-medium-sized afro, this to go with
a white buckskin Navaho surplice and blue velvet bellbottoms, the backward
and upside down white-on-white Strat just going ballistic at Woodstock. . . .

v
Having attended a Bulls game since then, we can honestly tell our great-
    grandchildren
that way back when in the previous millennium we stood in the presence of
    deities.
The fact is that mere mortals on coolie salaries like ours can still come into
    possession
of the sacred red and gold *tesserae* by a variety of means. (As Al Neri advised
    Michael
Corleone about the chances of killing Hyman Roth while Roth, a retired Jew
    living on a pension,
was under federal witness protection, obtaining Bulls tickets is *difficult, not
    impossible.*)
The father-in-law of our boss, who has season tickets, gets rushed, for
    example, at 6 p.m.
to Rush Presbyterian with gall stones the very evening the Bulls host the
    Lakers.
We win 19 of 24 hands at the hundred-dollar blackjack table and, for once,
have brains enough to immediately get off the boat and call Mr. B's Ticket
    Service,

whose number is right on our speed dial. It's our silver anniversary. Our first.
It's our twenty-first birthday. Our aunt works for TNT, or we go to
    kindergarten
with the grandson of one of the owners. Our boo is a Lovabull. We get straight
    A's
or maintain perfect attendance or buy the right raffle ticket or rewire the
    electricity
in the basement of a season-ticket holder, presenting a modest invoice in
    exchange for . . .
And as if the tickets aren't miracle enough, they happen to come with a pass
to the high-prestige parking lot next to Gate 3½. At this point, however,
we realize we have a big problem. Because the thing is, we've only got the
    deuce.
We could use about seventy-five, but at the very very least we need . . . three.
Do we take our middle or eldest daughter? Our spouse, who barely notices
unless Michael has a breakaway spike (most likely in a commercial), or our
    best friend,
a knowledgeable fanatic with whom we have watched every tenth of a
    second since 1986,
including the preseason games? Nine-year-old Jack or his twin brother
    Matthew?
The friend who loaned us twelve hundred dollars when we got laid off three
    years ago,
or the one who took us to a Sox game last week? Sometimes floor seats to a
    playoff game
are offered to us at face value, which is like being *paid* $2000 apiece
to go to the game of the year, but we have a prior engagement, a conflict
even a departmentful of tenured ethicists couldn't resolve. *We* have gall
    stones.
Or the tipoff is at 7:42, while the graduation ceremony for our firstborn
    namesake
begins at 6:30, the party for which twenty family members have flown into
    town at 8:00 sharp.
What calculus of utility can possibly determine what to do in such cases? . . .

So, do we optimistically park in a twelve-dollar lot, the better to negotiate
at close range, or try to suss out undercover detectives and fair ticket value
from inside our car? We opt for the latter because sidling up to our window
is a guy with a plaid corduroy hat and mad kickin' breath selling two for five
    hundred

in the seventeenth row of section 334; he's even considerate enough
to show us exactly where they are on his laminated seating chart. Now
the letter-equivalent of 334 was a pretty good place to sit—or even to stand
near the back of—in the steep, compressed, supercharged Stadium.
But we know that from the third level of the United Center, where the seats
are pitched so much less steeply and stacked behind luxury suites (in place of
the Stadium's generous balconies), the game is a virtual rumor.
We may as well lease our own skybox and watch the game from there on
        closed circuit.

There are other factors to weigh, but we don't have all night—although maybe
the price will come down if we stall Mr. Corduroy till just before tipoff,
when he can go buy himself *more* Nacho Cheese Doritos . . . While we struggle
to make up our mind, a well-dressed couple arrives alongside him.
A seven-word conversation ensues, money and tickets change hands,
Corduroy books 'round the corner. We watch the young couple parade
toward Gate 5 with unseemly spring in their step, their year made
with one swift transaction. For our part, there's nothing to do
but drive home with the radio on, listening as the Bulls go up by 14,
making plans for the money we've saved. Braces for Zoe? A couple
of half-decent suits—or (at the annual 40%-off sale) a single black-label
Armani? What about five golden rings? . . .
                                        Back in our livingroom,
los toros are up only two, and it looks like it might be a game.
We dash to the fridge and twist open a Honey Weiss, pricey
but more or less gratis compared to what we'd've paid for a room-
temperature Bud in the stadium. Michael buries a turnaround fade
from the baseline. Up four. Farting and sipping contentedly, we nestle
down into the Naugahyde. When we do have to pee, later on, we'll stroll
to our john at our leisure. In the meantime an Oakley 18–footer rims out,
Rodman the rebound. The Bulls slow it down, setting up triple-post
with Michael down low on the strong side, and four butter passes
lead to a Kukoc finger-roll in the paint over LJ. Late whistle.
After Toni clanks the first one, we notice his goatee has been trimmed
more than a little unevenly. When he sinks the second, PJ unleashes
the Dobermans, trapping Starks and denying the ball from the lanes.
After an ill-advised inbounds pass, a travel *Yo, Hue! Where's the call!* Pip
strips the Spalding from Patrick and lobs to Randy Brown for the oop.
And one. Even Red Kerr's vapid babbling can't diminish the pleasure we feel
as the Knicks burn another timeout and they cut to a witty commercial.

Maxine Chernoff

Tenderitis

I want to tell jokes
about tie salesmen and girls
named Dolores, whose letters
are always in French,
always the subjunctive mood.
Sadder than diamonds
that would spell your name,
you, whom the Indians called
Dies of Heartfelt Laughter.
Killing in a strange orange light,
muted as bees and humble.
The hum of blue weather
announces my proper angle,
and I am numb and kneeling
at the Shrine of Holy Women
Ironing Shirts. I, meaning you,
is a gesture, like a runaway
milkhorse, restless in ghost form.
I ask for the dumbness of tradition,
steering me toward a sideways reckoning,
an imperative satisfaction.
Please, when localities fail,
and the underbrush is lit
with false candles, tell me
what to do with history
that fashioned you at my feet.

How Lies Grow

The first time I lied to my baby, I told him that it was his face on the baby food jar. The second time I lied to my baby, I told him that he was the best baby in the world, that I hoped he'd never leave me. Of course I want him to leave me someday. I don't want him to become one of those fat shadows who live in their mothers' houses watching game shows all day. The third time I lied to my baby, I said, "Isn't she nice?" of the woman who'd caressed him in his carriage. She was old and ugly and had a disease. The fourth time I lied to my baby, I told him the truth, I thought. I told him how he'd have to leave me someday or risk becoming a man in a bow tie who eats macaroni on Fridays. I told him it was for the best, but then I thought, I want him to live with me forever. Someday he'll leave me. Then what will I do?

Lost and Found

I am looking for the photo that would make all the difference in my life. It's very small and subject to fits of amnesia, turning up in poker hands, grocery carts, under the unturned stone. The photo shows me at the lost and found looking for an earlier photo, the one that would have made all the difference then. My past evades me like a politician. Wielding a fly-swatter, it destroys my collection of cereal boxes, my childhood lived close to the breakfast table. Only that photo can help me locate my fourteen lost children, who look just like me. When I call the Bureau of Missing Persons, they say, "Try the Bureau of Missing Photos." They have a fine collection. Here's one of Calvin Coolidge's seventh wedding. Here's one of a man going over a cliff on a dogsled. Here's my Uncle Arthur the night he bought a peacock. Oh photo! End your tour of the world in a hot air balloon. Resign your job at the mirror-testing laboratory. Come back to me, you little fool, before I find I can live without you.

JEFF GUNDY

For the New York City Poet Who Informed Me that Few People Live This Way

1

We sat in the commons, my eyes scrunched against the smoke.
He hadn't asked me anything. He hadn't made small talk.
He kept reading. Finally he looked up, said he didn't understand.
I tried to explain. It was like being stuck in gravel.

More silence, more smoke. He didn't understand the next one,
either. He started telling me how there are no numbers
in nature, that one and one make two but one apple
and one apple make applesauce, or a nuclear explosion.

He wrote 1, 2, 3, ∞ on the page, paused, wrote 0, -1, $E = mc^2$,
something with Planck's constant in it. He started telling me
about Gödel's proof, but when I said, "Oh, undecidability,"
he sniffed and stopped. He lit another cigarette. I said

I'd be grateful for anything he could say about any of them.
He found the shortest one and said he liked it, it had
an incident and no abrupt transitions or metaphysical mush.
He found the one about small towns and said it was only

about one place, and I should put "small" and "town" in
the title. I didn't argue. What should he care about
fathers in church? Anyway the snack shop was closed,
he couldn't get a Coke, and I felt like it was my fault.

2

So what are you up to? Dead? Crammed into your study,
writing bitter quatrains about the Peloponnesian Wars?
Drinking beer after beer in some crosstown bar, feeling
like the bullseye in the target? Out here we've been fine,

mostly. My boys are growing, fighting, teaching us all
about power and margins and timing. If I thought
you'd do it I'd say find an atlas, pick a small dot,
rent a car: see if you can get there. If not, stop anyway.

We're out here, working and eating, playing games that
mean nothing, but make us stronger. An old machine
cleans the streets, wakes us to the dawn. We listen.
I remember your name. Nobody else here knows you from Adam.

Rain

And a stray face spins me back to the black-haired girl
I saw long ago and stood helpless
watching her pass, bareheaded in the rain,
the easy way she found, wet but not hunched
against it, hair damp and shining on her brow,
her shoulders. I wanted to give something
for the dark rain of that hair,
the quiet of her face, not angry or restless,
alert to each step, the crowded sidewalk . . .
But what? Words? Dark rain. Wet face.

She never saw me. We've tramped on down
our own dark tunnels now for years. What hapless watcher
at my gates would know her face, would let her in
without the password, find her a bed, say rest,
sleep, I'll be outside?

I know. It shouldn't matter
who's lovely in the rain and who isn't.
But it's not beauty or nostalgia or even lust
that's got me, I don't know what it is,
justice maybe, prisons and churches, the glowing creatures
in the center of the sun. Most days I think
I'm almost free, I don't miss a single meeting,
I don't hit squirrels with my bike. Most days

it doesn't rain, and nobody walks the streets
in black hair, a light jacket and a glaze
of shining water, rain beading and touching her
all over like the hand of someone very large
and very gentle, very far away.

ANA CASTILLO

The Toltec
c. 1955

My father was a Toltec.
Everyone knows he was *bad*.
Kicked the Irish-boys-from-Bridgeport's
ass. Once went down to South Chicago
to stick someone
got chased to the hood
running through the gangway
swish of blade in his back
the emblemed jacket split in half.

Next morning, Mami
threw it away.

Me & Baby
Chicago, c. 1984

It's me, the pregnant Puerto Rican girls, short Mexicans
with braids down to there, and all the babies in the world

waiting for our numbers to be called. At 3 p.m.,
there's an empty chair past Egberto with bad breath

from beer the night before, Marta and her sister with
strollers between them, autistic boy of the twisted cheeks,

and finally, me & baby get a seat. Women divided
from us by desks, type out cereal, milk, juice coupons,

government approved and labeled at the market. A woman
in back complains in Spanish; another wishes she had welfare.

An African with delicate tribal scars along her face
places her little one on my lap while she

goes to the bathroom. The Salvadoreñas, too glum,
having missed a day of work, don't say a word to anyone.

At 4:45 a man on the night shift left the kids with his wife. He
never lifted his eyes. We must have been an ugly sight.

Baby needs solids the doctor at the clinic has said.
i'll speak up when i get my chance. If they ask me for forms,

and doctor's written requests, i'll pound my fists
on those coupon covered desks. At 5 of 5 i kick the wall instead.

The office is officially closed, coupon books put away, clerks
freshen lipstick, nutritionist hangs her smock, her day ended.

And we, of the numbers uncalled, must come back, take a new
number, start again. Clear the entrance. If there are no

empty chairs, please don't block the way. Sorry, ma'am.
We open at 8. We'll see you tomorrow. Best to arrive temprano.

Women Are Not Roses

Women have no
beginning
only continual
flows.

Though rivers flow
women are not
rivers.

Women are not
roses
they are not oceans
or stars.

i would like to tell
her this but
i think she
already knows.

ELAINE EQUI

Things to Do in the Bible

Get drunk.
Walk on water.
Collect foreskins.
Pluck out an eye.

Build an ark.
Interpret dreams.
Kill your brother.
Don't look back.

Join a tribe.
Listen to clouds.
Live in a tent.
Quit your job.

Take to the hills.
Report to the king.
Raise the dead.
Seek the spirit.

Reap what you sow.
Count your blessings.
Gnash your teeth.
Fish for men.

Grow a beard.
Wear a cowl.
Ride a donkey.
Carry a torch.

Sit by a well.
Live to a ripe, old age.
Remain a virgin
and speak in tongues.

These are the words of the Lord.

Lesbian Corn

In summer
I strip away
your pale kimono.
Your tousled hair too,
comes off in my hands
leaving you
completely naked.
All ears and
tiny yellow teeth.

Being Sick Together

In the postmodern world
the sequel is always superior

to the original
and it is even possible

for someone like Tony Perkins
to meet a nice girl in Psycho III

a suicidal former nun
who is also tormented

by sexual fantasies
so that he can teach her something

old-fashioned as dancing
the fox trot

and she can offer him
a drink in her room.

At the Bates Motel
water drawn from the same tap

where famous shower scene began
now seems pleasantly refreshing.

RICHARD JONES

Portrait of My Father and His Grandson

Because I love my father,
I can see him turning away
from the river and the divers
and the policemen and the red lights;
I can see him walking back
to the house, follow him
down the long hallway
to the child's room;
I can see him bending over
the empty bed and lifting
the heavy white spread
and carrying it back
to the river's edge
to wrap around his grandson.
But even though I love them both,
I cannot see why this should happen,
or tell you what the boy saw
under the water, or how my father felt
standing by the river when the divers came up,
or where he found the strength to survive
that night, hugging the wet body,
wrapping it up against the cold,
carrying it through the darkness,
home.

Song of the Old Man

I might have died when I was young,
my body all muscle and desire,
and believed death was beautiful

but then I would have missed
the beauty of the body's
decline, how we fall

away like a flower,
surviving the season
to bloom just once,
throwing sweet scent into the air
and becoming a part of everything there.

A Beginning

Today I am walking in woods
where men with chain saws
are felling trees and other men
with guns are killing deer.
Today I have nothing to praise
and nothing to feel sorry for.
Today I refuse to make the sky
tender or the earth heroic.
Today I will not condemn the trail
leading to the garbage dump
or lose myself in the leaves' fiery colors.
Today I won't pretend to understand
the ways we care for one another.
Today I will simply stand
in these thick woods and love
how the branches of one tree
reach into the branches of another.

DAVID WOJAHN

The Assassination of Robert Goulet as Performed by Elvis Presley: Memphis, 1968

"That jerk's got no heart."
—E.P.

He dies vicariously on "Carol Burnett,"
Exploding to glass and tubes while singing "Camelot."

Arms outstretched, he dies Las Vegas-ed in a tux,
As the King, frenzied in his Graceland den, untucks

His .38 and pumps a bullet in the set.
(There are *three* on his wall, placed side by side.)

The room goes dark with the shot, but he gets the Boys
To change the fuses. By candlelight he toys

With his pearl-handled beauty. Lights back on,
But Goulet's vanished, replaced by downtown Saigon:

Satellite footage, the Tet offensive,
Bodies strewn along Ky's palace fences.

Above a boy whose head he's calmly blown apart,
An ARVN colonel smokes a cigarette.

"It's Only Rock and Roll but I Like It": The Fall of Saigon, 1975

The guttural stammer of the chopper blades
Raising arabesques of dust, tearing leaves
From the orange trees lining the Embassy compound:

One chopper left, and a CBS cameraman leans
From inside its door, exploiting the artful
Mayhem. Somewhere a radio blares the Stones,
"I like it, like it, yes indeed. . . ." Carts full
Of files blaze in the yard. Flak-jacketed marines
Gunpoint the crowd away. The overloaded chopper strains
And blunders from the roof. An ice-cream-suited
Saigonese drops his briefcase; both hands
Now cling to the airborne skis. The camera gets
It all: the marine leaning out the copter bay,
His fists beating time. Then the hands giving way.

Workmen Photographed inside the Reactor
    Chernobyl

It passes, you'll remember, through lead. Passes through
the protective suits that don't protect, passes through
every template, roil of hardened magma, each jutting

braincase of Medusan electric wire, each goggle, each mask,
each pike, each sandbag flung by helicopter seven years ago
to cool the meltdown, the pilots soon dead, passes through

the camera of Victoria Ivleva as her flash
picks out the shades in Circle IV, Circle V, Circle VII,
their bone white suits, a single ray of sunlight

slithering through the cracked reactor wall. Two hundred *rems*
per man per month. Passes through the windowpanes
of the empty concrete high rise forty miles away, the single

plastic eye and nylon lashes of a doll on a closet floor. *Each
thought is a rem*, she says, reloading the camera. Each thought
closer to the moment, the spiral more tightly wound:

the communications satellite exhausts its fuel,
the flawless colors of a soccer match in São Paulo
flooded by a gray screen's static hiss, the wreckage

alchemized to shooting stars, smoldering metal
littering Australian deserts. Each thought
coiled more tightly. L and I beneath the café awning

the morning of the news reports, the Plaza Mayor
in Salamanca, shouted headlines of *El País*.
And all morning the famous courtyard

of the Convent of Las Duenas—the capitals
sprout demons, horned dismembered sandstone heads,
sinners' faces laddering the columns in a double-

helix of damnation, cautionary images
for wealthy nuns of the Golden Age. This one
is eaten by his shriek. This one has become a bleeding tree.

And marble Dante, skullcapped at the fountain,
looking up from the *Comedia*. A cloud,
said the papers, pulsing westward. Each thought, each thought,

the spiral tightening to the plastic tube
lodged in my father's nostrils, *angina pectoris, emphysema,*
his jittery breathing in the next room. The oxygen machine,

umbilical hum and shudder. He has ten days to live.
Point where the circle disappears. The bedroom
I had as a child. Hum and shudder. . . .

I stand with the others as the gate
yawns open, chain link and barbed wire. The white
plastic suits swing from meat hooks in a hallway.

Step in, zip up. The mask, the skullcap,
the rubber gloves reaching up to the elbows,
the pike, the radiometer. Adjust the goggles.

One last breath, last glance at the trees.
Down the staircase to the pit. Each thought—
the pike before me, stabbing at the gloom.

Rajah in Babylon

We hanged our harps upon the willows in the midst thereof.
   —Psalm 137

Rajah doesn't like Nirvana but he seems
to tolerate Jimmy Cliff: "The Harder They Come"

is Rachael's little joke, and its chuffing from her boom box
as Rajah paces, his planetary back-

and-forth, manic orbits, exactly like Rilke's
panther. The bars and his stripes run parallel

and fuse, head abob like a marionette's,
the snare drum of his paws on the cement.

He's fasted for three days, and thinks that Rachael's
brought ten pounds of horse meat in her pail,

but his flared puzzled nostrils don't smell a thing
and Noelle bends down to the tranquilizer gun

while Rachael coos endearments meant
to slow him down so Noelle will get a decent shot.

Good Rajah Pretty Rajah Big Rajah—
Eyes wide, he turns, and Noelle aims and fires

and he shrieks and circles faster and we wait
while Jimmy croons that we can get it if we really want.

"Two minutes, tops," says Rachael, and by the time
the song is over he has wobbled and gone down.

He is one four-thousandth of the world's tigers.
To save them takes some drastic measures

and so the cage door's opened and we file
in, Bob and Noelle and Rachael

and me, and the tape slurs on to "Pressure Drop"
while Bob and Noelle strain to turn him on his back,

heaving till he's sprawling belly up,
the Maytals moaning as Rachael wipes

her brow, and fumbles with the electro-jack,
a miniature land mine, a low-tech

bristle of hose and wire. The down-sheathed penis
sprouts, pink and man-sized in her rubber gloves

and now the Melodians lay down beside
the Rivers of Babylon. *Oh the wicked*

carried us away, captivity. . . . The motor's
started, the penis clamped, the tiger

bright burning, his fearful symmetry
sprawled incandescent on the scat-pocked floor. Gingerly

I touch the ribs, the whorled sleeping flank,
stutter of heartbeat, Rachael scowling as she works,

and there we wailed as we / remembered Zion.
And slowly the liquid pearls in the flask, churn

and sputter as Rachael grins. Buttermilk
gold, *and there we wailed,* it streaks

the beaker's glassy walls, brimming and bound
for dry-ice burial, for resurrection in the wild,

Sumatra and some sleeping tigress. *By Babylon*
we wailed. Applause and the Melodians

fade. The bright liquid flares. *Oh Jerusalem,*
in this strange land we sing our song.

SANDRA CISNEROS

You Bring Out the Mexican in Me

You bring out the Mexican in me.
The hunkered thick dark spiral.
The core of a heart howl.
The bitter bile.
The tequila *lágrimas* on Saturday all
through next weekend Sunday.
You are the one I'd let go the other loves for,
surrender my one-woman house.
Allow you red wine in bed,
even with my vintage lace linens.
Maybe. Maybe.

For you.

You bring out the Dolores del Río in me.
The Mexican spitfire in me.
The raw *navajas,* glint and passion in me.
The raise Cain and dance with the rooster-footed devil in me.
The spangled sequin in me.
The eagle and serpent in me.
The *mariachi* trumpets of the blood in me.
The Aztec love of war in me.
The fierce obsidian of the tongue in me.
The *berrinchuda, bien-cabrona* in me.
The Pandora's curiosity in me.
The pre-Columbian death and destruction in me.
The rainforest disaster, nuclear threat in me.

The fear of fascists in me.
Yes, you do. Yes, you do.

You bring out the colonizer in me.
The holocaust of desire in me.
The Mexico City '85 earthquake in me.
The Popocatepetl/Ixtaccíhuatl in me.
The tidal wave of recession in me.
The Agustín Lara hopeless romantic in me.
The *barbacoa taquitos* on Sunday in me.
The cover the mirrors with cloth in me.

Sweet twin. My wicked other,
I am the memory that circles your bed nights,
that tugs you taut as moon tugs ocean.
I claim you all mine,
arrogant as Manifest Destiny.
I want to rattle and rent you in two.
I want to defile you and raise hell.
I want to pull out the kitchen knives,
dull and sharp, and whisk the air with crosses.
Me sacas lo mexicana en mi,
like it or not, honey.

You bring out the Uled-Nayl in me.
The stand-back-white-bitch in me.
The switchblade in the boot in me.

The Acapulco cliff diver in me.
The *Flecha Roja* mountain disaster in me.
The *dengue* fever in me.
The *¡Alarma!* murderess in me.
I could kill in the name of you and think
it worth it. Brandish a fork and terrorize rivals,
female and male, who loiter and look at you,
languid in your light. Oh,
I am evil. I am the filth goddess Tlazoltéotl.
I am the swallower of sins.
The lust goddess without guilt.
The delicious debauchery. You bring out
the primordial exquisiteness in me.
The nasty obsession in me.

The corporal and venial sin in me.
The original transgression in me.

Red ocher. Yellow ocher. Indigo. Cochineal.
Piñón. Copal. Sweetgrass. Myrrh.
All you saints, blessed and terrible,
Virgen de Guadalupe, diosa Coatlicue,
I invoke you.

Quiero ser tuya. Only yours. Only you.
Quiero amarte. Atarte. Amarrarte.
Love the way a Mexican woman loves. Let
me show you. Love the only way I know how.

I Am So in Love I Grow a New Hymen

Terrorists of the last
decade. Anarchists who fled
with my heart thudding on the back
bumper of a flatbed truck.
Nelson Algren impersonators.
Joe Hill detonators. *Los-más-
chingones-de-los-más-chingones-*
politically-correct-Marxist-tourists/voyeurs.
Olympic gold, silver, bronze love-
triathlons and several blue-
ribbon runner-ups to boot.
Forgot, forgotten, forget.
Past tense and no regrets.

No doubt you're Villa
and I'm Pershing's dizzy troops.
No doubt I'm eucalyptus and you
a California conflagration. No doubt
you're eucharist, Euclidean geometry,
World War II's Gibraltar strait,
the Chinese traders of Guangzhou,

Zapatistas breakfasting at Sanborn's,
Sassoferrato's cobalt blue,
Museo Poldi Pezzoli's insurance rate,
Gaudí's hammer against porcelain plates.

Ay, daddy, daddy, I
don't give a good goddamn. I
don't give
a good
god
damn.

Heart, My Lovely Hobo

Heart, my lovely hobo, you
remember, then, that afternoon in Venice
when all the pigeons rose flooding the piazza
like a vaulted ceiling. That was you
and you alone who grinned.
Fat as an oyster,
pulpy as a plum,
raw, exposed, naive,
dumb. As if love
could be curbed, and grace
could save you from the daily beatings.

Those blue jewels of flowers in the arbor
that the bees loved. Oh, there'll be other
flowers, a cat maybe beside the bougainvillea,
a little boat with flags glittering in the harbor
to make you laugh,
to make you spiral once more.
Not this throbbing.
This.

Loose Woman

They say I'm a beast.
And feast on it. When all along
I thought that's what a woman was.
They say I'm a bitch.
Or witch. I've claimed
the same and never winced.

They say I'm a *macha*, hell on wheels,
viva-la-vulva, fire and brimstone,
man-hating, devastating,
boogey-woman lesbian.
Not necessarily,
but I like the compliment.

The mob arrives with stones and sticks
to maim and lame and do me in.
All the same, when I open my mouth,
they wobble like gin.

Diamonds and pearls
tumble from my tongue.
Or toads and serpents.
Depending on the mood I'm in.

I like the itch I provoke.
The rustle of rumor
like crinoline.

I am the woman of myth and bullshit.
(True. I authored some of it.)
I built my little house of ill repute.
Brick by brick. Labored,
loved and masoned it.

I live like so.
Heart as sail, ballast, rudder, bow.
Rowdy. Indulgent to excess.
My sin and success—
I think of me to gluttony.

By all accounts I am
a danger to society.
I'm Pancha Villa.

LUIS J. RODRIGUEZ

Reflection on El Train Glass

Gaze penetrates through the glass
of El train window. It infringes
& infiltrates, a misdemeanor
against silence. I turn toward it.
The face in the haze refracting glare
in myriad directions; slicing into
working woman's tiredness, into
child's affront, into uniformed
man's wariness, into the uninterested
below city still-life.

A vise of sun rays grips a shape,
an innuendo of myself.
A caress of shade on the cheek.
I'm recalling the places I've been,
like flesh below the waters of a bath,
and I sleep into this transparent
world, sleep into a sort of flying,
into molds of day, into cinders
and the feel which doesn't feel, into
a stupor deeper than reflection.

Rant, Rave & Ricochet

Police killed her brother
for stealing a piece of chicken;

she says there's nothing
to do but squat. She's had

babies this way. Some nothing
more than arteries,

gray matter and fluid.
Three came out all right,

and were taken away
by bureaucrats. She's homeless.

She's been raped and almost killed.
They say she's mad. For her,

sanity is a crime.
"I'm not stuck on stupid,"

she exclaims, and welcomes the
chaos which crackles out

of social construct. It's
her only peace in the

piece of the street at war.
She rants & raves, but it's all

ricochet from the bullet
that has claimed her since birth.

She pulls at strands of hair
flooding a furrowed face,

declares herself twine,
thimble and an ace of hearts.

To the Police Officer Who Refused to Sit in the Same Room as My Son because He's a "Gang Banger":

How dare you!
How dare you pull this mantle from your sloven
sleeve and think it worthy enough to cover my boy.
How dare you judge when you also wallow in this mud.
Society has turned over its power to you,
relinquishing its rule, turned it over
to the man in the mask, whose face never changes,
always distorts, who does not live where I live,
but commands the corners, who does not have to await
the nightmares, the street chants, the bullets,
the early-morning calls, but looks over at us
and demeans, calls us animals, not worthy
of his presence, and I have to say: How dare you!
My son deserves to live as all young people.
He deserves a future and a job. He deserves
contemplation. I can't turn away as you.
Yet you govern us? Hear my son's talk.
Hear his plea within his pronouncement,
his cry between the breach of his hard words.
My son speaks in two voices, one of a boy,
the other of a man. One is breaking through,
the other just hangs. Listen, you who can turn away,
who can make such a choice; you who have sons
of your own, but do not hear them!
My son has a face too dark, features too foreign,
a tongue too tangled, yet he reveals, he truths,
he sings your demented rage, but he sings.
You have nothing to rage because it is outside of you.
He is inside of me. His horror is mine. I see what
he sees. And if my son dreams, if he plays, if he smirks
in the mist of moon-glow, there I will be, smiling
through the blackened, cluttered and snarling pathway
toward your wilted heart.

KEVIN STEIN

Past Midnight, My Daughter Awakened by Miles Davis' Kind of Blue

In the presence of blue, it's the eye
that signals to the brain that signals
to the heart, *slow down, slow down,*
a process of attenuation I hear
in Coltrane's notes, loping
then sprinting, then nearly gone,
Chambers' barely audible bass
holding sway amidst the fifties hiss.
It's then I think death must be like this,
its last beats sweeter because few,
the body closing doors and shutting windows,
locking up before the long buzz, crackle,
microphone hum. Then Miles and Cannonball
and Coltrane, horns whispering "So what,"
building in defiance until I wonder
at their swagger, their fear,
as I did at the woman in Jimmy's Bar,
who having nothing to lose, popped
the French heart medicine "experimental"
only tamely described. Quaffed them
with a Guinness, shoveled popcorn in,
and would not turn from those who stared.
Like me, birthday boy half in the bucket,
or those whose glass slipped from hand
to floor upon seeing her puffy face
the color of Franz Marc's horse. Still,
it's my mother's fault I can't think of blue
as forlorn: her kitchen and bath,
carpet and drapes, that starving goose
above her pale couch—all blue,
or better, some shade of calm embodied
by a thing we lounge upon, wash our hands in,

or do what we close the door to do in.
It's no miracle the sadness of the wretched
didn't come to mind studying the woman's
blue face, or watching the June delphinium
offer its trumpet of blossom in September,
horn of plenty, yellow throated surprise
as deft as my daughter, backlit
by stairwell light, hands on hips
in the manner young children take
with parents who've misbehaved.
Glancing at me, the chair I sit in,
our striped futon, even the cheap
Chagall taped to the wall, she says,
"I guess I'm doomed to love blue,"
a joke she knows will bring my laughter,
doomed to love what lifts and often
kills us—sailor's ocean, pilot's sky,
those eyes whose sheen I had not reckoned on.

Night Shift, after Drinking Dinner, Container Corporation of America, 1972

Through the cheap iron gate and its mythic
irony (for who would storm and sack
a box-making plant?); down the cigarette-stained

hall and past the super's all-glass office,
I lurched and reeled and had, as the boys
who play the ponies say, to piss like a racehorse.

It wasn't the urinous light, puddled
and wavering as if a mirage in some
bad Abbott and Costello Sunday movie;

not the yawing and clanging, the squeal
of machines in heat, for reproducing,
after all, is their anointed duty;

not the scent of sulphur and hot glue,
those belching and farting fork lifts,
not even "death valley" steaming cardboard.

It was a raspy *Jesus Christ* I heard
above the six pack hiss (Pabst Blue Ribbon,
a buck sixty-nine, cold), a voice which beckoned

me to Shipping where acid-tripping Bill
had metal-strapped his finger to a pallet.
Efficient, even when stoned, he'd stencilled:

SHIP TO: PITTSBURGH, PA / HEINZ 57
200 COUNT / SCORED / DOUBLE-NOTCHED.
That, my introduction to LSD and political subversion,

so little of either in my GM town:
alternators, headlamps, the domino theory,
"An Okie from Muskogee" our jukebox anthem.

What I knew of war I got from Cronkite's
daily tally, each lurid tone of death
on camera, that Vietnamese girl napalmed

and naked. This was what I watched—
mind you, watched, and took to saying "peace"
instead of good-bye, easy enough if your draft

number's 185. So it was when oh so wild Bill
lifted the stub to his lips and sucked it
as he would a paper cut, *Mr. Natural's*

going to keep me out of 'Nam, he said,
which meant: would keep him whole,
notwithstanding the lopped-off index finger;

which meant: no trigger, no Uncle Sam
poking his chest. He laughed
the bellyful laugh of shock,

the giddy electric giggle of lysergic acid.
We pried his finger from the skid,
buried it in a cup of ice, our ship

of state scuttled in rose waters.
There was beauty in the mind's eye,
which could afford to be inconsolably

clumsy with facts. "Keep on Truckin',"
said the little blotter acid man—
his boots huge, arm raised, finger pointed

to some constellation of loss
and promised rebirth. There was
irony, too, in our rush to hide the cup,

red-faced paramedics screaming,
"Where is it, man?"—how cleaving
may cleave a part unto the whole.

It Didn't Begin with Horned Owls Hooting at Noon

Though in them he heard   the weird symmetry
of loss and love's becoming,   a great silence
between one call and the   other's reply.
So he laid block, framed   studs into walls:
plumb, square, on line.   He stayed up late,
straightening bent nails   on the lip of a block
with his ballpeen hammer,   the way a contractor
with a sprung back had shown   him. Evenings
he went next door to talk,   toting his thermos
of bitter coffee and a picture   of his son
who's dying of AIDS. Son he'd   failed, son
he'd pounded on and never got   right. When he
was ready to hang sheet rock,   he penciled on
women with bulbous breasts   and legs
he'd spread wide, women bent   at the waist
as if in supplication to some   irremediable need

only his hand could quiet.   Then he hung
the rock with his women   facing him, sometimes
sawing them in two.   On the morning he finished
he rolled paint over   each and all of them.
Every wall white   in the room where his son,
forgiving him,   was coming home to wait.

In the Kingdom of Perpetual Repair

Sunday A.M. so early even FM crackles church service
        for shut-ins,
fire and brimstone fricatives torqued around a tongue
        as forked
as the red-one-with-tail's pitchfork, both useful tools
        for snaring souls
like me who've sworn off church pew for workbench,
        never mind my cursing
what I can't get right. The deck's three-legged table,

for instance, its mishmash of mismatched pine
        and close-out cedar
lifts in slight breeze then nosedives like a child's
        Easter kite,
salsa and beer sprawled from its swept wings. This should
        bring despair,
say, that of the preacher surveying his cracked flock—
        styptic pencils
and clip-on ties, clown dot rouge, and pantyhose bound

around muzzy melon bellies, the kiddies thwacked with shiny
        vinyl hymnals
he splurged collection money on—but *should* is not *does,*
        despite flimflam grammar,
and Christ, we love each other less for what we are than for
        what we might become.
I love it when the preacher claims to be the Lord's tool,
        wrench or saw
or claw hammer in the Big Guy's big hands, his vowels

sanding my soul's rusty hinges. Creak creak, a door opens.
    Creak creak
the organ hums a hymn amenable to each measure and rise
    of lives built
from the ground up only to be ground down like those
    fresh dead
the morning sermon mourns: So-Close Joe, loser of 237
    straight harness races,
lungs so scarred he wheezed from paddock to gate

only to foam home last; and lonely Colonel Bohart,
    retired U.S. Army,
who collapsed in bath holding Ike, his old stuffed dog
    with ruler built-in
for reasons only a man who loves equally his dog
    and his tools understands.
To wit: Bohart's homemade mailbox, exact size and girth
    of Ike,
designed to bark when its mouth-lid opens. Good dog.

No, good man, the more elusive creature in this church
    of break
and break anew. Creak creak, the hinges need oil.
    Creak creak,
my heart swings open with praise for losers we are
    and those we're not
by grace of a thousand fancy chances, blessed stretch
    by which we catch
Fate's hammer inches above the anvil of our head,

or failing that, still find among the cartoon stars its
    blow brings forth
our own brief comet, incandescent tale we believe
    is beautiful
because we've somehow made something of nothing.
    Only gods do that.
We elide to nothing: ice to mist, fist to dust.
    Praise this then:
that long undoing maps our single perfect act.

Sheryl St. Germain

Addiction

In Memory of My Brother, Jay St. Germain, 1958–1981

The truth is I loved it,
the whole ritual of it,
the way he would fist up his arm, then
hold it out so trusting and bare,
the vein pushed up all blue and throbbing
and wanting to be pierced,
his opposite hand gripped tight as death
around the upper arm,

the way I would try to enter the vein,
almost parallel to the arm,
push lightly but firmly, not
too deep,
you don't want to go through

the vein, just in,
then pull back until you see
blood, then

hold the needle very still, slowly
shoot him with it.
Like that I would enter him,
slowly, slowly, very still,
don't move,
then he would let the fist out,
loosen his grip on the upper arm—

and oh, the movement of his lips
when he asked that I open my arms.
How careful,
how good he was, sliding
the needle silver and slender
so easily into me, as though
my skin and veins were made for it,
and when he had finished, pulled
it out, I would be coming
in my fingers, hands, my ear lobes
were coming, heart, thighs,
tongue, eyes and brain were coming,
thick and brilliant as the last thin match
against a homeless bitter cold.

I even loved the pin-sized bruises,
I would finger them alone in my room
like marks of passion;
by the time I turned yellow,
my dreams were full of needles.

We both took lovers who loved
this entering and being entered,
but when he brought over the
pale-faced girl so full of needle hole
he had to lay her on her back
like a corpse and stick the needle
over and over in her ankle veins
to find one that wasn't weary
of all the joy, I became sick
with it, but

you know, it still stalks my dreams,
and deaths make no difference:
there is only the body's huge wanting.
When I think of my brother
all spilled out on the floor
I say nothing to anyone.
I know what it's like to want joy
at any cost.

DEAN YOUNG

Pleasure

One of those times I knew even then
I couldn't inhabit fully enough.
Lunch late, Duncan and Neal ordering Cobb Salad—
whatever whoever Cobb is—
and how wonderful to order something you've never heard of
even if the ingredients
are right there beside it
in their crisp assertive adjectives.
But what I ordered was corned beef.
Hot.
Our service strange:
our waiter takes our water off as if we've already left
as if to remind us how ephemeral all pleasures are
but then brought us coffee we didn't order
which we take.
Or took.
Time goes by in no time at all, confusing
all my tenses, Duncan's watch on Indiana time
keeps telling us we're late. Neal rattling on
about our chances in Bellingham,
shadows turning long and blue outside,
people in other booths leaning into each other,
feeding each other, inventing new forms
of procreation. In moments like these
the hothouse was invented. The kite.
The sandwich. I might have been lost
in the Delaware of my beloved's hair
as I rowed my heart to the restroom:
a long, odd way: out the restaurant and through
the lobby of a hotel I didn't know was there,
fussed-up with abstract art like sea gulls
thrown donuts in a storm, the concierge

atomizing her approval of where I asked to go,
of what I was about to do, had done, about
that whole arena of the body and its imperatives,
so why must I feel so guilty? Misery, misery
flush the automatic urinals as if I've wandered in
from a slide show of what the junta did
to the hill people. What livid stepparent
steps into my room and finds me with the Sunday-section bra ads?
Atrocities traipse across front pages
but creak creak goes the machinery of my heart
as I return to my table, as I swim back
to happiness, people making decisions solely
based on pleasure even though they choose low-cal,
even as they chew with their mouths open,
telling about the dreadful things their first husbands did,
the thing a sister said that hurt them, the time
they stepped on the urchin snorkeling
and that was the end of Florida.
Oh, it's all mixed up: the past, the present,
pain and pleasure and there's something
inexplicably sweet in my mouth considering
it's just perfectly okay corned beef,
it need not be the best I've ever had
and yes, yes, all over the world people
are suffering the basest sorts of deprivations
but don't we owe this pleasure our commitment,
our awe of this gift god's proffered us
or whatever we've replaced god with?
Creak, creak.
It's why we're given taste buds, so many nerves
in our lips and fingertips, why the piano, the cactus,
why women have clitorises, why and what for
frogs and pepper and the moon and no,
this isn't the light of wisdom,
it's the indirect lighting of joy,
of seduction, little fake candles on our tables
with bulbs shaped like flames and cars shaped
like flames, lovers shaped like flames
and the shoes of lovers.
Outside, above the road, eight-foot lips

declare desires we've just begun to formulate
in the test tubes of our yearning
and outside even further, there's a spot on the overpass
that must have required hanging upside down
to proclaim the beloved's name above the traffic:
spray paint,
only the first letter botched.
I remember being a boy in winter woods,
snow and women's underwear snagged in a tree;
oh, what mystery and a little menace like a good movie.
I thought one day I might be
if not exactly privy to a woman throwing her drawers in a tree
then something comparable. It's why we're given
tongues and hands for unbuttoning, clasping
and unclasping. It's for doing round-the-world
and putting on the hot mustard yourself.
It's for reaching for the check not fast enough.
There must be an aesthetic not based on death.
There's a small bird called Pure Flame.
There's a tomato called Pride.
There's Duncan, there's Neal, there's me.
There're free matches by the door.

Rothko's Yellow

What I don't understand is the beauty.
The last attempts of the rain, my shoulders
aching from all afternoon with the ladders
and the hour with her. I watch the rainbow
until I have to focus so hard I seem
to create it. Thinking of her watching
this storm, wanting him. This lightning.
This glut in the gutters. Now only
the yellow left. Now the blue
seeped out. The purple gone. The red
gone. People downstairs playing Bach,
the quiet, attenuated Bach. She must
have tried and tried. The holes drilled in.

The small man in the movie who looked
like laughter would kill him. The carnation
farmer who left snared birds for the woman
he loved. Who would hang himself after
stitching her ribbon to his chest.
What I don't understand is the beauty.
I remember the theatre in Berkeley where
we sat eating cucumbers, watching the colossal
faces played over with colossal loss.
I would get off early and meet her outside,
her hair always wet. All last night
I listened to the students walk by until 3,
only the drunk left, the rebuffed and
suddenly coupled. What did I almost
write down on the pad by my bed
that somehow lowered me into sleep? One morning
when she and I still lived together,
the pad said only, cotton. Cotton.
Sometimes it's horrible, the things said
outright. But nothing explains the beauty,
not weeping and shivering on that stone bench,
not kneeling by the basement drain.
Not remembering otherwise, that scarf she wore,
the early snow, her opening the door
in the bathing light. She must have tried
and tried. What I don't understand is the beauty.

Upon Hearing of My Friend's Marriage Breaking Up, I Envision Attack from Outer Space

Even in September noon, the ground hog
casts his divining shadow: summer will never
end and when it does it will never come again.
I've only the shadows of doubts, shadows
of a notion. The leaves turn in tarnished
rain like milk. Hearts, rotund with longing,
explode like dead horses left in a creek,
our intentions misunderstood, misrepresented

like that day they turned the candles
upside down, thumped them out and we all
lost our jobs. Nothing personal. Handshakes around.
Of course we're not guilty
of what we've been accused of
but we're guilty of so much else, what's it matter,
I heard on the radio. I hate the radio,
how it pretends to be your friend.
You could be eating, you could be driving around
and then you're screaming, What, what did that fucker say
but by then it's someone else with the voice
of air conditioning saying, Take cover,
storm on the way. It's amazing
word hasn't gotten back to us from irritated
outer space how some creatures of spine and light
have finally had enough. Shut up, they beep back
but we're so dense, so unevolved, we think
it's just the usual interference: Bill next door
blending his Singapore Slings during Wheel
of Fortune. Right now they're working on something
that'll make our fillings fall out,
turn our checking accounts to dust,
something far more definitive.
There's a man starting his mower in the bedroom.
There's a woman burning photos in a sink.
I hate the phone, how it pretends to be
your friend, but I called you anyway,
got some curt, inchoate message that means
everyone's miserable, little shreds of your heart
rain down on me, twitching like slivered worms.
Upstairs, they're overflowing the tub again,
they're doing that Euripidian dance. I knew
a guy in college who stuck his head through a wall.
It seemed to decide something, to make us all
feel grateful, restored to simple things:
cars starting, cottage cheese, Larry, Curly, Mo.
It was, of course, a thin wall, a practice wall,
a wall between nowhere and nowhere's bedroom,
nothing like that 16th century woodcut
where the guy pokes through the sky into

the watchback of the cosmos. Tick, tick.
The cosmos gives me the creeps.
I like a decent chair where you can sit
and order a beer, be smiled at while you wait
for a friend who just had his sutures removed,
who rolls a quarter across his knuckles
to get them working again.

White Crane

I don't need to know any more about death
from the Japanese beetles
infesting the roses and plum
no matter what my neighbor sprays
in orange rubber gloves.
You can almost watch them writhe and wither,
pale and fall like party napkins
blown from a table just as light fades,
and the friends,
as often happens when light fades,
talk of something painful, glacial, pericardial,
and the napkins blow into the long grass.
When Basho writes of the long grass,
I don't need to know it has to do with death,
the characters reddish-brown and dim,
shadows of a rusted sword, an hour hand.
Imagine crossing mountains in summer snow
like Basho, all you own
on your back: brushes, robe,
the small gifts given in parting it's bad luck to leave behind.
I don't want to know what it's like to die on a rose,
sunk in perfume and fumes,
clutching,
to die in summer with everything off its knees,
daisies scattered like eyesight by the fence,
gladiolas open and fallen in mud,
weighed down with opening and breeze.
I wonder what your thoughts were, Father,

after they took your glasses and teeth,
all of us bunched around you like clouds
knocked loose of their moorings,
the white bird lying over you,
its beak down your throat.
Rain, heartbeats of rain.

LI-YOUNG LEE

I Ask My Mother to Sing

She begins, and my grandmother joins her.
Mother and daughter sing like young girls.
If my father were alive, he would play
his accordion and sway like a boat.

I've never been in Peking, or the Summer Palace,
nor stood on the great Stone Boat to watch
the rain begin on Kuen Ming Lake, the picnickers
running away in the grass.

But I love to hear it sung;
how the waterlilies fill with rain until
they overturn, spilling water into water,
then rock back, and fill with more.

Both women have begun to cry.
But neither stops her song.

This Room and Everything in It

Lie still now
while I prepare for my future,
certain hard days ahead,
when I'll need what I know so clearly this moment.

I am making use
of the one thing I learned
of all the things my father tried to teach me:
the art of memory.

I am letting this room
and everything in it
stand for my ideas about love
and its difficulties.

I'll let your love-cries,
those spacious notes
of a moment ago,
stand for distance.

Your scent,
that scent
of spice and a wound,
I'll let stand for mystery.

Your sunken belly
is the daily cup
of milk I drank
as a boy before morning prayer.

The sun on the face
of the wall
is God, the face
I can't see, my soul,

and so on, each thing
standing for a separate idea,
and those ideas forming the constellation
of my greater idea.
And one day, when I need
to tell myself something intelligent
about love,

I'll close my eyes
and recall this room and everything in it:
My body is estrangement.
This desire, perfection.
Your closed eyes my extinction.
Now I've forgotten my
idea. The book

on the windowsill, riffled by wind . . .
the even-numbered pages are
the past, the odd-
numbered pages, the future.
The sun is
God, your body is milk . . .

useless, useless . . .
your cries are song, my body's not me . . .
no good . . . my idea
has evaporated . . . your hair is time, your thighs are song . . .
it had something to do
with death . . . it had something
to do with love.

Eating Together

In the steamer is the trout
seasoned with slivers of ginger,
two sprigs of green onion, and sesame oil.
We shall eat it with rice for lunch,
brothers, sister, my mother who will
taste the sweetest meat of the head,
holding it between her fingers
deftly, the way my father did
weeks ago. Then he lay down
to sleep like a snow-covered road
winding through pines older than him,
without any travelers, and lonely for no one.

The Cleaving

He gossips like my grandmother, this man
with my face, and I could stand
amused all afternoon
in the Hon Kee Grocery,

amid hanging meats he
chops: roast pork cut
from a hog hung
by nose and shoulders,
her entire skin burnt
crisp, flesh I know
to be sweet,
her shining
face grinning
up at ducks
dangling single file,
each pierced by black
hooks through breast, bill,
and steaming from a hole
stitched shut at the ass.
I step to the counter, recite,
and he, without even slightly
varying the rhythm of his current confession or harangue,
scribbles my order on a greasy receipt,
and chops it up quick.

Such a sorrowful Chinese face,
nomad, Gobi, Northern
in its boniness
clear from the high
warlike forehead
to the sheer edge of the jaw.
He could be my brother, but finer,
and, except for his left forearm, which is engorged,
sinewy from his daily grip and
wield of a two-pound tool,
he's delicate, narrow-
waisted, his frame
so slight a lover, some
rough other
might break it down
its smooth, oily length.
In his light-handed calligraphy
on receipts and in his
moodiness, he is

a Southerner from a river-province;
suited for scholarship, his face poised
above an open book, he'd mumble
his favorite passages.
He could be my grandfather;
come to America to get a Western education
in 1917, but too homesick to study,
he sits in the park all day, reading poems
and writing letters to his mother.

He lops the head off, chops
the neck of the duck
into six, slits
the body
open, groin
to breast, and drains
the scalding juices,
then quarters the carcass
with two fast hacks of the cleaver,
old blade that has worn
into the surface of the round
foot-thick chop-block
a scoop that cradles precisely the curved steel.

The head, flung from the body, opens
down the middle where the butcher
cleanly halved it between
the eyes, and I
see, foetal-crouched
inside the skull, the homunculus,
gray brain grainy
to eat.
Did this animal, after all, at the moment
its neck broke,
image the way his executioner
shrinks from his own death?
Is this how
I, too, recoil from my day?
See how this shape
hordes itself, see how

little it is.
See its grease on the blade.
Is this how I'll be found
when judgement is passed, when names
are called, when crimes are tallied?
This is also how I looked before I tore my mother open.
Is this how I presided over my century, is this how
I regarded the murders?
This is also how I prayed.
Was it me in the Other
I prayed to when I prayed?
This too was how I slept, clutching my wife.
Was it me in the other I loved
when I loved another?
The butcher sees me eye this delicacy.
With a finger, he picks it
out of the skull-cradle
and offers it to me.
I take it gingerly between my fingers
and suck it down.
I eat my man.

The noise the body makes
when the body meets
the soul over the soul's ocean and penumbra
is the old sound of up-and-down, in-and-out,
a lump of muscle chug-chugging blood
into the ear; a lover's
heart-shaped tongue;
flesh rocking flesh until flesh comes;
the butcher working
at his block and blade to marry their shapes
by violence and time;
an engine crossing,
re-crossing salt water, hauling
immigrants and the junk
of the poor. These
are the faces I love, the bodies
and scents of bodies
for which I long

in various ways, at various times,
thirteen gathered around the redwood,
happy, talkative, voracious
at day's end,
eager to eat
four kinds of meat
prepared four different ways,
numerous plates and bowls of rice and vegetables,
each made by distinct affections
and brought to table by many hands.

Brothers and sisters by blood and design,
who sit in separate bodies of varied shapes,
we constitute a many-membered
body of love.
In a world of shapes
of my desires, each one here
is a shape of one of my desires, and each
is known to me and dear by virtue
of each one's unique corruption
of those texts, the face, the body:
that jut jaw
to gnash tendon;
that wide nose to meet the blows
a face like that invites;
those long eyes closing on the seen;
those thick lips
to suck the meat of animals
or recite 300 poems of the T'ang;
these teeth to bite my monosyllables;
these cheekbones to make
those syllables sing the soul.
Puffed or sunken
according to the life,
dark or light according
to the birth, straight
or humped, whole, manqué, quasi, each pleases, verging
on utter grotesquery.
All are beautiful by variety.
The soul too

is a debasement
of a text, but, thus, it
acquires salience, although a
human salience, but
inimitable, and, hence, memorable.
God is the text.

CARLOS CUMPIÁN

Armadillo Charm

I

Armadillos are flattened on roads every week,
ending up like some cold drunk Indians
that lie down on warm dark asphalt after
trips back from fiery-watering holes.

Smart armadillos amble jobless,
happy not to work in a zoo, they stroll
plush river grass and smooth red pebble paths,
far from fast two-legged foreigners.

II

Armadillos want to be around when the earth smears
the last mad zig-zag road from her body,
armadillos are patient, armadillos count
every wind stir roaring off solar coasters,
bringing layers of fine star dandruff to land,
that's why they look like dried-up
sailors or the last face of thirsty travelers,
armadillos are prone to tropical leprosy,
like lost botanists they go skinning themselves
raw while roaming hungry in the dark.

Before the sky master tossed sparks to bake all creation
with tell-tale universal panther carbon, nothing big had died
yet, truly a nadir niche for four-legged fossils, though not too
bad for fishes, it nearly killed calorie-starved armadillo.

III

Armadillo, ugly craggy creature, with twenty tribes across the hemisphere,
armadillo, with few friends from beginning to end:
the hairy tree sloth, and rapacious ant eater,

each claiming to be his pal, sharing a pre-Ice-Age pedigree
with the armored rascal, each sticking to the same survival
diet since making the Paleocene,
peg-tooth armadillo got hot under his sixty million year-old
scapular collar and became a cranium-hard tourist walking backwards—
going south to north, before entering borderland Texas.

Gringos discovered Armadillo in the mid-nineteenth century,
the indigenous people had always known him,
but history started with the newcomers ripe for independence,
Alamo insurance, Austin honky-tonks, accordion *conjunto*-polka suds,
salsa music, blue eyed Baptists, plastic saints on dashboards,
chile-flavored beans and King Ranch cowboys trained by *vaqueros*
raised on tacos of onion-soaked armadillo,
available only in south *Texaztlán,*
giving the chicken-colored meat cult status.

IV
Armadillos are fond of colorful flowers, thorns pose no problem,
and armadillos love dark dirt body bugs, slugs and worms
on steamy leaves and bright powdery pistils-to-petals.
There are no obese armadillos.
Armadillo has no patent on this diet, so some of us
wanting to slim down just might like to try it. You go first.

Armadillo kitsch means being flayed for book ends, salt shakers or
decorative baskets to please some schmucks passing through airports,
armadillos become rustic *canastas* filled with pecans and
pomegranates after eyes are shredded by twenty-two caliber bullets,
there's no graveside music for their passing,
no lead-lined casket for a charade with eternity,
not a moment of ritual magic,
nothing cushions armadillo death when shells, cars or trucks
splatter red guts like gastral litter on subtropical scrublands.

V
Armadillo prefers his original name in Nahuatl *Ayotochtli,*
a combination of turtle and rabbit,
looking like a hedgehog in an obsidian helmet,
sturdy enough to become an instrument,

complete with strings for *charango*-mountain music,
Ayotochtli, Ayotochtli, Ayotochtli,

"Ah, don't touch me," he seems to say,
balling up after he burrows away
at speeds pushing fifty,
armadillos have lived like charmed moving stones
for generations, so don't knickknack them to extinction,
be compassionate compadres
adopt one.

Estrellitas

Julian and Mia
sat outside
abuela's casa,
watching heaven's
sparklers hang quietly
in the bay of darkness.

Thinking they'd miss
one or a dozen
flashing tips,
falling from a
hidden angel's scepter,
each tried not to blink,
and kept their chins lifted
like moon-struck coyotes.

With sore eyes and
stiff necks they were
just about to stop,
when the top of
the vast night sky
beaded up briefly
like a woodland moccasin
then rained bright
plumed cinders.

Lucia Perillo

Dangerous Life

I quit med school when I found out the stiff they gave me
had Book Nine of *Paradise Lost* and the lyrics
to "Louie, Louie" tattooed on the inside of her thighs.

That morning as the wind was mowing
little ladies on a street below, I touched a bunsen burner
to the Girlscout sash whose badges were the measure of my worth.

Careers . . .
Cookery, Seamstress
and *Baby Maker* all gone up in smoke.

But I kept the merit badge marked *Dangerous Life,*
for which, if you remember, the girls were taken to the woods
and taught the mechanics of fire,

around which they had us dance with pointed sticks
lashed into crucifixes that we'd wrapped with yarn and wore
on lanyards round our necks, calling them "The Eyes of God."

Now my mother calls the payphone outside my walk up, raving
about what people think of a woman: thirty, unsettled,
living on foodstamps, coin-op laundromats & public clinics.

Some nights I take my lanyards from their shoebox, practice baying
those old campsongs to the moon. And remember how they told us
that a smart girl could find her way out of anywhere, alive.

The Body Mutinies

When the doctor runs out of words and still
I won't leave, he latches my shoulder and
steers me out doors. Where I see his blurred hand,
through the milk glass, flapping goodbye like a sail
(& me not griefstruck yet but still amazed: how
words and names—medicine's blunt instruments—
undid me. And the seconds, the half seconds
it took for him to say those words.) For now,
I'll just stand in the courtyard, watching bodies
struggle in then out of one lean shadow
a tall fir lays across the wet flagstones,
before the sun clears the valance of gray trees
and finds the surgical-supply shop window
and makes the dusty bedpans glint like coins.

Needles

So first there's the chemo: three sticks, once a week,
        twenty-six weeks.
Then you add interferon: one stick, three times a week,
        forever.
And then there's the blood tests. How many blood tests?
        (Too many to count.)
Add all the sticks up and they come down to this: either
        your coming out clean
or else . . . well, nobody's talking
        about the B side,
an *or else* that plows through your life like a combine
        driven at stock-car speed,
shucking the past into two piles: *things that mattered*
        and *things that didn't.*
And the first pile looks so small when you think of
        everything you haven't done—
never seeing the Serengeti or Graceland, never running
        with the bulls in Spain.

Not to mention all the women you haven't done yet!—
    and double that number of breasts.
Okay—
    you've got a woman, a good woman make no mistake.
But how come you get just one woman when you're getting
    many lifetimes' worth of sticks?
Where was the justice in that? You feel like someone
    who's run out of clean clothes
with laundry day still half a week away; all those women
    you tossed in the pile
marked *things that didn't matter,* now you can't help but
    drag them out.
Like the blonde on trail crew who lugged the chain saw
    on her shoulder up a mountain
and bucked up chunks of blighted trees, how could you
    have forgotten
how her arms quaked when the saw whined and the muscles
    went liquid in her quads,
or the sweaty patch on her chest where a mosaic formed
    of shiny flies and moss?
Or that swarthy-haired dancer, her underpants hooked
    across her face like the Lone Ranger,
the one your friends paid to come to the table, where
    she pawed and made you blush:
How come yer getting married when you could be muff-diving
    every night?
At college they swore it was John Dewey, they swore
    by the quadruped Rousseau,
and it took cancer to step up and punch your gut
    before you figured
that all along immortal truth's one best embodiment
    was just
some sixteen-year-old tabledancing on a forged ID
    at Ponders Corners.
You should have bought a red sports car, skimmed it under
    pale descending arms at the railroad crossing,
the blonde and brunette beside you under its moonroof
    & everything smelling of leather—
yes yes—this has been your flaw: how you have always
    turned away from the moment

your life was about to be stripped so the bone of it
    lay bare and glittering.
You even tried wearing a White Sox cap to bed, but its bill
    nearly put your wife's eye out.
So now you're left no choice but going capless, scarred;
    you must stand erect;
you must unveil yourself as a bald man in that most
    treacherous darkness.
You remember the first night your parents left town, left
    you home without a sitter.
Two friends came over and one of them drove the Mercury
    your dad had parked stalwartly
in the drive (you didn't know how yet)—took it down
    to some skinny junkie's place
in Wicker Park, cousin of a friend of a cousin, friend
    of a cousin of a friend,
what did it matter but that his name was Sczabo.
    Sczabo!—
As though this guy were a skin disease, or a magician
    about to make doves appear.
What he did was tie off your friends with a surgical tube,
    piece of lurid chitterling
smudged with grease along its length. Then needle, spoon—
    he did the whole bit,
it was just like in the movies, only your turn turned you
    chicken (or were you defiant?—)
Somebody's got to drive home, and that's what you did
    though you'd never
made it even as far as the driveway's end before your dad
    put his foot over the transmission hump
to forestall some calamity he thought would compromise
    the hedges.
All the way back to Evanston you piloted the Mercury
    like General Montgomery in his tank,
your friends huddled in the back seat, spines coiled,
    arms cradled to their ribs—
as though each held a baby being rocked too furiously
    for any payoff less than panic.
It's the same motion your wife blames on some blown-out
    muscle in her chest

when at the end of making love she pitches violently,
    except instead of saying
something normal like *god* or *jesus* she screams *ow! ow!*
    and afterwards,
when you try sorting out her pleasure from her pain,
    she refuses you the difference.
Maybe you wish you took the needle at Sczabo's place—
    what's one more stick
among the many you'll endure, your two friends not such
    a far cry from being women,
machines shaking and arching in the wide back seat
    as Sczabo's doves appeared—
or so you thought then, though now you understand
    all the gestures the body will employ
just to keep from puking. Snow was damping the concrete
    and icing the trees,
a silence stoppered in the back of your friends' throats
    as you let the Mercury wheel pass
hand over hand, steering into the fishtails, remembering
    your dad's admonition:
when everything goes to hell the worst you can do
    is hit the brakes.

Skin

Back then it seemed that wherever a girl took off her clothes
    the police would find her—
in the backs of cars or beside the dark night ponds, opening
    like a green leaf across
some boy's knees, the skin so white and taut beneath the moon
    it was almost too terrible,
too beautiful to look at, a tinderbox, though she did not know.
    But the men who came
beating the night rushes with their flashlights and thighs—
    they knew. About Helen,
about how a body could cause the fall of Troy and the death
    of a perfectly good king.
So they read the boy his rights and shoved him spread-legged

against the car
while the girl hopped barefoot on the asphalt, cloaked
    in a wool rescue blanket.
Or sometimes girls fled so their fathers wouldn't hit them,
    their white legs flashing as they ran.
And the boys were handcuffed just until their wrists had welts
    and let off half a block from home.

God, for how many years did I believe there were truly laws
    against such things,
laws of adulthood: no yelling out of cars in traffic tunnels,
    no walking without shoes,
no singing any foolish songs in public places. Or else
    they could lock you in jail
or, as good as condemning you to death, tell both your lower-
    and upper-case Catholic fathers.
And out of all these crimes, unveiling the body was of course
    the worst, as though something
about the skin's phosphorescence, its surface as velvet as
    a deer's new horn,
could drive not only men but civilization mad, could lead us
    to unspeakable cruelties.
There were elders who from experience understood these things
    much better than we.
And it's true, remembering I had that kind of skin does drive me
    half-crazy with loss.
Skin that to me now so much resembles a broad white lily
    on the first morning it unfurls.

ELISE PASCHEN

Between the Acts
   at Chicago's Lyric Opera

Tonight at *Antony and Cleopatra*,
I met Nicole, again,
between the acts in the Green Room.
(How many years had it been?)

It was awkward shaking hands (offer
a kiss, instead?) because we both
held flutes of Veuve Cliquot.
She pours it on. "How you have grown!

You look just like your mother,
but you inherited your father's
eyes and his coloring," she says,
blue-eyed, blond-haired, and smiling.

She too has changed, now middle-aged
and married to a high society
orthodontic surgeon. They have
a five-year-old daughter, the age

I was when I first met Nicole
at my grandmother's Christmas feast.
She was nineteen, alone, and new
in town, spoke English with a thick

Swedish accent and was employed
at a Chicago hair salon.
While trimming my half sister's hair,
she was invited home

for Christmas dinner.
What better present could my sister
(no doubt relieved her stepmother
and I had moved out East)

have offered to our father?
The next summer I left
my mother to fly west; my sister
left hers, flew east, and we

landed, mid-country, at
our father's summer cottage
above Lake Michigan.
Nicole had moved in.

—⧟—

After the opera, my parents
and I sit at our kitchen table.
It's Christmas break. My father teases
my mother about a card she's

received from one of the boyfriends
she had during their separation.
All I can remember about
the man is the gift he gave me,

a fluffy snow kitten perched on
a heart-shaped cushion (probably
delivered on Valentine's Day).
I ask my father whether they

had ever met. My father answers:
"Yes, once, at dinner. All I could
think was that your mother was wearing
her new mink coat. I was so mad

because I had just given it
to her for Christmas."
They're playing Frank Sinatra.
I hug my parents goodnight,

and leave them in the kitchen—
holding hands, in love, laughing.

12 East Scott Street

We move back to my father's home
when I can press the highest button
of our slow Otis elevator.

My mother unclasps her lizard
Kelly handbag and fishes out
a ring of incandescent keys.

This is the only place that smells
like home. We travel down the hallway
hung with clippings about my mother.

She pulls open the top right drawer
(my chin just clears the top)
of her mahogany bureau.

Home is my mother finding inside
her drawer a snapshot of a blond
posing naked against beach boulders.

My mother covers with her thumbs
the bottom half of the snapshot,
evenly asks, "Is this Nicole?"

I hold my breath and wonder whether
to answer yes. My mother takes
the photograph between her thumb

and forefinger, quarters the picture,
quartering and quartering
the bits into the wastepaper basket.

Home is my mother. Home is mother
with airplane smell on all her clothes,
when she unsnaps each suitcase, trunk,

when she unfolds her nicely folded
St. Laurent blouses, jackets, dresses,
positioning the arms, the shoulders

on hanger after hanger in
her half of their well-arranged closet,
when she lines up her panties, bras,

stockings, handkerchiefs, purses, gloves
in dresser drawers, beginning at
the top, then working her way down.

REGINALD SHEPHERD

A Man Named Troy

Here are the homeless black men begging small coins
on the corner, and to the left are the instructive ruins
of others' wars, nine layers of rubble
struggling for the site of one lost city. Here is
some blond man stalled halfway down a slope
called realism in a long white car. It's called
America, where all the accidents
are built to last, where all the alabaster
and chipped marble anyone could ever use
is quarried and carried away. (Achilles is killed
by Apollo the butcher of heroes, who doesn't care
whose side he slaughters, doesn't recall
from one day's lethal sunlight to another: Apollo
who prophesied long life, beauty, and the love
of many men and women, then
forgot.) He wasn't born yet, somehow
he's responsible. He's just reading the paper
in an afternoon café, reading random
pages of unwritten history, his
or whose. He's history, him or me or someone
illegible, all too readable. Who wrote that, here.

And lined-up lighted windows aren't the eyes
of trains hurtling toward the underground entrance
of hell, the El looking into someone's living room
from up and out, just like the gods, who don't
take public transportation, who never look
before they leap from some whitewashed trestle
or another, with only one or two mortals
to break their fall. (Apollo fell
into the tenth year of the Trojan War, landed
atop an Anatolian trading town and the old queen

cried *Oimoi,* kneeling on the burnt ramparts
where the last missiles landed: no quarter
given, none expected. He broke
their ancient backs and walked to Rome. A god's feet
should never touch the ground.) The stars
aren't streetlights: lowered on their nylon strings
and hovering second-story window height, they just look
that way. Here are the windows looking away,
averted from the chain of cars that sideswipe them
and miss. Here is some man in a white T-shirt (a color
we collaborated on) watching a documentary, drowned out
by the clatter of passing traffic.

There were blind days a blond man's toss of head
to shake the careless hair back into place
above the half-closed sky-blue eyes (late Mediterranean
breakers beaten white against an Asian shore, late afternoon
sky shaking off slight rain) seemed the whim
of some Greek god: all force, gesture,
grace, the consecrated body with no mind
at all. *Why is there nothing in thy face?* Here
is a man (but never him) sitting by a plate glass window
as if in a museum, still life with stranger
seen through glass: Clark Street, the El scaffolding,
all of Chicago the just backdrop for this history
play: blank page I'm reading into, white text or
white skin. (Is skin burning paper, palimpsest, the written
over only, face again?) Now he's translating lines
about Achilles' wrath, white waves
folded over to expose the virtual wound.
(The mourners beg for mercy and Apollo
only shakes his perfectly formed head.)
Here are the homeless black men begging
drachmas and quarters on the corner
of this place soon to be called the new world.

West Willow

For Christopher Cutrone

Morning traffic murmurs like an ocean
out my open window. Now it looks like rain, whatever rain
that hasn't fallen looks like, scrawled over the illegible,
sky moving south from Evanston with thunder in its gray
felt pockets. Happiness, I've heard, is easy, joy written
on the earth, russet and sorrel leaves, fruit
fallen past ripeness darkest where the rot has set in.
And who wouldn't wish to live forever in the sensual
world, but not just yet? In bed at ten A.M.,
I asked for the authenticity of forms and the day
gave me this twig twisted from its branch, this broken bracelet
stripped of charms, a tear shaped like September
in the yellowed shade. Who wouldn't wish this sky
on anyone, clouds squandering their slate-gray
on potential weather? I walked out into the street
where life resumes its absorbing routines (I admit now
they mean nothing to me, people hurrying
to labor, people hurrying to leisure), crushed cochineal
small berries into the sidewalk. Even crows and starlings
wouldn't eat them. *If the fruit lasts long enough to fall, it's bitter
through and through.* I picked one up and crushed its globe
between two well intentioned fingers, it smelled of nothing
at all. These are my hands, these are love, that fails
and tries again tomorrow afternoon, as clumsy, as incapable
of making any single thing whole. These are my hands,
that have no power to hurt anyone, that wake
each day with no memory and begin again, lightly touching
this thing, touching inaccurately that. Rain shivers
in its several voices all night long, the scenery's submerged
in liquid air, white atmosphere awash in generalities.
How clean I can become. Now the trees lining the parking lot
are bending over solicitously, everything the wind moves through
is whispering *now, now,* and patting me on the shoulder
like small rain. It looks like this. Wherever love is found
(bent penny cured to ruddle, rust, raw chestnut
half cracked open), my hands are stained with it.

ALLISON JOSEPH

Traitor

What did that girl on the playground mean
when she hissed *you ain't black* at me,

pigtails bouncing, her hands
on her bony hips? She sucked her teeth,

stared at me with such contempt
that I wanted to hide in my mother's

skirts, wanted to scurry to my house's
hall closet, safe among the great

dark coats. *You talk funny,* she said,
all proper, as if pronunciation

was a sin, a scandal, a strike
against the race only a traitor

would perform, an Uncle Tom sellout.
Somehow I'd let her down by not

slurring, I'd failed her by not
letting language laze on its own,

its sound unhurried. I'd said
isn't rather than *ain't*,

called my mother *mom* instead
of *momma,* pronounced *th* distinctly

so no one would confuse *them*
with *dem, those* with *dose.*

Your momma talk that funny?
the girl demanded, her face

in my face now, her nose
inches from mine, her eyes

lit by something near hate,
but more ferocious, a kind

of disgust mixed with pity,
disdain. *We're from Canada,*

I said, and the girl's eyes
went wide, as if I'd said

cantaloupe, or *harpoon,*
or some nonsense word like

*abracadabra. There must not be
no black folks in Canada then,*

she sneered, leaning in further,
pushing on my chest with one

bony finger, pinning me there
like a bug to a fly screen,

pressing me so hard that
my lower lip started to tremble

on its own, a sign of weakness
she laughed a mocking, heavy

laugh at, telling me *go on and cry,
white girl, cry till your momma*

can hear, pushing me so I toppled
onto my back, ripping the pants

my mother warned me not to rip.
She stood over me, laughing

like she'd just seen the world's
best clown, laughing though I

was just as dark as she,
my hair in the same

nappy plaits, my skin
the same rough brown.

In the Bookstore

Here I find refuge, though the woman
behind the counter looks at me

as if I can't read, regarding me
as just another colored girl

who might steal her store
out from under her, who might

rip pages from paperbacks,
ruin hardcovers with rough

handling. But her suspicion
can't stop me, however she looks

at me she won't stir from
her chair, afraid as I'm afraid,

both of us moving but not
moving, me shuffling

through tight aisles,
her pencil tapping, tapping.

She waits for me to figure out
whatever it is I want,

will be glad to silently ring up
my sale, hand me my small sack.

But I'm intent on lingering,
shifting my weight from one foot

to another, taking book after book
in my hands, holding each one

a long moment before I replace it,
before I hand her the one I'll take

back with me to the Bronx,
where rumor has it no one reads

unless it's the *New York Post*'s
daunting, garish headlines.

I'm 21, with twenty dollars and two
subway tokens in my pocket, greedy

for the life of the mind,
that energy, needing it enough

so when this woman hands me my change
I hiss a whispered *thank you,*

make sure my eyes catch hers
for one second of indictment,

one moment where I'm right, she's wrong,
and there are still dollars in my palm.

On Sidewalks, on Streetcorners, as Girls

Just who was Miss Mary Mack,
all dressed in black, with her stalwart buttons
up and down her back, her patient request
for fifty cents to see some bedraggled circus elephant
jump a fence? As children, we never asked
who she was, content instead to clap out her story
in pairs, our hands meeting, then parting
in quick motions. When we sang
We're going to Kentucky, we're going to the Fair,
to see the señorita with flowers in her hair,
we'd shake our little girl hips in time
with the melody, but we never stopped to ask
what a lovely *señorita* was doing at a fair,
and we possessed no knowledge of where
Kentucky was, didn't even know
what one did at a fair—children who only
knew cinderblock and cement,
corner storefronts, brick high-rises.
We sang about Miss Lucy
and her prized steamboat,
the steamboat destined for heaven
and Miss Lucy for hell;
sang *rumble to the bottom,*
rumble to the top,
one girl in the midst of the circle
twirling and twirling until she stopped,
finger pointed at the next girl
who would shake her stuff in front
of us, our chants heard in every
schoolyard, every parking lot,
everywhere small dark girls
could gather to hear their voices swell
in nonsense rhyme, neighborhood chant.
Hands and feet would stomp out rhythms
inherited from older sisters—story-songs
about seeing London, seeing France,
sassy songs about someone's mama
doing wrong, acting crazy.

No one would dare take away
our homemade streetcorner music,
so we'd spend every afternoon after school
and every shred of summer daylight
riffing, scatting, improvising,
unafraid to tell each other
shake it to the east,
shake it to the west,
shake it to the one
you love the best.

Quraysh Ali Lansana

The Woolworth's Poem
For Russ and Tod

I

we rode summer on ten speeds
bike routes to the courthouse lawn
where parking meter hitching posts
lined melting, technicolor days.

II

we knew every corner
from the bird droppings in the basement
to the scent of musty popcorn.

III

we laughed in the face of history.
him, golden locked and chubby nosed.
me, bubbling hot fudge.
we dared lunch counters innocently.
so close some thought us lovers
we were.

IV

Tod gave me a coffee mug
on the last day of business
before it became a museum.
he sat where freedom's students
wore ketchup and abuse
in a pre-jordan north carolina.
it is a simple mug.
opaque, speckled clay.
rounded handle.

sides geometrically balanced. sturdy.
it meant a lot to him
to give it to me.
it meant a lot to me to have it.

v
the parakeets and canaries are no more.
silence creeps the arthritic escalator.
those fat, pasty, sandwich fingers
labor now in snaptight kitchens
across town, their tenderness lost.

Contributors

Michael Anania's poetry collections include *The Color of Dust, Riversongs, The Sky at Ashland,* and *Selected Poems.* He is also the author of a novel, *The Red Menace,* and a collection of essays, *In Plain Sight.* Anania was the poetry editor of *Audit,* the poetry and literary editor of the Swallow Press in Chicago, and a contributing editor to *TriQuarterly.* He is a professor of English at the University of Illinois at Chicago.

James Ballowe has published the poetry collection *The Coal Miners* (1979) and has edited *George Santayana's America: Essays on Literature and Culture* (1967). He is also the recipient of two Illinois Arts Council awards for poetry and one for creative nonfiction.

Ray Bradbury spent his childhood in Waukegan. His publications include the poetry collections *When Elephants Last in the Dooryard Bloomed* and *Where Robot Mice and Robot Men Run Round in Robot Towns: New Poems, Both Light and Dark,* as well as the celebrated novels *Fahrenheit 451* and *The Martian Chronicles.*

Gwendolyn Brooks grew up in Chicago, attending Englewood High School and graduating from Wilson Junior College. She supplemented her own reading in the moderns with the instruction of Inez Cunningham Stark, a socialite and reader for *Poetry* magazine. With the awarding of the 1949 Pulitzer Prize for her volume *Annie Allen,* Brooks became the first African American to receive that honor. Brooks published an astounding array of poetry collections ranging in style from traditional lyric forms to those of improvisational jazz and spoken language. Brooks also worked tirelessly and enthusiastically with young writers, devoting particular attention to the social and artistic needs of Chicago's African American community. For many years Brooks served admirably as Poet Laureate of Illinois.

Debra Bruce's *What Wind Will Do* was published in 1997. She has received grants from the National Endowment for the Arts and the Illinois Arts Council. Her second book of poetry, *Sudden Hunger,* won the 1989 Carl Sandburg Award. Bruce is a professor of English at Northeastern Illinois University.

Paul Carroll was born in Chicago and educated at Mt. Carmel High School and the University of Chicago. The former editor and publisher of *Big Table,* he taught for many years at the University of Illinois at Chicago. His books include *The Luke Poems* (1971), *New and Selected Poems* (1979), and *The Garden of Earthly Delights* (1985). He was the winner of the Chicago Poets Award.

Ana Castillo is the author of the novels *The Mixquiahuala Letters, Sapogonia,* and, most recently, *So Far from God.* She is also the author of *Massacre of the Dreamers: Essays on Xicanisma.* She has received an American Book Award, a Carl Sandburg Award, and a Mountains and Plains Booksellers Award for her fiction and a National Endowment for the Arts fellowship for her poetry.

Maxine Chernoff has published six collections of poetry. *New Faces of 1952* won the 1985 Carl Sandburg Award. *American Heaven,* one of her four books of fiction, was runner-up for the Bay Area Book Reviewers' Award. She chairs the Creative Writing Program at San Francisco State University and coedits *New American Writing* with Paul Hoover.

Sandra Cisneros, a poet and fiction writer, grew up in Chicago's Mexican American community and was educated at Loyola University and the University of Iowa's Writers' Workshop. Cisneros's books include *The House on Mango Street* (1984) and *Woman from Hollering Creek* (1991).

Carlos Cumpián is the author of *Coyote Sun* (1990), a collection of Chicano poetry, and *Latino Rainbow* (1994), a book of poetry for children. Cumpián has been awarded two Community Arts Assistance Grants from the City of Chicago Department of Cultural Affairs and has been honored for his poetry by the Illinois State Library. An active promoter of poetry, he teaches and organizes several reading series in the Chicago area.

John Dickson entered the grain business at nineteen and stayed in it for over forty years, mostly as a member of the Chicago Board of Trade. His first collection, *Victoria Hotel* (1980), won a Friends of Literature Award. The recipient of a National Endowment for the Arts fellowship, he has published two other collections, *Waving at Trains* (1986) and *The Music of Solid Objects* (1997).

George Dillon won the Pulitzer Prize at age twenty-two for *The Flowering Stone* (1932). His only other collection was *Boy in the Wind* (1927). Dillon served as the editor of *Poetry* magazine, on and off, from 1937 to 1949.

Stuart Dybek was born and raised in Chicago. He is the author of two books of fiction and a collection of poems, *Brass Knuckles*. He has received two National Endowment for the Arts grants, a Guggenheim Fellowship, and a Whiting Writer's Award. He teaches at Western Michigan University.

Jim Elledge has published four collections of poetry among his ten books. The most recent, *Into the Arms of the Universe: Poems and Prose Poems,* won the 1994 Stonewall chapbook competition for gay and lesbian poets. His fifth collection, *The Chapters of Coming Forth by Day,* was published in 2001.

Elaine Equi is the author of many books, including *Surface Tension, Decoy,* and, most recently, *Voice-Over.* Her work has also been featured in such anthologies as *The Best American Poetry 1989, The Best American Poetry 1995,* and *The Norton Anthology of Postmodern American Poetry.* She lives in New York City.

Dave Etter, an Illinois resident since 1958—in Evanston, Geneva, Lily Lake, Elburn, and, currently, Lanark—has held editorial positions with Encyclopedia Britannica and Northwestern and Northern Illinois University presses. He has published twenty-five collections of poetry, has contributed to many magazines and anthologies, and has had his work translated into German, Polish, and Japanese. His prizes include the Carl Sandburg, Society of Midland Authors, and Illinois Sesquicentennial awards.

Kenneth Fearing, a prototypical hard-nosed newspaper reporter in Chicago during the 1920s, developed a unique poetic style that embraced the distinctive idioms, slang, and staccato rhythms of American speech. The most important of his seven collections of poems are *Angel Arms, Stranger at Coney Island,* and *Afternoon of a Pawn Broker.*

Calvin Forbes has taught at the School of the Art Institute since 1991. He has written two books, *Blue Monday* and *From the Book of Shine,* and a forthcoming collection, *The Shine Poems.* He is the recipient of National Endowment for the Arts and Fulbright fellowships.

Lucia Cordell Getsi's *Intensive Care* (1992) won the Capricorn Prize for Poetry. Illinois Author of the Year in 1994, she has received one National Endowment for the Arts fellowship, three Illinois Arts Council fellowships, two Fulbright fellowships (for study in Germany and in Austria), and the Ann Stanford Prize. She is Distinguished Professor of English and Comparative Literature and the codirector of the creative writing program at Illinois State University.

Reginald Gibbons has won poetry fellowships from the Guggenheim Foundation, the National Endowment for the Arts, and the Illinois Arts Council. He has won the Carl Sandburg Award for poetry and the Anisfield-Wolf Award for fiction. From 1981 to 1997 he was the editor of *TriQuarterly*. In 1989, he helped to found the Guild Complex in Chicago and presently serves on its board of directors.

Albert Goldbarth was born in Chicago and currently lives in Wichita, Kansas. His most recent collections are *Troubled Lovers in History* (poems) and *Dark Waves and Light Matter* (essays).

Bruce Guernsey is a professor of English and Board of Governors Distinguished Professor at Eastern Illinois University. Among his collections of poetry is *January Thaw*. The recipient of fellowships from the National Endowment for the Arts and the Illinois Arts Council, he has published poems in magazines such as *Poetry* and the *American Scholar*. He has held Fulbright lectureships in Portugal and Greece and recently sailed around the world with Semester at Sea.

Dan Guillory is the author of two books of essays, *Living with Lincoln: Life and Art in the Heartland* (1989) and *When Waters Recede: Rescue and Recovery after the Great Flood* (1997), as well as a book of poetry, *The Alligator Inventions* (1992). He is a professor of English at Millikin University.

Jeff Gundy's books include *Rhapsody with Dark Matter, Inquiries, Flatlands,* and *A Community of Memory: My Days with George and Clara* (creative nonfiction). Born and raised in central Illinois, he teaches at Bluffton College in Ohio, where he has received three Ohio Arts Council grants.

Susan Hahn was born in Chicago, has two degrees from Northwestern University, and has lived and worked in Illinois all her life. Her books of poetry are *Harriet Rubin's Mother's Wooden Hand* (1991), *Incontinence* (1993)—winner of the 1994 Society of Midland Authors Award—*Confession* (1997), and *Holiday* (2001). She is the recipient of several Illinois Arts Council awards and fellowships and is the cofounder/editor of TriQuarterly Books and the editor of *TriQuarterly* magazine.

Ernest Hemingway, born and raised in Oak Park, became an international celebrity following the publication of his first novel, *The Sun Also Rises* (1926). His distinguished career as a journalist, novelist, and short story writer brought him numerous awards, including the Pulitzer Prize and the 1954 Nobel Prize for Literature.

David Hernandez's *Rooftop Piper* was published in 1991. For many years he performed his poetry to the accompaniment of his band, Street Sounds.

Daryl Hine, a native of British Columbia, studied classics and philosophy at McGill University in Montreal before moving to Chicago, where he served as the editor of *Poetry* from 1968 to 1978. Hine has taught at the University of Chicago, Northwestern University, and the University of Illinois. His poems are imbued with classical learning and strict metrical control, most evident in the collection *Daylight Saving.*

Edward Hirsch was born in Chicago in 1950 and educated at Grinnell College and the University of Pennsylvania. His first book, *For the Sleepwalkers* (1981), won the Lavan Younger Poets Award from the Academy of American Poets and the Delmore Schwartz Memorial Prize from New York University. His second collection, *Wild Gratitude* (1986), received the National Book Critics Circle Award. His subsequent poetic works include *The Night Parade* (1989), *Earthly Measures* (1994), and *On Love* (1998).

Paul Hoover has written *Viridian* (1997), the book-length poem *The Novel* (1990), and *Idea* (1987), which won the Carl Sandburg Award. Editor of *Postmodern American Poetry: A Norton Anthology* (1994), the definitive collection of American avant-garde poetry since 1950, he has also authored a novel, *Saigon, Illinois* (1988). With Maxine Chernoff, he edits *New American Writing.*

Angela Jackson, a poet, playwright, and storyist, is the recipient of National Endowment for the Arts and Illinois Arts Council fellowships. A graduate of Northwestern University, she has published *Solo in the Boxcar Third Floor E* (1985) among other poetry collections.

Richard Jones is the author of *Country of Air, At Last We Enter Paradise, A Perfect Time,* and six other poetry volumes. For two decades he has edited *Poetry East,* and since 1990 he has been a professor of English and the director of the creative writing program at DePaul University. The recipient of Illinois Arts

Council awards and fellowships for poetry, he currently lives in Evanston with his wife and son.

Rodney Jones is the author of *The Story They Told Us of Light* (1980), *The Unborn* (1985), *Transparent Gestures* (1989), *Apocalyptic Narrative* (1993), *Things That Happen Once* (1996), and *Elegy for the Southern Drawl* (1999). He has received a Guggenheim Fellowship, the Jean Stein Award of the American Academy of Arts and Letters, and the National Book Critics Circle Award. He lives in Carbondale and teaches at Southern Illinois University.

Allison Joseph is the author of *What Keeps Us Here* (1992), *Soul Train* (1997), and *In Every Seam* (1997). She teaches at Southern Illinois University, home to the first M.F.A. program in creative writing at a public university in the state.

Brigit Pegeen Kelly has published two books of poems. Her first, *To the Place of Trumpets* (1988), was part of the Yale Series of Younger Poets. Her second, *Song*, was the 1994 Lamont Poetry Selection of the Academy of American Poets.

Mary Kinzie is the author of three critical books, most recently *A Poet's Guide to Poetry* (1998). She has published *Autumn Eros* (1991), *Ghost Ship* (1996), and three other poetry collections. In addition, she is the founding director of the creative writing program at Northwestern University and the recipient of a Guggenheim Fellowship.

John Knoepfle's many collections include *Rivers into Islands* (1965), *Poems from the Sangamon* (1985), and *Selected Poems* (1985). The winner of the Mark Twain Award and the Illinois Author of the Year Award, Knoepfle is also the recipient of a National Endowment for the Arts fellowship. Along with James Wright and Robert Bly, he has translated the works of César Vallejo, including the influential collection of translations *Twenty Poems of César Vallejo* (1962).

Quraysh Ali Lansana is the author of *Southside Rain* (1999) and a poetry chapbook, *Cockroach Children: Corner Poems and Street Psalms* (1995). *Passage,* his poetry video collaboration with Kurt Heintz, won the first Bob Award from WTTW-TV, Chicago's public television station. He has collaborated extensively with musicians in jazz, blues, reggae, and traditional West African idioms.

Li-Young Lee, who was born in Jakarta, Indonesia, currently lives in Chicago. His first collection, *Rose* (1986), won the Delmore Schwartz Memorial Poetry Award; his second, *The City in which I Love You* (1990), was the Lamont Poetry

Selection of the Academy of American Poets. He has also received a Guggenheim Fellowship and a Whiting Foundation Writing Award.

Janet Lewis was born in Oak Park and was a classmate of Ernest Hemingway. Educated at the University of Chicago, where she met the young poet Yvor Winters, she moved to Paris in 1921 and worked at the American consulate. She subsequently returned to the United States and married Winters. Her major poetry collections include *The Indians in the Woods; The Wheel in Midsummer; The Earth-Bound; Poems, 1924–1944; The Ancient Ones; Poems Old and New, 1918–1978;* and *The Dear Past.*

Laurence Lieberman is the author of eleven books of poetry, including *Compass of the Dying* (1999) and *Dark Songs: Slave House and Synagogue* (1996). His most recent book of criticism is *Beyond the Muse of Memory* (1995). The editor of the University of Illinois Poetry Series since its inception in 1971, Lieberman has received National Endowment for the Arts and Yaddo fellowships. He teaches at the University of Illinois at Urbana-Champaign.

Vachel Lindsay spent his early writing years seeking an audience by distributing his work on the streets of Springfield. An artist, poet, social reformer, and motion picture critic, Lindsay was a mainstay in the Chicago Renaissance. Once having achieved literary recognition, Lindsay ceaselessly toured the United States and England, presenting his poetry and social consciousness in performances that offered near-vaudeville flair.

Archibald MacLeish was born in the Chicago suburb of Glencoe. His epic *Conquistador* (1932) won the Pulitzer Prize, as did *JB: A Play in Verse* (1959). MacLeish served as Librarian of Congress from 1939 to 1944 and later as assistant secretary of state in 1944–45. He taught for many years at Harvard University.

Haki R. Madhubuti is a recipient of National Endowment for the Arts and National Endowment for the Humanities fellowships. He has received an Illinois Arts Council Literary Award and the Distinguished Writers Award from the Middle Atlantic Writers Association. In 1991, he received an American Book Award and was named Author of the Year by the Illinois Association of Teachers of English. In 1995 he was awarded the Gwendolyn Brooks/Alaine Locke Literary Excellence Award from the U.S. Organization of Los Angeles.

Michael David Madonick currently teaches writing at the University of Illinois. He has received an Academy of American Poets Prize, the New Jersey Council on the Arts Distinguished Artist Award, an Illinois Arts Council award, and an Illinois Arts Council fellowship.

Edgar Lee Masters was raised in two small Illinois towns, Petersburg and Lewiston. He attended Knox College for one year before passing the bar exam. While practicing law, he became deeply involved in the Chicago Renaissance movement. A poet, novelist, and biographer of Abraham Lincoln, Vachel Lindsay, Walt Whitman, and Mark Twain, Masters achieved immediate and lasting acclaim for his *Spoon River Anthology* (1915), a collection that cast a critical eye on the constraints and foibles of life in small-town America.

James McManus is the author of six books of fiction and three books of poems—*Antonio Salazar Is Dead, Great America,* and *Spike Logic.* His novel *Going to the Sun* received the 1997 Society of Midland Authors and Carl Sandburg awards. He has been a fellow of the Guggenheim, Shifting, and Rockefeller foundations, the Illinois Arts Council, and the National Endowment for the Arts.

Ralph J. Mills Jr. is a professor emeritus at the University of Illinois at Chicago. *Living with Distance* (1979), which won the Society of Midland Authors Award, and *March Light* (1983), which received the Carl Sandburg Award, are among his poetry collections. He has also published critical articles, monographs, two volumes of essays on contemporary American poets, as well as editions of Theodore Roethke's letters and selected prose.

Harriet Monroe served as founder and editor of the little magazine *Poetry,* established in Chicago in 1912. That magazine served not only as the heart of the literary resurgence known as the Chicago Renaissance but also contributed largely to modernism's international appeal. Monroe demonstrated a keen eye for fresh talent. Her editorial choices include, for example, T. S. Eliot's "The Love Song of J. Alfred Prufrock" and Ezra Pound's "To Whistler, American." Monroe's own poetry, like that of many she published, evolved from decorous nineteenth-century forms to the more compressed and imagistic mode of the modernist era.

Lisel Mueller's most recent book of poetry is *Alive Together: New and Selected Poems* (1996), which received the Pulitzer Prize. Among her other five books are *The Private Life,* chosen as the 1975 Lamont Poetry Selection by the Academy of American Poets, and *The Need to Hold Still,* winner of the 1980 National Book Award.

G. E. Murray won the Devins Award from the University of Missouri Press for his collection *Repairs* in 1979. In 1992, he published *Walking the Blind Dog*. For nearly three decades Murray has worked as a corporate communications consultant, with extensive experience in western Europe and Japan. These involvements serve as backdrops for his long "mystery poem" *Oils of Evening: Journeys in the Art Trade*.

Georg Nikolic was born in Serbia and came to the United States in 1970. He is the author of four books of poetry; two have been translated into English by Charles Simic: *Three Slavic Poets* (with Joseph Brodsky and Tymoteusz Karpowicz, 1975) and *Key to Dreams according to Djordje* (1978). He has won numerous literary awards, including one from the Academy of American Poets in 1977. He is the publisher of Elpenor Books in Chicago.

John Frederick Nims received his Ph.D. from the University of Chicago. He taught at the University of Illinois's Urbana-Champaign and Chicago campuses. He received a Guggenheim Fellowship, a National Foundation of Arts and Humanities fellowship, an American Academy of Arts and Letters fellowship, a Creative Arts Citation from Brandeis University, an Academy of American Poets fellowship, the Aiken Taylor Award for Modern American Poetry, and the Melville Cane Award from the Poetry Society of America among many others.

Elder Olson taught for many years at the University of Chicago. Among his poetry collections are *Last Poems, Plays and Poems*, and *Olson's Penny Arcade*, which was given the Society of Midland Authors Award. Chief among his works of literary criticism are *The Poetry of Dylan Thomas* and *On Value Judgments in the Arts and Other Essays*.

Elise Paschen's collection of poems, *Infidelities* (1996), received the Nicholas Roerich Poetry Prize. Her poems have appeared in the *New Yorker*, the *New Republic*, *The Nation*, and *Poetry*, among other magazines, and in many anthologies. She is the former executive director of the Poetry Society of America and the coeditor of *Poetry in Motion* (1996) and teaches in the M.F.A. writing program at the School of the Art Institute.

Lucia Perillo's first collection, *Dangerous Life*, won the Norma Faber Award from the Poetry Society of America. Her second, *The Body Mutinies*, was greeted with the Verna Emery Poetry Award and the Balcones Prize. A former park ranger, she now teaches at Southern Illinois University in Carbondale.

Sterling Plumpp is a professor in the departments of African American studies and English at the University of Illinois at Chicago. The winner of the 1983 Carl Sandburg Award for *The Mojo Hands Call, I Must Go,* he has also had poems published in many U.S., South African, and French magazines.

Henry Rago began editing *Poetry* in 1955, when he succeeded Karl Shapiro. His first book of poetry, *The Travelers,* was published in 1949. A teacher and reviewer, Rago lectured and read his poems at universities in several countries.

Eugene Redmond is a professor of English, the chair of the Creative Writing Committee, and the editor of *Drumvoices Revue* at Southern Illinois University at Edwardsville. In 1976 he was named Poet Laureate of East St. Louis and in 1993 won an American Book Award for *The Eye in the Ceiling.*

Carolyn M. Rodgers has been published in *Essence, Ebony,* and the *Black Scholar.* Her volumes of poetry include *The Heart as Ever Green, We're Only Human,* and *A Train Called Judah.* She is currently an instructor with Chicago City College.

Luis J. Rodriguez is the author of the memoir *Always Running: La Vida Loca, Gang Days in L.A.* (1993), which won a Carl Sandburg Award and a *Chicago Sun-Times* Book Award and was chosen as a *New York Times* Notable Book. *Poems across the Pavement* (1989) won the Poetry Center Book Award from San Francisco State University and *The Concrete River* (1991) won the PEN West/Josephine Miles Award for Literary Excellence. He is also the recipient of a Lila Wallace–Reader's Digest Writers' Award and a Lannan Foundation Literary Fellowship.

Paulette Roeske's *Divine Attention* (1995) was the recipient of the Carl Sandburg Award. Her other publications include *Breathing under Water* (1988) and a chapbook, *The Body Can Ascend No Higher,* which won the 1992 Illinois Writers, Inc. Competition. She has been recognized with fellowships from the Illinois Arts Council, the Fulbright Foundation, and the Japan Foundation. She is a professor of English at the College of Lake County in Grayslake.

Alane Rollings has published *Transparent Landscapes* (1984), *In Your Own Sweet Time* (1989), *The Struggle to Adore* (1994), and *The Logic of Opposites* (1998), among other collections. She lives in Chicago with her husband, author Richard Stern.

Carl Sandburg, a native of Galesburg, sprang to national fame with the 1914 publication of his poem "Chicago" in Harriet Monroe's *Poetry* magazine. In quick succession followed four volumes that cemented his reputation as a Midwestern poet of the people: *Chicago Poems* (1914), *Cornhuskers* (1918), *Smoke and Steel* (1920), and *Slabs of the Sunburnt West* (1922). A journalist, populist, socialist, and author of a stunning multivolume biography of Abraham Lincoln, Sandburg was also a driving figure in the Chicago Renaissance.

Dennis Schmitz's books include *We Weep for Our Strangeness* (1969), *Goodwill, Inc.* (1976), *String* (1980), *Singing* (1985), *Eden* (1989), and *About Night: Selected and New Poems* (1993). Among his many awards are the Discovery Award, a National Endowment for the Arts fellowship, a Guggenheim Fellowship, and the Shelley Memorial Award, given by the Poetry Society of America for career achievement.

Maureen Seaton is the author of *Furious Cooking* (1996)—winner of the Iowa Prize for Poetry—*Exquisite Politics* (1997)—a collaboration with poet Denise Duhamel, and two other poetry books. She is the recipient of an Illinois Arts Council grant, a National Endowment for the Arts fellowship, and the Lambda Literary Award.

Karl Shapiro won the 1945 Pulitzer Prize for his collection *V-Letter.* Between 1950 and 1956, Shapiro edited *Poetry,* leaving that post to teach at the University of Nebraska. In addition to poetry, Shapiro also authored a number of striking critical works, including the influential *In Defense of Ignorance* and *The Poetry Wreck: Selected Essays, 1950–1970.*

Reginald Shepherd's books are *Wrong* (1999), *Angel, Interrupted* (1996), and *Some Are Drowning* (1994). He has won fellowships from the National Endowment for the Arts and the Illinois Arts Council, among other honors.

Barry Silesky is the author of *One Thing That Can Save Us, The New Tenants,* and a biography, *Ferlinghetti: The Artist in His Time.* He has twice won an Illinois Arts Council fellowship and has been a finalist three times.

Maura Stanton's books of poetry include *Snow on Snow* (part of the Yale Series of Younger Poets), *Cries of Swimmers* (1991), *Tales of the Supernatural* (1988), and *Life among the Trolls* (1998). Her novel, *Molly Companion,* set in South America, was reprinted in Spanish as *Rio Abajo.* She is currently the Ruth Lilly Professor of Poetry at Indiana University.

Kevin Stein is the author of five books, including *Chance Ransom* (2000) and *Bruised Paradise* (1996). His collection *A Circus of Want* won the 1992 Devins Award. Stein's books of criticism include *Private Poets, Worldly Acts,* essays on poetry and history. A recipient of fellowships granted by the National Endowment for the Arts and the Illinois Arts Council, he is Caterpillar Professor of English at Bradley University.

Sheryl St. Germain has received two National Endowment for the Arts fellowships, a National Endowment for the Humanities fellowship, and the Ki Davis Award from the Aspen Writers Foundation. Her books include *Going Home, The Mask of Medusa, Making Bread at Midnight, How Heavy the Breath of God,* and *The Journals of Scheherazade.* She has also published *Je Suis Cadien,* a book of translations of the Cajun poet Jean Arceneaux's works..

Lucien Stryk is the prize-winning author of more than two dozen volumes of poetry, translations, and editorial collections, including *The Penguin Book of Zen.* His most recent collection is *And Still Birds Sing: New and Collected Poems.* He taught for many years at Northern Illinois University.

Michael Van Walleghen is the author of five books of poetry, the most recent of which is *The Last Neanderthal* (1998). He has a Borestone Mountain Poetry Award and a Pushcart Prize. His second book, *More Trouble with the Obvious,* was the Lamont Poetry Selection of the Academy of American Poets. He has been the recipient of two National Endowment for the Arts writing fellowships and several grants from the Illinois Arts Council. He teaches at the University of Illinois at Urbana-Champaign.

Martha Vertreace's most recent books are *Light Caught Bending* and *Second Mourning.* Both won Scottish Arts Council Grants. Her other publications are *Second House from the Corner, Under a Cat's-Eye Moon, Oracle Bones, Cinnabar, When Night Becomes a Lion,* and a children's book, *Kelly in the Mirror.* Vertreace has earned four Illinois Arts Council Literary Awards and an Illinois Arts Council fellowship.

Yvor Winters was born in Chicago in 1900 but spent part of his childhood in Seattle and the foothills of Southern California. He attended the University of Chicago, but after contracting tuberculosis moved to New Mexico to convalesce. He eventually took his B.A. and M.A. degrees at the University of Colorado and his doctorate at Stanford University, where he taught until his death in 1968. Although he published a major poetry collection, *The Giant Weapon,* he is perhaps best remembered for his classic critical studies *In Defense of Reason* and *The Function of Criticism.*

David Wojahn is the author of *Mystery Train* (1990), *Late Empire* (1994), *The Falling Hour* (1997), and two other collections. His first collection, *Icehouse Lights,* was part of the Yale Series of Younger Poets. He has received fellowships from the National Endowment for the Arts, the Provincetown Fine Arts Work Center, and the Illinois Arts Council. Awarded the Amy Lowell Traveling Poetry Scholarship, the William Carlos Williams Book Award, and the George Kent Memorial Prize, he teaches at Indiana University and in the low-residency M.F.A. in Writing Program at Vermont College.

Dean Young's four poetry collections include *First Course in Turbulence* (1999) and *Strike Anywhere,* which won the 1995 Colorado Prize. He is the recipient of fellowships from the National Endowment for the Arts, Stanford University, and the Provincetown Fine Arts Work Center.

Acknowledgments

Michael Anania: "The Fall," "The Judy Travaillo Variations," "Interstate 80," and "On the Conditions of Place" are from *Selected Poems* (Wakefield, R.I.: Moyer Bell, 1994). © 1994 Moyer Bell/Asphodel Press. Reprinted with the permission of Moyer Bell/Asphodel Press.

James Ballowe: "Starved Rock" and "The Coal Miners" are from *The Coal Miners* (Peoria: Spoon River Poetry Press, 1979). © 1979 by James Ballowe. Reprinted with the permission of the poet.

Ray Bradbury: "Byzantium I Come Not From" is from *Where Robot Men and Robot Mice Run Round in Robot Towns: New Poems, Both Light and Dark* (New York: Alfred A. Knopf, 1978). Reprinted by permission of Don Congdon Associates, Inc. Copyright © by Ray Bradbury.

Gwendolyn Brooks: "The Coora Flower" and "Uncle Seagram" are from *Children Coming Home* (Chicago: The David Company, 1991). © 1991 by The David Company, Chicago. "The Lovers of the Poor," "We Real Cool," and "A Bronzeville Mother Loiters in Mississippi. Meanwhile, a Mississippi Mother Burns Bacon," are from *The Bean Eaters* (New York: Harper, 1960). © 1960 by Gwendolyn Brooks. "The Near-Johannesburg Boy" is from *The Near-Johannesburg Boy and Other Poems* (Chicago: Third World Press, 1986). © 1986 by Gwendolyn Brooks. "The Mother" and "Gay Chaps at the Bar" are from *A Street in Bronzeville* (New York: Harper, 1945). © 1945 by Gwendolyn Brooks. "To Black Women" is from *To Disembark* (Chicago: Third World Press, 1981). © 1981 by Gwendolyn Brooks. "Malcolm X" and the excerpt from "The Blackstone Rangers" are from *In the Mecca* (New York: Harper and Row, 1968). © 1968 by Gwendolyn Brooks. All poems are reprinted with the permission of the poet.

Debra Bruce: "Plunder" first appeared in *Atlantic Monthly* (May 1998). Reprinted with the permission of the poet. "Prognosis" is from *What Wind Will Do* (Oxford: Miami University Press of Ohio, 1997). © 1997 by Debra Bruce. Reprinted with the permission of Miami University Press and the poet.

Dan Guillory: The excerpt from "Snowpoems" is reprinted with the permission of the poet.

Jeff Gundy: "For the New York City Poet Who Informed Me that Few People Live This Way" appeared in *Flatlands*, published by Cleveland State University Poetry Center in 1995 (CSU Poetry Series XLVI). Reprinted with the permission of Cleveland State University Poetry Center. "Rain" first appeared in *Poetry Northwest*. Reprinted with the permission of the poet.

Susan Hahn: "Nijinsky's Dog" and "Confession" are from *Confession* (Chicago: University of Chicago Press, 1997). © 1997 by Susan Hahn. Reprinted with the permission of the poet. "Perennial" first appeared in *Poetry*. © 1998 by the Modern Poetry Association. Reprinted by permission of the editor of *Poetry*. "Incontinence" is from *Incontinence* (Chicago: University of Chicago Press, 1993). © 1993 by Susan Hahn. Reprinted with the permission of the poet.

Ernest Hemingway: "Champs d'Honneur," "Valentine," "The Lady Poet with Footnotes," and "The Age Demanded" are from *88 Poems* by Ernest Hemingway, edited by Nicholas Gerogiannis, copyright © 1979 by the Ernest Hemingway Foundation and Nicholas Gerogiannis, reprinted by permission of Harcourt, Inc.

David Hernandez: "Rooftop Piper" and "Workers" are from *Rooftop Piper* by David Hernandez. Copyright © 1991 by David Hernandez (Tia Chucha Press, 1991, Chicago).

Daryl Hine: "Man's Country" is from *Daylight Saving* by Daryl Hine. Copyright © 1978 Daryl Hine. Reprinted with the permission of Scribner, a division of Simon & Schuster. "Lines on a Platonic Friendship" is from *Selected Poems* by Daryl Hine. Copyright © 1955, 1980 Daryl Hine. Reprinted with the permission of Scribner, a division of Simon & Schuster, and Oxford University Press Canada.

Edward Hirsch: "Husband and Wife" is from *On Love* by Edward Hirsch. Copyright © 1998 by Edward Hirsch. Reprinted by permission of Alfred A. Knopf Inc. "For the Sleepwalkers" is from *For the Sleepwalkers* by Edward Hirsch. Copyright © 1981 by Edward Hirsch. Reprinted by permission of Alfred A. Knopf Inc. "American Apocalypse" is from *The Night Parade* by Edward Hirsch. Copyright © 1989 by Edward Hirsch. Reprinted by permission of Alfred A. Knopf Inc. "Wild Gratitude" is from *Wild Gratitude* by Edward Hirsch. Copyright © 1985 by Edward Hirsch. Reprinted by permission of Alfred A. Knopf Inc.

Paul Hoover: "Family Romance," "Theoretical People," and "Letter to Einstein Beginning Dear Albert" are reprinted with the permission of the poet.

Ralph J. Mills Jr.: "For Lorine Niedecker in Heaven" is from *March Light* (West Lafayette, Ind.: Sparrow Press, 1983). Reprinted with the permission of Sparrow Press. "Water Lilies" is from *A Window in Air* (Wakefield, R.I.: Asphodel Press/Moyer Bell Ltd., 1993). "Evening Song" is from *In Wind's Edge* (Wakefield, R.I.: Asphodel Press/Moyer Bell Ltd., 1997). These poems are reprinted with the permission of Asphodel Press.

Harriet Monroe: "The Meeting," "These Two," "Rubens," and "The Garden" are from *The Difference and Other Poems* (New York: Macmillan, 1925). © 1925 by Harriet Monroe. Reprinted with the permission of Ann Monroe Howe.

Lisel Mueller: "Alive Together," "Highway Poems," "Another Version," "Naming the Animals," "Monet Refuses the Operation," "Triage," and "Curriculum Vitae" are from *Alive Together: New and Selected Poems* by Lisel Mueller. Copyright © 1996 by Lisel Mueller. All rights reserved. Reprinted with the permission of Louisiana State University Press.

G. E. Murray: "The Rounds" and "On Being Disabled by Light at Dawn in the Wilderness" are from *Walking the Blind Dog*. © 1992 by G. E. Murray. Reprinted with the permission of the University of Illinois Press and the poet. "American Cheese" is from *Repairs* (Columbia: University of Missouri Press, 1979). © 1979 by G. E. Murray. Reprinted with the permission of the poet. "Art of a Cold Sun" is from *Oils of Evening: Journeys in the Art Trade*. Copyright 1995 by G. E. Murray. Reprinted with the permission of Lake Shore Publishing and the poet.

Georg Nikolic: "Under the Ninth Sky" and "Key to Dreams" are reprinted with the permission of the poet.

John Frederick Nims: "Love Poem" and "The Young Ionia" are from *Selected Poems* (Chicago: University of Chicago Press, 1982). Copyright © 1982 John Frederick Nims. Reprinted with the permission of the University of Chicago Press. "Tide Turning" is from *The Kiss: A Jambalaya*. Copyright © 1982 by John Frederick Nims. Reprinted by permission of Houghton Mifflin Company. All rights reserved. "Trick or Treat" is from *The Six-Cornered Snowflake and Other Poems*. Copyright © 1990 by John Frederick Nims. Reprinted by permission of New Directions Publishing Corp.

Elder Olson: "The Presence" is from *Last Poems* (Chicago: University of Chicago Press, 1984). © 1984 by Elder Olson.

Elise Paschen: "Between the Acts" and "12 East Scott Street" are from *Infidelities* (Ashland, Ore.: Story Line Press, 1996). © 1996 by Elise Paschen. Reprinted with the permission of Story Line Press.

Lucia Perillo: "Dangerous Life" is from *Dangerous Life* by Lucia Maria Perillo. Copyright 1989 by Lucia Maria Perillo. Reprinted with the permission of Northeastern University Press. "The Body Mutinies," "Needles," and "Skin"

Index of Poems and Poets

The Pebble: Old and New Poems
Mairi MacInnes (2000)

Chance Ransom
Kevin Stein (2000)

House of Poured-Out Waters
Jane Mead (2001)

The Silent Singer: New and Selected
   Poems
Len Roberts (2001)

The Salt Hour
J. P. White (2001)

National Poetry Series

Eroding Witness
Nathaniel Mackey (1985)
Selected by Michael S. Harper

Palladium
Alice Fulton (1986)
Selected by Mark Strand

Cities in Motion
Sylvia Moss (1987)
Selected by Derek Walcott

The Hand of God and a Few Bright
   Flowers
William Olsen (1988)
Selected by David Wagoner

The Great Bird of Love
Paul Zimmer (1989)
Selected by William Stafford

Stubborn
Roland Flint (1990)
Selected by Dave Smith

The Surface
Laura Mullen (1991)
Selected by C. K. Williams

The Dig
Lynn Emanuel (1992)
Selected by Gerald Stern

My Alexandria
Mark Doty (1993)
Selected by Philip Levine

The High Road to Taos
Martin Edmunds (1994)
Selected by Donald Hall

Theater of Animals
Samn Stockwell (1995)
Selected by Louise Glück

The Broken World
Marcus Cafagña (1996)
Selected by Yusef Komunyakaa

Nine Skies
A. V. Christie (1997)
Selected by Sandra McPherson

Lost Wax
Heather Ramsdell (1998)
Selected by James Tate

So Often the Pitcher Goes to Water until
   It Breaks
Rigoberto González (1999)
Selected by Ai

Renunciation
Corey Marks (2000)
Selected by Philip Levine

Other Poetry Volumes

Local Men and *Domains*
James Whitehead (1987)

Her Soul beneath the Bone: Women's
   Poetry on Breast Cancer
Edited by Leatrice Lifshitz (1988)

Days from a Dream Almanac
Dennis Tedlock (1990)

Working Classics: Poems on Industrial
   Life
*Edited by Peter Oresick and Nicholas
   Coles* (1990)

Composed in 9/13 Utopia
with Utopia display
by Jim Proefrock
at the University of Illinois Press
Designed by Paula Newcomb
Manufactured by Thomson-Shore, Inc.

University of Illinois Press
1325 South Oak Street
Champaign, IL 61820-6903
www.press.uillinois.edu